# THE

# 50 GREATEST PLAYERS

## IN

# BUFFALO BILLS

## HISTORY

### ROBERT W. COHEN

LYONS
PRESS

ESSEX, CONNECTICUT

## ALSO AVAILABLE IN THE 50 GREATEST PLAYERS SERIES

An imprint of Globe Pequot, the trade division of
The Rowman & Littlefield Publishing Group, Inc.
4501 Forbes Blvd., Ste. 200
Lanham, MD 20706
www.rowman.com

Distributed by NATIONAL BOOK NETWORK

British Library Cataloguing in Publication Information available

**Library of Congress Cataloging-in-Publication Data**
Names: Cohen, Robert W., author.
Title: The 50 greatest players in Buffalo Bills history / Robert W. Cohen.
Description: Essex, Connecticut : Lyons Press, [2023] | Series: 50 greatest players series |
Includes bibliographical references.
Identifiers: LCCN 2023010074 (print) | LCCN 2023010075 (ebook) | ISBN 9781493071135
(cloth) | ISBN 9781493071203 (epub)
Subjects: LCSH: Buffalo Bills (Football team)--History. | Football players--United
States–Biography.
Classification: LCC GV956.B83 C64 2023 (print) | LCC GV956.B83 (ebook)
LC record available at https://lccn.loc.gov/2023010074
LC ebook record available at https://lccn.loc.gov/2023010075

♾™ The paper used in this publication meets the minimum requirements of American National
Standard for Information Sciences—Permanence of Paper for Printed Library Materials, ANSI/
NISO Z39.48-1992.

# CONTENTS

# ACKNOWLEDGMENTS

I wish to thank Kate Yeakley of RMYauctions.com, George A. Kitrinos, Mark Cromwell, Keith Allison, Jeffrey Beall, Guy Harbert, Erik Drost, and Matthew D. Britt, each of whom generously contributed to the photographic content of this work.

# INTRODUCTION

## THE BILLS LEGACY

Founded in 1960 as a charter member of the newly formed American Football League (AFL), the Buffalo Bills primarily came to be through the efforts of Detroit insurance salesman and automobile heir Ralph C. Wilson Jr., who held a stake in the National Football League's (NFL) Detroit Lions at the time. Offered a franchise in the upstart league by its founder, Lamar Hunt, Wilson jumped at the opportunity to have a team of his own, telling Hunt, "Count me in. I'll take a franchise anywhere you suggest."

Given his choice of six cities—Miami, Buffalo, Cincinnati, St. Louis, Atlanta, or Louisville—Wilson initially expressed an interest in placing his team in Miami, before city officials there rejected his proposal due to the lack of success the Miami Seahawks had experienced in the short-lived All-America Football Conference (AAFC) some years earlier. Subsequently turning to general contractor and Buffalo resident George E. Schaaf, with whom he had served in World War II, Wilson received assurances from his old navy buddy that the city was ripe for professional football. And with powerful Buffalo attorney Paul Crotty and mutual friend Pat McGroder negotiating an advantageous deal that offered him full control of Civic Stadium, a 36,500-seat arena, and a deep discount on rent, Wilson decided that Upstate New York was his best option.

Originally opened in 1937 and previously serving as the backdrop for football, baseball, soccer, and NASCAR events (it also had a racetrack), Wilson rechristened Civic Stadium as the War Memorial Stadium and set about finding a name for his new team. Yielding to public sentiment, Wilson ultimately elected to assign his team the same moniker that had been used more than a decade earlier by the AAFC's Buffalo Bills, who had been named after famed western frontiersman Buffalo Bill Cody. Having settled on a home and name for his new team, Wilson assigned head coaching duties to the innovative Buster Ramsey, a World War II veteran and former NFL player who had spent the previous eight seasons serving as defensive coordinator for the Detroit Lions teams that had won three NFL championships.

In the AFL's inaugural season of 1960, the Bills took up residence in the league's Eastern Division, which they shared with the Boston Patriots, Houston Oilers, and New York Titans (who later became known as the Jets). Meanwhile, the Los Angeles Chargers, Oakland Raiders, Denver Broncos, and Dallas Texans (who later became known as the Chiefs after they moved to Kansas City) comprised the infant circuit's Western Division.

Experiencing very little success their first two seasons, the Bills posted a losing record in both 1960 and 1961, before finishing third in the division with a mark of 7-6-1 under new head coach Lou Saban in 1962. But with Saban, a former Cleveland Browns player who had spent the previous decade serving as both an assistant and head coach at the college and pro levels, leading the way, the Bills soon emerged as the infant league's best team, capturing three straight division titles and two AFL championships from 1964 to 1966. Particularly outstanding in 1964, the Bills compiled a record of 12-2 during the regular season, outscoring their opponents by a combined margin of 400-242 along the way, before defeating the San Diego Chargers, 20-7, in the AFL championship game. After posting a regular-season mark of 10-3-1 the following year, the Bills laid claim to their second straight league championship by defeating the Chargers in the title game once again, this time by a score of 23-0. The Bills subsequently won their third straight division title in 1966 by compiling a record of 9-4-1 under Joe Collier, the team's former linebackers and defensive backs coach who replaced Saban at the helm after the two-time AFL Coach of the Year unexpectedly left Buffalo to become head coach at the University of Maryland. But the Bills came up short in the playoffs, suffering a 31-7 defeat at the hands of the Kansas City Chiefs in the AFL championship game.

The league's most difficult team to score against during their championship run, the Bills relied heavily on their exceptional defense to thwart the opposition. Featuring standout linemen Tom Sestak, Ron McDole, and Jim Dunaway, perennial All-AFL linebacker Mike Stratton, hard-hitting safety George Saimes, and shutdown corner Butch Byrd, the Buffalo defense made life extremely difficult for opposing offenses, surrendering fewer than 20 points per game for three straight seasons. However, the Bills also possessed a considerable amount of talent on the other side of the ball, with running backs Cookie Gilchrist and Wray Carlton giving them one of the league's most potent rushing attacks, speedy wide receiver Elbert Dubenion ranking among the circuit's top deep threats, and superb linemen Billy Shaw, Stew Barber, and Al Bemiller opening up huge holes for Gilchrist and Carlton and providing excellent protection for quarterback Jack Kemp, who did an expert job of running the offense.

Unfortunately, diminished play from some of the team's aging veterans ultimately brought the Bills' period of dominance to an end. After finishing third in the AFL East with a record of 4-10 in 1967, the Bills compiled an overall mark of just 13-54-3 over the course of the next five seasons, as control of the team passed from Collier to John Rauch, to Harvey Johnson, and finally back to Lou Saban, who returned to Western New York in 1972. Meanwhile, the NFL-AFL merger prior to the start of the 1970 campaign placed the Bills in the newly constructed AFC East, which they shared with the Jets, Patriots, Miami Dolphins, and Baltimore Colts, who came over from the old NFL.

Things finally began to turn around for the Bills shortly after they adopted a new home venue in 1973. With War Memorial Stadium seating only 36,500 patrons and in rapid decay by the late 1960s, Ralph Wilson threatened to move his team elsewhere if construction on a new stadium did not begin immediately. Finally acquiescing to Wilson's wishes after he began fielding offers from Seattle, Tampa, and Memphis, city government leaders built a new open-air facility in the Buffalo suburb of Orchard Park that featured a seating capacity of over eighty thousand. Originally called Rich Stadium and later renamed Ralph Wilson Stadium, New Era Field, and Bills Stadium, the facility now known as Highmark Stadium has served as the Bills' home for the last fifty years.

Finding their new surroundings very much to their liking, the Bills posted three consecutive winning records under Lou Saban from 1973 to 1975, advancing to the playoffs as a wild card in 1974 after going 9-5 during the regular season. However, they ended up losing to the eventual Super Bowl champion Pittsburgh Steelers, 32-14, in the opening round of the postseason tournament.

Certainly, O. J. Simpson served as the driving force behind the success the Bills experienced during this three-year period. Although it took Simpson some time to adjust to life as a pro after the Bills selected him with the first overall pick of the 1969 NFL Draft, he eventually established himself as one of the greatest running backs ever, leading the league in rushing four times and becoming the first player in NFL history to gain more than 2,000 yards on the ground in a season. Yet Simpson received a considerable amount of help from his teammates, with offensive linemen

Joe DeLamielleure and Reggie McKenzie gaining Pro Bowl recognition on multiple occasions and quarterback Joe Ferguson proving to be a solid game manager.

With Simpson eventually wearing down and Lou Saban handing in his resignation after the team got off to a 2-3 start in 1976, the Bills struggled terribly the next few seasons, going a combined 17-43 from 1976 to 1979 under head coaches Jim Ringo (1976–1977) and Chuck Knox (1978–1979). But, with Joe Cribbs replacing Simpson as lead back, Joe Ferguson developing into one of the league's better passers, and nose tackle Fred Smerlas and left end Ben Williams excelling along the defensive front, the Bills experienced a brief resurgence under Knox in 1980 and 1981, winning one division title and making consecutive playoff appearances, although they lost in the divisional round of the postseason tournament both times, suffering a 20-14 defeat at the hands of the San Diego Chargers the first year, before falling to the Cincinnati Bengals, 28-21, in the second after edging out the Jets, 31-27, in the wild card game one week earlier.

The 1982 campaign ushered in another dark period in franchise history that lasted the next six seasons, with the Bills failing to post a winning record and compiling an overall mark of just 27-61 from 1982 to 1987 under head coaches Knox (1982), Kay Stephenson (1983–1985), Hank Bullough (1985–1986), and Marv Levy, who replaced Bullough at the helm midway through the 1986 season. However, Levy, a shrewd judge of talent who coached at the collegiate level for many years before going to the Canadian Football League and later coaching the Kansas City Chiefs from 1978 to 1982 and the Chicago Blitz of the United States Football League (USFL) in 1984, brought to Buffalo a brilliant football mind and a winning attitude that helped him and new general manager Bill Polian build a perennial contender before long. Following the USFL's demise in 1986, the Bills also welcomed into the fold special teams coach Bruce DeHaven, quarterback Jim Kelly, and center Kent Hull, all of whom ended up making a huge impact on the organization for many years. Acquiring several excellent players through the NFL Draft as well, the Bills selected running back Thurman Thomas in 1988, one year after they drafted cornerback Nate Odomes and linebackers Cornelius Bennett and Shane Conlan.

Having added those players to a solid nucleus that included standout offensive linemen Jim Ritcher and Joe Devlin, special teams demon Steve Tasker, and defensive stalwarts Fred Smerlas, Darryl Talley, Mark Kelso, and Bruce Smith, who went on to establish himself as the greatest pass-rusher in the game, the Bills emerged as the AFC's dominant team in 1988, beginning an extraordinary six-year run during which they advanced to the playoffs each season, captured five division titles, and appeared in the Super Bowl an unprecedented four straight times. Unfortunately, they ultimately came up short in the playoffs each season, losing in the divisional round of the postseason tournament once, the conference championship game once, and the Super Bowl all four times.

After finishing first in the AFC East with a regular-season record of 12-4 in 1988, the Bills defeated the Houston Oilers, 17-10, in the opening round of the playoffs. However, they subsequently lost to the Cincinnati Bengals by a score of 21-10 in the AFC Championship Game. Although the Bills posted a mark of just 9-7 the following season, they again captured the division title. But this time the Cleveland Browns defeated them, 34-30, in their first-round playoff matchup.

Fielding perhaps their finest team in 1990, the Bills finished the regular season with a record of 13-3, outscoring their opponents by a combined margin of 428-263 over the course of the campaign after switching to a no-huddle, hurry-up offense. Continuing their exceptional play in the postseason, the Bills beat the Miami Dolphins, 44-34, in the divisional round of the playoffs, before routing the Los Angeles Raiders, 51-3, in the AFC Championship Game. But even though the Bills entered Super Bowl XXV as heavy favorites to defeat the New York Giants, they ended up suffering a heartbreaking 20-19 defeat at the hands of their NFC counterparts when placekicker Scott Norwood's 47-yard field goal attempt in the closing seconds sailed just right of the goalpost upright.

After winning their fourth consecutive division title in 1991 by again going 13-3 during the regular season and scoring a then-franchise record 458 points, the Bills earned their second straight trip to the Super Bowl by defeating the Chiefs, 37-14, in the divisional round of the playoffs, before edging out the Broncos, 10-7, in the AFC Championship Game. But they subsequently faltered on Super Sunday, this time losing to Washington by a score of 37-24.

Although the Bills failed to win the division title for the first time in five years in 1992, their regular-season record of 11-5 earned them a spot in the playoffs as a wild card. However, with backup quarterback Frank Reich subbing for an injured Jim Kelly, the Bills appeared to be on the verge of exiting the postseason tournament quickly when they fell behind the Houston Oilers, 35-3, early in the third quarter of the AFC's wild card game. Displaying hearts of champions, the Bills subsequently rallied behind Reich, scoring the next 35 points to take the lead late in the fourth quarter, before winning the game in overtime, 41-38. The Bills extraordinary effort, which became known as "The Comeback," represented the largest come-from-behind victory in NFL history for the next three decades. Carrying their momentum over to the next two games, the Bills earned their third consecutive Super Bowl berth by defeating Pittsburgh, 24-3, in the divisional round of the playoffs and then outscoring Miami, 29-10, in the AFC Championship Game. But the season again ended on a sour note when Dallas ran roughshod over the Bills in Super Bowl XXVII, defeating them by a score of 52-17.

Reclaiming the top spot in the AFC East in 1993, the Bills compiled a regular-season record of 12-4, before advancing to the Super Bowl for the fourth straight time by registering victories over the Raiders (29-23) and Chiefs (30-13) in the playoffs. But although they put up more of a fight against Dallas than they did the previous year, the Bills again lost to the Cowboys in the Super Bowl, this time by a score of 30-13.

Even though the Bills won another division title and made the playoffs in four of the next six seasons, the 1993 campaign marked the end of their period of dominance in the AFC. With Darryl Talley moving on to Atlanta at the end of 1994, Cornelius Bennett signing with the Falcons one year later, Jim Kelly and Kent Hull retiring at the end of 1996, and Thurman Thomas and Andre Reed starting to show signs of wear-and-tear by the mid-1990s, the Bills failed to seriously contend for the conference championship the rest of the decade, advancing beyond the wild card round of the playoffs only in 1995, when Pittsburgh defeated them in the divisional round, 40-21.

Choosing to announce his retirement after the Bills finished just 6-10 in 1997, Marv Levy left head-coaching duties in the hands of Buffalo defensive coordinator Wade Phillips, who had previously served as head coach in Denver for two years. Easily the most successful head coach in franchise history, Levy left the Bills after leading them to eight playoff appearances, six division titles, four conference championships, and an overall regular-season record of 112-70 in his eleven and-a-half years in charge.

Experiencing a moderate amount of success under Phillips from 1998 to 2000, the Bills advanced to the playoffs twice, as Doug Flutie and Rob Johnson took turns starting at quarterback. But Phillips received his walking papers from Ralph Wilson when he refused to fire one of his assistants after the team finished 8-8 in 2000. Shortly thereafter, general manager John Butler, who had taken over for Bill Polian when the latter was relieved of his duties at the end of 1992, departed for San Diego. One year later, Wilson announced his retirement as president of the Bills, turning over control of the team to former Pittsburgh Steelers executive Tom Donahue, who, over the course of the next five seasons, made several poor personnel decisions that caused the franchise to lapse into an extended period of mediocrity. In addition to gutting the team of much of its on-field talent, Donahue replaced Wade Phillips as head coach with former Tennessee Titans defensive coordinator Gregg Williams, who led the Bills to an overall record of 17-31 from 2001 to 2003. Then, after firing Williams, Donahue hired former Pittsburgh Steelers offensive coordinator Mike Mularkey, who directed the Bills to an overall mark of 14-18 over the course of the next two seasons.

Having watched the disaster unfold from afar, Ralph Wilson retook control of the team's operations in 2006. After handing Donahue his walking papers, Wilson talked Marv Levy into coming out of retirement and assuming the role of general manager on a short-term basis. Levy retained his post for the next two years, before retiring for good and turning GM responsibilities over to his former assistant Russ Brandon, who replaced Mike Mularkey as head coach with Bills defensive coordinator Dick Jauron. Continuing to struggle under Jauron the next three seasons, the Bills finished 7-9 each year, causing management to replace him with defensive coordinator Perry Fewell on an interim basis midway through the 2009 campaign. The Bills underwent further changes at season's end, with Ralph Wilson promoting Russ Brandon to CEO. Brandon then replaced himself as GM with former San Diego Chargers general manager Buddy Nix, who, in turn, hired Chan Gailey as head coach. Faring no better under Gailey, who had previously served as offensive coordinator in Kansas City and head coach in Dallas, the Bills compiled an overall record of just 16-32 over the course of the next three seasons, prompting Gailey and his entire staff to be relieved of their duties at the end of 2012.

In the end, the organization's lack of stability in the front office and constant coaching changes made it extremely difficult for the Bills to establish any sort of continuity on the playing field, contributing greatly to the lack of success they experienced throughout the period. However, the organization's inability to find a suitable replacement for Jim Kelly at quarterback also proved to be a huge factor. With ten different men starting behind center for the Bills from 2001 to 2014, they often found themselves placing near the bottom of the NFL rankings in points scored and total offense. Only from 2002 to 2004, when Drew Bledsoe took most of the snaps, did the Bills have one of the league's better signal callers. Yet, even in mediocrity, the Bills generally fielded representative teams that featured at least a handful of excellent players, with standout performers such as offensive lineman Ruben Brown, wide receiver Eric Moulds, running back Fred

Jackson, defensive lineman Kyle Williams, and cornerbacks Nate Clements and Terrence McGee gracing their roster at different times.

With Ralph Wilson in failing health, he ceded most of his power to Russ Brandon on January 1, 2013, naming him team president. Still, Wilson continued to consult with Brandon on team and league operations until he passed away at the age of ninety-five on March 25, 2014. The NFL's oldest owner at the time of his death, Wilson remained heavily involved with the running of the Bills for more than five decades.

Following Wilson's passing, his assets, including the team, were placed into a trust governed by his widow, Mary Wilson; his niece, Mary Owen; Bills chief financial officer, Jeff Littman; and attorney Eugene Driker. A little over one year later, the trust sold the team to Buffalo Sabres owner Terrence Pegula and his wife, Kim, for a reported $1.4 billion in cash.

Since purchasing the Bills, the Pegulas have gradually restored the team to prominence by hiring the right people to run it, both on and off the field. While Russ Brandon remained in control of the day-to-day operations of the team, Doug Whaley replaced Buddy Nix as GM early in 2013, a season in which the Bills finished just 6-10 under new head coach Doug Marrone. After Marrone guided the team to a 9-7 record the following year, ownership denied his request for a contract extension, choosing, instead, to name recently-fired New York Jets head coach Rex Ryan head man. Ryan continued to coach the Bills for most of the next two seasons before being relieved of his duties during the latter stages of the 2016 campaign after leading them to an overall record of 15-16.

Following the firing of Ryan, the Bills named former Carolina Panthers defensive coordinator Sean McDermott their new head coach and replaced GM Doug Whaley with Panthers assistant general manager Brandon Beane. Although the Bills showed little improvement under that duo the next two seasons, compiling records of 9-7 and 6-10, respectively, they began their ascension to elite status shortly after they selected quarterback Josh Allen with the seventh overall pick of the 2018 NFL Draft and Kim Pegula assumed the role of team president when Russ Brandon abruptly handed in his resignation shortly thereafter.

A playoff team in each of the last four seasons, the Bills have captured three straight division titles and made one appearance in the AFC Championship Game. After advancing to the postseason as a wild card in 2019 by posting a regular-season record of 10-6, the Bills suffered a hard-fought 22-19 defeat at the hands of the Houston Texans in the opening round of the playoffs. With the addition of star wide receiver Stefon Diggs and the maturation of Allen into a top-tier quarterback in 2020, the Bills established themselves as one of the NFL's premier teams, winning their first division title in twenty-five years by going 13-3 during the regular season, before defeating the Indianapolis Colts, 27-24, and the Baltimore Ravens, 17-3, in the playoffs. However, the Kansas City Chiefs ended the Bills' dream of advancing to the Super Bowl when they defeated them, 38-24, in the AFC Championship Game. After capturing their second straight AFC East title by posting a regular-season mark of 11-6 in 2021, the Bills routed the Patriots, 47-17, in the wild card round of the playoffs. Seeking revenge against the Chiefs the following week in their divisional round playoff game matchup, the Bills appeared to be on their way to another appearance in the conference championship game when a 19-yard touchdown pass from Josh Allen to Gabriel Davis with just thirteen seconds left in regulation put them up by 3 points. But in the thirteen seconds that remained, Patrick Mahomes navigated his team downfield for a game-tying field goal that sent the contest into overtime. And just a few minutes later, Mahomes hit tight end Travis Kelce with an 8-yard TD pass in the corner of the end zone that gave the Chiefs a 42-36 win in OT, once again causing the Bills season to end in heartbreak.

Battling through injuries and a frightful experience in which defensive back Damar Hamlin nearly lost his life when he suffered cardiac arrest during a Week 17 matchup with the Cincinnati Bengals, the Bills repeated as AFC East champions in 2022, finishing the regular season with a record of 13-3 for the second time in three years. But after the Bills barely squeaked by the Miami Dolphins, 34-31, in the opening round of the postseason tournament, their season ended in disappointing fashion the following week when they lost to the Bengals, 27-10.

Nevertheless, with one of the league's stingiest defenses and a potent offense led by Allen and Diggs, the Bills figure to be perennial contenders for conference championship honors in the years ahead. Their next AFC title will be their fifth. They have also won thirteen division titles and two league championships. Featuring a plethora of exceptional performers through the years, the Bills have inducted twenty-three players into their Wall of Fame, three of whom have had their numbers retired by the team. Meanwhile, nine members of the Pro Football Hall of Fame spent at least one full season in Buffalo, with seven of those men wearing a Bills uniform during many of their peak seasons.

## FACTORS USED TO DETERMINE RANKINGS

It should come as no surprise that selecting the fifty greatest Buffalo Bills players ever presented quite a challenge. Even after narrowing the field down to a mere fifty men, I still needed to devise a method of how to rank them. Certainly, Bruce Smith, O. J. Simpson, Jim Kelly, Thurman Thomas, Andre Reed, and Josh Allen would appear at, or near, the top of virtually all lists, although their order of appearance might vary from list to list. However, several other outstanding performers have gained general recognition throughout the years as being among the greatest players ever to wear a Bills uniform: Billy Shaw, Joe DeLamielleure, Fred Smerlas, Darryl Talley, and Kyle Williams. But how does one compare players who lined up on opposite sides of the ball with any degree of certainty? Furthermore, how does one differentiate between the pass-rushing and run-stopping skills of front-seven defenders Bruce Smith and Cornelius Bennett and the ball-hawking skills of defensive backs Butch Byrd and Tony Greene? And, on the offensive end, how can a direct correlation be made between the contributions made by standout lineman Kent Hull and skill position players such as Joe Cribbs and Fred Jackson? After initially deciding who I wanted to include on my list, I then had to determine the criteria needed to formulate my final rankings.

The first thing I examined was the level of dominance a player attained during his time with the Bills. How often did he lead the league in a major statistical category? Did he ever capture league MVP honors? How many times did he earn a trip to the Pro Bowl or a spot on the All-Pro Team?

I also chose to assess the level of statistical compilation a player achieved while wearing a Bills uniform. I reviewed where he ranked among the team's all-time leaders in those statistical categories most pertinent to his position. Of course, using statistics as a gauge has its inherent flaws. The level of success a team experiences rushing and passing the ball is impacted greatly by the performance of its offensive line. There really is no way to quantifiably measure the level of play reached by each individual offensive lineman. Conversely, the play of the offensive line affects tremendously the statistics compiled by a team's quarterback and running backs. Furthermore, the NFL did not keep an official record of defensive numbers, such as tackles and quarterback sacks, until the 1980s (although the Bills kept their own records prior to that). In addition, when examining the statistics compiled by offensive players, the era during which a quarterback, running back, or wide receiver competed, must be factored into the equation.

To illustrate my last point, rule changes instituted by the league office have opened up the game considerably since the turn of the century. Quarterbacks are accorded far more protection than ever before, and officials have also been instructed to limit the amount of contact defensive backs are allowed to make with wide receivers. As a result, the game has experienced an offensive explosion, with quarterbacks and receivers posting numbers that players from prior generations rarely even approached. That being the case, one must place the current numbers Josh Allen has compiled in his career in their proper context when comparing him to earlier Bills quarterbacks Joe Ferguson and Jim Kelly. Similarly, the statistics posted by Lee Evans and Stefon Diggs must be viewed in moderation when comparing them to previous Bills wideouts Elbert Dubenion and Andre Reed.

Other important factors I had to consider were the overall contributions a player made to the team's overall success, the degree to which he improved the fortunes of the club during his time in Buffalo, and the manner in which he impacted the team, both on and off the field. While the number of championships and division titles the Bills won during a player's years with the team certainly factored into the equation, I chose not to deny a top performer his rightful place on the list if his years in western New York happened to coincide with a lack of overall success by the club. As a result, the names of players such as Nate Clements and Aaron Schobel will appear in these rankings.

One other thing I should mention is that I only considered a player's performance while playing for the Bills when formulating my rankings. That being the case, the names of standout performers such as Ron McDole and LeSean McCoy, both of whom had many of their finest seasons with other teams, may appear lower on this list than one might expect. Meanwhile, the names of Hall of Famers James Lofton and Terrell Owens are nowhere to be found.

Having established the guidelines to be used throughout this book, the time has come to reveal the fifty greatest players in Bills history, starting with number 1 and working our way down to number 50.

# 1

## BRUCE SMITH

lthough Bruce Smith received stiff competition from O. J. Simpson, Thurman Thomas, and Jim Kelly for first place in these rankings, his status as arguably the greatest pass-rusher in the history of the game enabled him to finish just ahead of his three closest rivals for the top spot. The NFL's all-time sack leader, Smith recorded more sacks and forced more fumbles than any other player in franchise history, while also registering the second-most tackles in team annals. Capable of taking over a game all by himself, Smith earned Pro Bowl and All-Pro honors eleven times each with his dominant play at right-defensive end, which helped lead the Bills to six division titles and four AFC championships. A two-time NFL Defensive Player of the Year and four-time AFC Defensive Player of the Year, Smith also earned spots on the NFL 1980s and 1990s All-Decade Teams, a No. 58 ranking on *The Sporting News'* 1999 list of the 100 Greatest Players in NFL History, and a No. 31 ranking on the NFL Network's 2010 list of the NFL's 100 Greatest Players. Later named to the NFL 100 All-Time Team in 2019, Smith received the additional honors of having his No. 78 retired by the Bills and gaining induction into the Pro Football Hall of Fame in his very first year of eligibility.

Born in Norfolk, Virginia, on June 18, 1963, Bruce Bernard Smith grew up in the middle-class neighborhood of Poplar Hall, where he spent his youth idolizing his father. Recalling the lessons he learned from his dad during his formative years, Smith said, "People talk about athletes being role models. I think of my father as being a role model and a hero in my life. My father was a minimum-wage worker when I was growing up. So was my mother. And they didn't look for any excuses to get away from their responsibilities of being a parent. He would work eight or 10 hours a day at his job, come home, and find a way to muster up the energy to take me to a baseball or basketball practice. When I think about people with character and integrity, he's the first person who comes to my mind."

Bruce Smith recorded more sacks than any other player in NFL history.
Courtesy of George A. Kitrinos.

Eventually establishing himself as a star in multiple sports at Booker T. Washington High School, Smith excelled in baseball, basketball, football, and wrestling, with childhood friend, Andre Smith, remembering, "In high school, he used to play both ways, and nobody could stop him. In baseball, he could hit the ball. In basketball, it was total domination. You did not dare come in the middle. He was just so big—so demanding. And he wouldn't give up ground."

After earning All-State honors in football and basketball in high school, Smith accepted an athletic scholarship to Virginia Polytechnic Institute and

State University (Virginia Tech), where he became known before long as "The Sack Man." Recording career totals of 46 sacks and 71 tackles for loss at Virginia Tech, Smith gained All-America recognition twice and won the Outland Trophy as the nation's top lineman his senior year.

Subsequently selected by the Bills with the first overall pick of the 1985 NFL Draft, Smith performed relatively well as a rookie, registering 6.5 sacks, 48 tackles, and 4 fumble recoveries for a team that won just two games for the second straight year. Nevertheless, Smith's work habits and overall play left something to be desired, with Marv Levy saying years later, "He was overweight, self-indulgent, didn't have great practice habits, all of those things."

However, Smith, who spent most of the year playing at 310 pounds, experienced a metamorphosis the following off-season, with the help of two individuals who inspired him to improve himself, both on and off the field.

In discussing the changes that Smith underwent, Marv Levy stated, "Two people had quite an impact in turning him around. One was his coveted teammate, Darryl Talley. He gave him that proverbial kick in the butt to get going. But the other, in the off-season, he went back to Virginia Tech to finish his degree, which is good, and there he met a woman counselor who put him on the right track in every respect. Boy, he dropped weight at the urging of her and Darryl, shaped up, got ready, his principles changed. He turned out to not only be the greatest player; he married that woman. And what a wife she was, his wife Carmen."

Recalling the reasons behind his transformation, Smith stated, "I wouldn't say there was fear. I would say there was an extreme amount of pressure. When I ballooned up to 310 pounds, I quickly realized I wasn't going to become the player that I wanted to be. I made some adjustments. That's when I got it, and when you get it, that's when special things happen."

Altering his diet completely, the 6'4" Smith shed some 35 pounds to get down to 275, which he maintained for the rest of his career. Dramatically improving his performance in 1986, a much leaner Smith gained Second-Team All-AFC recognition by ranking among the league leaders with 15 sacks, while also making 63 tackles and forcing 3 fumbles. Continuing his outstanding play during the strike-shortened 1987 campaign, Smith garnered Pro Bowl, First-Team All-AFC, and First-Team All-Pro honors by recording 12 sacks and 78 tackles in just twelve games, prompting United Press International (UPI) to also name him its NFL Defensive Player of the Year for the first of four times.

Although Smith experienced a minor setback in 1988, appearing in only twelve contests after receiving a four-game suspension for violating the

NFL's substance abuse policy, he performed well enough to earn Pro Bowl, First-Team All-Pro, and UPI NFL Defensive Player of the Year honors for the second straight time. After gaining Pro Bowl and All-Pro recognition again in 1989 by registering 13 sacks and 88 tackles, Smith turned in the most dominant performance of his career the following season, when he earned official NFL Defensive Player of the Year honors from the Associated Press and a fourth-place finish in the league MVP voting by recording 19 sacks, 101 tackles, and 4 forced fumbles.

Virtually impossible to stop because of his rare combination of size and speed, Smith proved to be too fast for most offensive linemen to block one-on-one and far too strong for running backs or tight ends to handle.

In discussing his longtime teammate's freakish athletic ability, former Bills center Kent Hull said, "You're talking about a guy who is stronger than a 300-pounder and faster than a linebacker. His speed around the corner is unreal. And if you move out, he'll take one step up field, spin inside, and he's gone."

Recalling the time Smith picked up Colts offensive tackle Chris Hinton and slammed him to the ground, Darryl Talley, who developed tremendous chemistry with his teammate on the right side of the Bills defense, stated, "I had a catbird's seat and saw an individual do things a lot of people couldn't imagine. Let's put it this way: when you see a guy grab an All-Pro tackle that's 320 pounds and launch him five yards, what would you think?"

Hall of Fame offensive tackle Art Shell commented, "All you can do with a guy like that is try and stay in front of him and hope the quarterback gets rid of the damn ball quick enough."

Former NFL defensive lineman Jim Jeffcoat said of Smith, "He makes things happen. He can get triple- or double-teamed, but he's still going to make things happen. He's just one of those rare kinds of athletes."

An extremely instinctive player, Smith received praise for his ability to quickly diagnose plays from former Bills defensive coordinator and head coach Wade Phillips, who stated, "Like most great players, he sees things and reacts quicker to them than average players. . . . I can say I've never had anybody better than Bruce."

Although Smith built his reputation largely on his ability to apply pressure to opposing quarterbacks, he gradually developed into an outstanding run defender as well, with Marv Levy saying during the latter stages of the Hall of Fame lineman's career, "Early in his career, he wanted to get every sack he could, and his run defense would suffer. Seven or eight years ago, he began to take great pride in his run defense."

Levy also spoke of Smith's strong work ethic and leadership ability, stating, "Bruce likes to do things quietly, when he doesn't think people see him, like working out every week on his day off. I guess he feels if people think he has stayed so good for so long on natural talent alone, so be it. . . . The best leadership anybody can provide is by example. And the way he prepared it spilled over on the other players."

Levy then added, "I've said this before, so I might as well say it again: I think he's the greatest defensive end who's ever played the game."

After appearing in all but four nonstrike games the Bills played his first six years in the league, Smith missed most of the 1991 season with knee problems. However, he returned the following season to begin a seven-year stretch during which he recorded a total of 86 sacks, earning in the process Pro Bowl and All-Pro honors each year. Particularly outstanding in 1992, 1993, and 1996, Smith registered 14 sacks and 89 tackles in the first of those campaigns, before recording 14 sacks and 108 tackles in the second. Three years later, Smith earned AP NFL Defensive Player of the Year honors for the second time by finishing second in the league with 13.5 sacks, while also making 90 tackles.

However, after the thirty-six-year-old Smith registered just 7 sacks and 45 tackles in 1999, the Bills released him at the end of the year due to salary cap constraints. Smith, who, during his time in Buffalo, recorded 171 sacks, 1,054 tackles, 35 forced fumbles, 14 fumble recoveries, 2 interceptions, and 1 touchdown, amazingly compiled that lofty sack total despite spending several seasons playing in a 3-4 defense. Quick to point out his tremendous feat, Smith, of whom Darryl Talley once said, "He's the best, and he'll tell you he's the best and mean it," stated, "When you're able to accomplish that in a 3-4 defense, you have to sit back, shake your head, and say, 'That's pretty darn impressive.' It's incredible, to be quite honest with you."

After being released by the Bills, Smith signed with Washington, for whom he recorded another 29 sacks over the course of the next four seasons, before announcing his retirement at the end of 2003. In addition to holding the NFL record for most career sacks (200), Smith ranks eighth all-time with 43 forced fumbles. Meanwhile, Smith's career total of 279 games played places him second in league history only to Minnesota's Jim Marshall among defensive ends.

Returning to his home state following his playing days, Smith became a large-scale hotel designer in Virginia Beach, where he heads his own real estate development company, Bruce Smith Enterprises. Although Smith exercises regularly and appears to be in good shape physically, he stated during a 2016 interview, "I look good, but I'm in pain. There's not a day that goes by that I'm not in pain. Multiple joints and things that I experience on a daily basis. It can be very frustrating sometimes and painful, but I'm very blessed. God has been good."

## BILLS CAREER HIGHLIGHTS

**Best Season**

Smith earned NFL Defensive Player of the Year honors in both 1990 and 1996, and either of those seasons would make an excellent choice for the best of his career. In addition to setting a single-season franchise record that still stands by recording 19 sacks in the first of those campaigns, Smith registered 101 tackles, which represents the second-highest total of his career. Meanwhile, Smith recorded 13.5 sacks, 90 tackles, and a league-leading 5 forced fumbles in 1996. Since the Bills won the AFC Championship and Smith recorded more sacks and tackles in 1990, we'll identify that as his finest season.

**Memorable Moments/Greatest Performances**

- Recorded the first two sacks of his career during a 27-20 loss to the Minnesota Vikings on September 29, 1985.
- Earned AFC Defensive Player of the Week honors for the first of eight times by recording 3 sacks and forcing a fumble, which he recovered in the end zone for a touchdown, during a 27-3 win over the Indianapolis Colts on December 13, 1987.
- Contributed to a 37-14 victory over the Jets on October 17, 1988, by registering 2.5 sacks.
- Turned in another dominant performance against the Jets on October 22, 1989, sacking quarterback Ken O'Brien three times during a lopsided 34-3 victory.
- Got to quarterback Jeff George four times during a 31-7 win over Indianapolis on December 9, 1990, earning in the process AFC Defensive Player of the Week honors.
- Starred against the Colts once again on September 20, 1992, recording 3 sacks during a convincing 38-0 Bills victory.
- A sack and interception during a 19-10 win over the Jets on October 24, 1993, earned him AFC Defensive Player of the Week honors.

- Contributed to the Bills 29-23 victory over the Los Angeles Raiders in the divisional round of the 1993 playoffs by sacking quarterback Jeff Hostetler twice.
- Equaled his single-game high by recording 4 sacks during a 15-7 win over the Houston Oilers on September 18, 1994.
- Turned in an exceptional all-around effort against Kansas City on October 30, 1994, earning AFC Defensive Player of the Week honors by sacking Joe Montana twice, forcing a fumble, and recovering another during a 44-10 rout of the Chiefs.
- Led the Bills to a 17-10 win over the Patriots on September 8, 1996, by sacking Drew Bledsoe three times.
- Gained recognition as AFC Defensive Player of the Week by recording 2 sacks during a 24-17 win over the Eagles on November 10, 1996, with his sack of Ty Detmer on a 4th and goal play from the Buffalo 3-yard line in the closing moments preserving the victory.
- Earned that distinction again by recording 2.5 sacks during a 9-6 win over the Colts on October 20, 1997.
- Earned AFC Defensive Player of the Week honors for the last time by registering a sack and forcing a fumble during a 26-21 win over the 49ers on October 4, 1998.

## Notable Achievements

- Scored one defensive touchdown
- Finished in double digits in sacks twelve times
- Recorded more than one hundred tackles twice
- Led NFL in forced fumbles twice
- Finished second in NFL in sacks three times
- Led Bills in sacks thirteen times
- Holds Bills single season record for most sacks (19 in 1990)
- Holds Bills career records for most sacks (171) and most forced fumbles (35)
- Ranks among Bills career leaders with 1,054 tackles (2n$^d$), 14 fumble recoveries (2nd), and 217 games played (2nd)
- Ranks first in NFL history with 200 career sacks
- Ranks eighth in NFL history with 43 forced fumbles
- Six-time division champion (1988, 1989, 1990, 1991, 1993, and 1995)
- Four-time AFC champion (1990, 1991, 1992, and 1993)
- Eight-time AFC Defensive Player of the Week

- Six-time AFC Defensive Player of the Month
- Two-time AP NFL Defensive Player of the Year (1990 and 1996)
- Four-time UPI NFL Defensive Player of the Year (1987, 1988, 1990, and 1996)
- Two-time PFWA NFL Defensive Player of the Year (1993 and 1996)
- 1993 NEA NFL Defensive Player of the Year
- Four-time AFC Defensive Player of the Year (1987, 1988, 1990, and 1996)
- Eleven-time Pro Bowl selection (1987, 1988, 1989, 1990, 1992, 1993, 1994, 1995, 1996, 1997, and 1998)
- Eight-time First-Team All-Pro selection (1987, 1988, 1990, 1993, 1994, 1995, 1996, and 1997)
- Three-time Second-Team All-Pro selection (1989, 1992, and 1998)
- Ten-time First-Team All-AFC selection (1987, 1988, 1989, 1990, 1992, 1993, 1994, 1995, 1996, and 1997)
- 1986 Second-Team All-AFC selection
- Pro Football Reference All-1990s First Team
- NFL 1980s All-Decade Second Team
- NFL 1990s All-Decade First Team
- Named to NFL 100 All-Time Team in 2019
- Number 58 on *The Sporting News'* 1999 list of the 100 Greatest Players in NFL History
- Number 31 on the NFL Network's 2010 list of the NFL's 100 Greatest Players
- Number 78 retired by Bills
- Inducted into Bills Wall of Fame in 2008
- Inducted into Pro Football Hall of Fame in 2009

# 2

# O. J. SIMPSON

S ome may object to the idea of placing O. J. Simpson second on this list due to the unconscionable acts he allegedly committed long after his playing career ended. Nevertheless, the level of excellence Simpson attained during his time in Buffalo made it impossible to rank him any lower. One of the most dynamic running backs in NFL history, Simpson won four rushing titles, becoming in 1973 the first player to gain more than 2,000 yards on the ground in a single season. A member of the Bills from 1969 to 1977, Simpson rushed for more than 1,000 yards five times, amassed more than 1,000 all-purpose yards seven times, and surpassed 2,000 yards from scrimmage twice, earning in the process six Pro Bowl selections, five First-Team All-Pro nominations, and one NFL MVP award. Also named AFC Offensive Player of the Year once and conference Player of the Year twice, Simpson earned the additional honors of being awarded spots on the NFL's 75th Anniversary Team and the NFL 100 All-Time Team, being accorded a No. 26 ranking on *The Sporting News'* 1999 list of the 100 Greatest Players in NFL History and a No. 40 ranking on the NFL Network's 2010 list of the NFL's 100 Greatest Players, and gaining induction into the Pro Football Hall of Fame the first time his name appeared on the ballot. Yet despite his many achievements and the tremendous popularity he enjoyed during his playing career and throughout the early stages of his retirement, Simpson remains one of the most tragic figures in the history of American sports.

Born in San Francisco, California, on July 9, 1947, Orenthal James Simpson grew up with his three siblings in the housing projects of the Potrero Hill neighborhood barely knowing his father, who, after leaving the family in 1952, worked as a drag queen, announced he was gay, and eventually died of aids. Raised by his mother, Eunice, who worked as a hospital administrator, Simpson developed rickets as a toddler and wore braces on his legs until the age of five, leaving him pigeon-toed and bowlegged.

O. J. Simpson won four rushing titles during his time in Buffalo.
Courtesy of RMYAuctions.com

Something of a problem during his early teenage years, Simpson joined a street gang called the Persian Warriors at the age of thirteen and ultimately spent some time at the San Francisco Youth Guidance Center, where he received anger management assistance. Later described by his childhood sweetheart and first wife, Marguerite, as a "really awful person then," Simpson also experienced troubles in school, often engaging in fistfights and suffering numerous suspensions. However, following his third arrest, Simpson decided to mend his ways after his uncle Hollis, with the help of a youth counselor at the local Booker T. Washington Center, arranged a meeting one afternoon between him and his childhood hero, Willie Mays. Recalling how his conversation with the Hall of Fame Giants outfielder changed his life, Simpson told *Sports Illustrated*, "I had an entirely different outlook on everything after that day with Willie Mays. I can't really say that it turned my life around, just like that. I honestly believe that I would have made it on my own. But that time with Mays made me realize that my dream was possible. Willie wasn't superhuman. He was an ordinary person, so there was a chance for me."

Eventually emerging as a standout athlete at Galileo High School, Simpson ran track, played baseball, and starred at running back and defensive back for the school's football team, earning All-City honors with his outstanding play on the gridiron. But, with Simpson struggling in the classroom, he received little interest from college recruiters, forcing him to spend two years at the City College of San Francisco (CCSF), a local junior college. Performing brilliantly at CCSF over the course of the next two seasons, Simpson scored 26 touchdowns and averaged almost 10 yards per carry as a freshman, before earning Junior College All-America honors his sophomore year.

Subsequently recruited far more heavily by Division I schools, Simpson accepted an athletic scholarship to the University of Southern California, where his accomplishments on the football field made him a legend. After leading the Trojans to the national championship and earning a runner-up finish in the Heisman Trophy voting as a junior by leading the nation with 1,543 yards rushing and 13 touchdowns, Simpson took his game to another level his senior year, when en route to winning the Heisman and being named the College Athlete of the Year by both the AP and UPI, he gained 1,880 yards on the ground and scored 23 touchdowns. Excelling in track as well, Simpson served as a member of the USC sprint relay team that broke the world record in the 4 x 110-yard relay at the NCAA track championships in Provo, Utah, on June 17, 1967.

Entering the 1969 NFL Draft as the most highly touted running back prospect in years, Simpson came off the board quickly, with the Bills selecting him with the first overall pick. However, following his arrival in Buffalo, Simpson inexplicably found himself being used very much as a decoy by new Bills head coach John Rauch, who often assigned him blocking and receiving duties at the expense of running the football. Recalling Rauch's questionable strategy, Bills tight end Paul Costa stated, "We knew he [Simpson] had a lot of ability, but the way Rauch was using him was weird. There was no rhyme or reason to it. You've got a rookie running back, and he's got a lot to learn, and you've got a coach that's insecure, so they didn't really hit it off. . . . He didn't use him right—decoy, wide receiver, and all that."

Although Rauch failed to take full advantage of his tremendous running ability, Simpson earned Pro Bowl honors in 1969 by rushing for 697 yards, amassing 1,040 yards from scrimmage, finishing third in the league with 1,569 all-purpose yards, and scoring 5 touchdowns for a Bills team that won just four games. With Simpson missing six games the following year from a knee injury, the Bills fared no better, finishing the season with a record of just 3-10-1. Meanwhile, Simpson gained only 488 yards on the ground, accumulated 960 all-purpose yards, and scored 6 touchdowns, one of which came on a 95-yard kickoff return.

Frustrated with his misuse and lack of overall production, Simpson said during the 1971 preseason, "The last two years, I was playing football just for the money. I couldn't wait for the season to end so I could get out of Buffalo and go back home. Well, man, I finally realized that was no way to be. I had to get my mind right and go to work."

Hoping for better things under new head coach Harvey Johnson, both Simpson and the Bills found themselves being terribly disappointed with the team winning just one game and Simpson rushing for 742 yards, amassing 904 yards from scrimmage and 1,011 all-purpose yards, and scoring 5 TDs.

However, Simpson finally began to realize his full potential after ownership fired Johnson at the end of the year and replaced him with former Denver Broncos head coach Lou Saban, who had previously coached the Bills from 1962 to 1965, leading them to back-to-back AFL championships in 1964 and 1965. Making his intentions known upon his return to Buffalo prior to the start of the 1972 season, Saban declared, "We have a great runner, a game-breaker who is a big-play athlete. I intend to use him."

Flourishing under Saban the next five seasons, Simpson posted the following numbers from 1972 to 1976 (note that any numbers printed in bold throughout this book indicate that the player led the NFL in that statistical category that year):

1972: **1,251** Yds Rushing, 27 Recs, 198 Rec Yds, 1,449 Yds from Scrimmage, 6 TDs

1973: **2,003** Yds Rushing, 6 Recs, 70 Rec Yds, **2,073** Yds from Scrimmage, 12 TDs

1974: 1,125 Yds Rushing, 15 Recs, 189 Rec Yds, 1,314 Yds from Scrimmage, 4 TDs

1975: **1,817** Yds Rushing, 28 Recs, 426 Rec Yds, **2,243** Yds from Scrimmage, **23** TDs

1976: **1,503** Yds Rushing, 22 Recs, 259 Rec Yds, **1,762** Yds from Scrimmage, 9 TDs

In addition to leading the NFL in rushing in all but one of those seasons, Simpson topped the circuit in yards from scrimmage three times, all-purpose yards and rushing touchdowns twice each, and touchdowns, points scored, and yards per rushing attempt once each, averaging more than 5 yards per carry on three separate occasions. A Pro Bowl, First-Team All-Pro, and First-Team All-AFC selection all five years, Simpson also earned NFL MVP and Offensive Player of the Year honors in 1973, when he became the first player to surpass 2,000 yards rushing in a season. Two years later, Simpson gained recognition as AFC Offensive Player of the Year by setting personal bests in yards from scrimmage, touchdowns, and points scored. Meanwhile, the Bills posted a winning record three times, winning nine games twice and advancing to the playoffs as a wild card in 1974.

Certainly, Buffalo's rebuilt offensive line, which included perennial All-Pros Joe DeLamielleure and Reggie McKenzie, contributed greatly to the success Simpson experienced throughout the period, as McKenzie acknowledged when he said, "You know, when I got to Buffalo, they were starting to call O. J. 'Stutter-step' because he was stepping back because he had no blocking." And with Simpson acquiring the nickname "Juice" (short for "Orange Juice," as in O. J.), the Bills' front five became known as the "Electric Company," since they "turned on the Juice."

Nevertheless, much of Simpson's success could be attributed to his extraordinary natural ability, which set him apart from other runners. Blessed with exceptional speed, the 6'1", 212-pound Simpson hit holes quickly and proved to be virtually impossible to bring down once he broke into the open field. Capable of outrunning even the league's swiftest defensive backs, Simpson also displayed outstanding strength, balance, and cutback ability. Marveling at his onetime teammate's elusiveness, former Bills center Mike Montler said, "I played with him four years, and I'd be willing to bet I could count on one hand the number of times he was actually tackled."

Quarterback Joe Ferguson, who spent much of his time in Buffalo handing the ball off to Simpson, stated, "It was amazing to hand the ball off to him and watch him move with his balance and vision and football wisdom."

Claiming that the snow and frigid temperatures at Rich Stadium seemed to have little effect on Simpson, Joe DeLamielleure said, "I can't fail to mention how amazing Simpson played in bad weather. While other guys were slipping and sliding in an inch of water—or half a foot of snow—on the field, O. J. could plant and cut as if it were dry as a bone."

Simpson's greatness on the football field and engaging personality helped make him one of the sport's most popular and recognizable figures. Further increasing his notoriety by appearing in a handful of movies and television commercials during the mid-1970s, Simpson became almost as well-known for running through airports as part of a TV advertisement for Hertz Rent-a-Cars, which represented something of a breakthrough in terms of the marketing of African American athletes.

But, as Simpson's popularity surged, his string of brilliant seasons ended in 1977, when, sidelined for much of the year by an injury, he rushed for only 557 yards, amassed just 695 yards from scrimmage, and failed to score a single touchdown. Dealt to his hometown San Francisco 49ers following the conclusion of the campaign for five future draft picks, Simpson spent two years playing on the West Coast, failing to regain his earlier form, before retiring at the end of 1979 with career totals of 11,236 rushing yards, 2,142 receiving yards, 13,378 yards from scrimmage, 14,368 all-purpose yards, and 76 touchdowns, with his 11,236 yards gained on the ground representing the second-highest total in NFL history at the time. As a member of the Bills, Simpson rushed for 10,183 yards and 57 touchdowns, made 175 receptions for 1,924 yards and 12 TDs, amassed 12,107 yards from scrimmage, accumulated 13,097 all-purpose yards, and scored 70 touchdowns.

Following his retirement from football, Simpson remained in the public eye for several more years, doing color commentary on ABC's "Monday Night Football" and NBC's NFL coverage, while also accumulating a total of thirty-one film credits in television and cinema. However, Simpson found himself being thrust into the spotlight for all the wrong reasons in June 1994, when, two years after divorcing his second wife, Nicole Brown, authorities accused him of murdering her and her good friend, Ron Goldman, at her Los Angeles home.

After leading police on a car chase through the freeways of Los Angeles, which the entire nation viewed on television, Simpson, who had a history of physically abusing and making death threats toward Brown, eventually surrendered to law enforcement officers. A controversial, highly publicized, and racially charged "trial of the century" ensued that ended with Simpson being acquitted of all charges, even though evidence presented at the trial linked him to the murders. But, with Simpson later found liable for both deaths in a civil lawsuit, he was ordered to pay $33.5 million to the families of the victims.

Running afoul of the law again in 2007, Simpson and some associates broke into a Las Vegas hotel room and stole memorabilia that he claimed belonged to him. Convicted of armed robbery and kidnapping, Simpson received a sentence of thirty-three years' imprisonment, with a minimum of nine years without parole. After serving his minimum sentence at the Lovelock Correctional Center in Nevada, Simpson was released on parole on October 1, 2017. Granted early release from his parole by the Nevada Division of Parole and Probation on December 14, 2021, the seventy-six-year-old Simpson now lives quietly in Las Vegas, where he participates in memorabilia signings and playing golf.

## BILLS CAREER HIGHLIGHTS

### Best Season

Simpson posted the best overall numbers of his career in 1975, earning AFC Offensive Player of the Year honors by leading the league with 1,817 yards rushing, 2,243 yards from scrimmage, 16 rushing TDs, 23 touchdowns, 138 points scored, and a rushing average of 5.5 yards per carry. Nevertheless, the 1973 campaign is generally considered to be Simpson's signature season. En route to earning NFL Player of the Year and league MVP honors, Simpson topped the circuit in five different offensive categories, including yards rushing (2,003), yards from scrimmage (2,073), and rushing touchdowns (12). He also averaged a career-high 6.0 yards per carry, which placed him second in the league rankings to Miami's Mercury Morris.

### Memorable Moments/Greatest Performances

- Went over 100 yards rushing for the first time as a pro during a 41-28 win over the Denver Broncos on September 28, 1969, gaining 110 yards on 24 carries, while also making 5 receptions for 45 yards and 1 touchdown.
- Led the Bills to a 28-3 victory over the Miami Dolphins on November 16, 1969, by rushing for 72 yards and making 3 receptions for 81 yards and 2 touchdowns, scoring one of those on a 55-yard pass from Jack Kemp. Also had a kickoff return of 73 yards, giving him a total of 226 all-purpose yards on the day.
- Topped that performance on October 4, 1970, amassing 303 all-purpose yards and scoring 2 touchdowns during a 34-31 win over the Jets. In addition to rushing for 99 yards and 1 touchdown, made 3 receptions

for 63 yards and accumulated 141 yards on special teams, scoring a second TD on a 95-yard kickoff return.

• Contributed to a 45-10 win over the Patriots on November 1, 1970, by carrying the ball 17 times for 123 yards and one TD, which came on a 56-yard run early in the second quarter.

• Rushed for 189 yards and recorded a career-long 94-yard touchdown run during a 38-21 loss to the Steelers on October 29, 2972.

• Rushed for 250 yards and 2 touchdowns during a 31-13 win over the Patriots in the opening game of the 1973 regular season, scoring one of his TDs on an 80-yard run.

• Led the Bills to a 27-26 victory over the Philadelphia Eagles on October 7, 1973, by carrying the ball 27 times for 171 yards and 1 touchdown.

• Followed that up by rushing for 166 yards and 2 touchdowns during a 31-13 win over the Colts on October 14, 1973, scoring one of his TDs on a 78-yard run.

• Continued his banner year by rushing for 157 yards and 2 touchdowns during a 23-14 win over the Kansas City Chiefs on October 29, 1973.

• Moved to within striking distance of the magical 2,000-yard mark by rushing for 219 yards and 1 touchdown during a 37-13 win over the Patriots on December 9, 1973. One week later, during a 34-14 win over the Jets in the regular-season finale, became the first player in NFL history to gain more than 2,000 yards on the ground in a season when he carried the ball thirty-four times for 200 yards and 1 touchdown.

• Began the 1975 campaign in fine fashion, rushing for 173 yards and 2 touchdowns during a 42-14 victory over the Jets in the opening game of the regular season.

• In Week 2, followed that up by rushing for 227 yards and 1 touchdown during a 30-21 win over the Pittsburgh Steelers, scoring his TD on an 88-yard run.

• Led the Bills to a 38-31 victory over the Baltimore Colts on October 12, 1975, by carrying the ball thirty-two times for 159 yards and 1 touchdown.

• On November 9, 1975, rushed for 123 yards, made 3 receptions for 71 yards, and scored 3 TDs, the longest of which came on a 44-yard run, although the Bills lost to the Colts, 42-35.

• The following week, carried the ball seventeen times for 197 yards and 2 touchdowns during a 33-24 loss to the Cincinnati Bengals on November 17, 1975.

- Six days later, gained only 69 yards on the ground during a 45-31 win over the Patriots, but scored a career-high 4 touchdowns, scoring twice on short runs and twice on short passes from Joe Ferguson.
- Continued to be a thorn in the side of the Patriots during a 34-14 Bills win on December 14, 1975, rushing for 185 yards and 1 touchdown, which came on a 63-yard run.
- Had a huge game against the Detroit Lions on November 25, 1976. Though losing 27-14, rushed for a career-high 273 yards and 2 touchdowns, the longest of which came on a 48-yard scamper.
- Turned in another exceptional effort in a losing cause on December 5, 1976, rushing for 203 yards and 1 touchdown during a 45-27 loss to the Dolphins, scoring his TD on a 75-yard run.

## Notable Achievements

- Rushed for more than 1,000 yards five times, topping 1,500 yards three times and 2,000 yards once
- Amassed more than 1,000 yards from scrimmage six times, topping 2,000 yards twice
- Surpassed 1,000 all-purpose yards seven times
- Scored more than 10 touchdowns twice
- Scored more than 100 points once (138 in 1975)
- Led NFL in rushing attempts three times, rushing yards four times, yards from scrimmage three times, all-purpose yards twice, rushing touchdowns twice, touchdowns once, points scored once, and rushing average once
- Finished second in NFL in rushing attempts once, all-purpose yards once, and rushing average twice
- Finished third in NFL in rushing attempts once, rushing yards once, yards from scrimmage once, and all-purpose yards once
- Led Bills in rushing nine times
- Holds Bills single-season records for most yards rushing (2,003 in 1973), yards from scrimmage (2,243 in 1975), rushing touchdowns (16 in 1975), and touchdowns (23 in 1975)
- Ranks among Bills career leaders with 2,123 rushing attempts (2nd), 10,183 yards rushing (2nd), 12,107 yards from scrimmage (3rd), 13,097 all-purpose yards (3rd), 57 rushing touchdowns (2nd), 70 touchdowns (3rd), and 420 points scored (7th)
- Four-time NFL Offensive Player of the Week
- 1973 NFL Offensive Player of the Year

- 1973 NFL MVP
- 1973 Bert Bell Award winner as NFL Player of the Year
- Two-time AFC Player of the Year (1972 and 1973)
- 1975 AFC Offensive Player of the Year
- Six-time Pro Bowl selection (1969, 1972, 1973, 1974, 1975, and 1976)
- Five-time First-Team All-Pro selection (1972, 1973, 1974, 1975, and 1976)
- Five-time First-Team All-AFC selection (1972, 1973, 1974, 1975, and 1976)
- Pro Football Reference All-1970s First Team
- NFL 1970s All-Decade First Team
- Named to NFL's 75th Anniversary All-Time Team in 1994
- Named to NFL 100 All-Time Team in 2019
- Number 26 on *The Sporting News'* 1999 list of the 100 Greatest Players in NFL History
- Number 40 on the NFL Network's 2010 list of the NFL's 100 Greatest Players
- Inducted into Bills Wall of Fame in 1980
- Inducted into Pro Football Hall of Fame in 1985

# 3

# THURMAN THOMAS

The only player in NFL history to lead the league in total yards from scrimmage in four straight seasons, Thurman Thomas accomplished the feat from 1989 to 1992, a period during which he served as one of the key figures on Bills teams that won three division titles and three AFC championships. The NFL's finest all-purpose back for much of his career, Thomas excelled as both a runner and a receiver out of the backfield, rushing for more than 1,000 yards eight times, while also surpassing 50 receptions and 500 receiving yards four times each. The Bills' all-time leading rusher, Thomas also amassed more yards from scrimmage, all-purpose yards, and rushing touchdowns that anyone else in team annals, with his magnificent all-around play earning him five Pro Bowl selections, five All-Pro nominations, and a spot on the NFL 1990s All-Decade Second Team. A member of Bills teams that won six division titles and four conference championships in all, Thomas earned the additional distinctions of winning one NFL MVP award, having his No. 34 retired by the organization, and being named to both the Bills Wall of Fame and the Pro Football Hall of Fame.

Born in Houston, Texas, on May 16, 1966, Thurman Lee Thomas got his start in organized football at Missouri City Junior High School, before moving on to Willowridge High School, whom he led to the Texas Class 4A State Title in 1983.

Offered an athletic scholarship to Oklahoma State University, Thomas spent four seasons starring in the Cowboys' offensive backfield, gaining All-America and Big Eight Conference Offensive Player of the Year recognition twice each by rushing for 4,847 yards, amassing 5,445 yards from scrimmage, and scoring 43 touchdowns. A teammate of future Hall of Fame running back Barry Sanders his final two seasons, Thomas performed especially well in his sophomore and senior years, finishing fourth in the nation with 1,650 yards rushing in the first of those campaigns. Then, after gaining 741 yards on the ground as a junior in 1986 despite tearing the

Thurman Thomas led the NFL in total yards from scrimmage in four straight seasons.
Courtesy of George A. Kitrinos.

ACL in his left knee during the offseason, Thomas returned to top form in 1987, finishing third in the country with 1,613 yards rushing.

Looking back on how his college career impacted him once he reached the pros, Thomas said, "I think what got me to the top was that my last two years in college, I had to work really hard to get my game to where I wanted it to be because I had a guy behind me whose name was Barry Sanders. With him being behind me and not wanting him to take my job, if he ran

10 100-yard sprints, I had to run 11—just to keep that edge. I think that helped me once I got into the pros."

Despite his outstanding play at OSU, Thomas ended up falling to the second round of the 1988 NFL Draft due to concerns over his previously injured knee. Finally selected by the Bills with the 40th overall pick, Thomas nearly dropped even further, with Marv Levy recalling, "Thurman Thomas was a good running back, but we had him red starred [on the team's draft board], which means, 'Don't pick him—injury problem.' He had a bad, torn-up knee. He couldn't finish his previous season. Six running backs went off the draft board in the first round."

Levy continued, "Now we're in the second round and finally get a pick. Elijah Pitts, our running backs coach, says, 'Marv, we need this guy, Thurman. I've seen him play. I've never seen anyone like him.' . . . I called the Oklahoma State head coach and asked, 'How about him? How are his knees?' He said, 'His knee's healed, I'm telling you!' I said, 'All right, go ahead, take him.' He gained more yards in his career than the other six running backs combined."

Meanwhile, as the Bills deliberated carefully before making their decision, Thomas grew increasingly angry, remembering, "Not only am I a little disappointed, but I'm a little pissed off too because now, in my mind, I'm thinking of all these teams that have told me, and that I've talked to, they pretty much lied to me."

Arriving in Buffalo with a huge chip on his shoulder, Thomas made it his mission to prove all those teams wrong. Getting off to an excellent start his rookie year, Thomas helped the Bills capture the AFC East title for the first of four straight times by rushing for 881 yards, amassing 1,089 yards from scrimmage, and scoring 2 touchdowns. Taking his game up a notch in 1989, Thomas began an extraordinary five-year run during which he compiled the following numbers:

1989: 1,244 Yds Rushing, 60 Recs, 669 Rec Yds, **1,913** Yds from Scrimmage, 12 TDs

1990: 1,297 Yds Rushing, 49 Recs, 532 Rec Yds, **1,829** Yds from Scrimmage, 13 TDs

1991: 1,407 Yds Rushing, 62 Recs, 631 Rec Yds, **2,038** Yds from Scrimmage, 12 TDs

1992: 1,487 Yds Rushing, 58 Recs, 626 Rec Yds, **2,113** Yds from Scrimmage, 12 TDs

1993: 1,315 Yds Rushing, 48 Recs, 387 Rec Yds, 1,702 Yds from Scrimmage, 6 TDs

The NFL's most complete running back throughout the period, Thomas finished either first or second in the league in yards from scrimmage all five years, topped the circuit in all-purpose yards three times, and placed in the league's top three in rushing on four occasions. Named NFL MVP and NFL Offensive Player of the Year in 1991, Thomas also earned Pro Bowl, All-Pro, and First-Team All-AFC honors each year. Meanwhile, the Bills made five playoff appearances and won four division titles and four AFC championships.

Although the Bills of the early-1990s became known for their fast-paced offense that predicated much of its success on the throwing arm of Jim Kelly, Thomas helped keep opposing defenses honest with his ability to gain huge chunks of yardage on the ground. A huge contributor in the passing game as well, the versatile Thomas possessed superb pass-receiving skills and run-after-catch ability, making him extremely effective in all phases of the "no-huddle" offense.

Praising the 5'10", 200-pound Thomas for the tremendous overall contributions he made to the Bills on offense, former teammate Steve Tasker said, "He was a great receiver out of the backfield. He was Marshall Faulk before Marshall Faulk. He was the prototype of today's NFL running back, and he started playing in the late eighties. He was a guy that was ahead of his time."

Called "the most versatile running back to ever play the game" by longtime teammate Cornelius Bennett, Thomas, said Jim Kelly, "had every phase of the game down to a T. Thomas could do it all."

Meanwhile, Marv Levy spoke of his star running back's strength and exceptional balance, saying, "He had balance the likes of which I don't think I've ever seen in a player. When you banged into Thurman Thomas, you didn't knock him down—you moved him over."

Although not particularly vocal, Thomas proved to be one of the Bills' team leaders as well, with Jim Kelly stating, "Thurman wasn't the guy in the locker room who would stand up and say a lot, but when he got on the football field, that's when his leadership came out. Things he would say to offensive linemen on the sidelines and things he would say in the huddle. He'd say things on the field that would keep us going. Behind the scenes, the attitude he brought to the game once he was on the football field was something not many people had a chance to see."

Thomas continued to perform at an elite level for three more years, rushing for more than 1,000 yards, amassing more than 1,200 yards from scrimmage, and scoring at least 8 touchdowns three straight times from 1994 to 1996, before his skills began to diminish. After gaining just 643 yards on the ground, accumulating only 851 yards from scrimmage, and scoring just 1 TD in 1997, Thomas assumed a backup role in Buffalo the next two seasons. Released by the Bills following the conclusion of the 1999 campaign, Thomas signed with the Miami Dolphins, with whom he spent one injury-marred season, before announcing his retirement.

In explaining why he chose to retire when he did, Thomas later said, "I figured I had played 13 years and, when I tore my knee up in 2000, I was ready to go—I wasn't going to be one of those athletes that hangs on for a number of years and not be able to perform the way I wanted to perform. . . . To me, I still had a life to live, and I wanted to be able to walk. At the time I hurt my knee, I was 34 years old and ready to go. I knew what I had in store for me. I've got a beautiful wife of 28 years and four lovely kids, so I wanted to spend the rest of my life with them and be able to do things with them. I knew that day would come, so I prepared myself for it, and that made it a lot easier."

Leaving the game with career totals of 12,074 rushing yards, 472 pass receptions, 4,458 receiving yards, 16,532 yards from scrimmage, 65 rushing touchdowns, and 88 total TDs, Thomas compiled virtually all those numbers during his time in Buffalo. In addition to being the only player to lead the NFL in yards from scrimmage four straight times, Thomas is one of only six running backs in league history to surpass 400 receptions and 10,000 rushing yards, and one of only five backs to gain more than 1,000 yards on the ground in eight consecutive seasons.

Following his playing days, Thomas, who signed a ceremonial one-day contract with the Bills on February 27, 2001, that allowed him to officially retire as a member of the team, launched Legends Energy, a power solutions company that NRG Energy later acquired, and became president of a telecommunications and construction company. Eventually returning to Western New York, Thomas established a sports training facility, began hosting a weekly sports show for the Bills, and became an ambassador for the organization. Thomas has also served as vice president of the New York State Tourism Board since 2014.

Unfortunately, several years after he left the game, Thomas began experiencing uncontrollable mood swings and the inability to focus for long periods of time, which brought fear and uncertainty into his life. The victim of several head injuries during his playing career, Thomas said at the District School Board of Niagara's Concussion Summit in 2016, "Still, to this day, I can't control my mood swings. On so many days, I have to apologize to my family for them. I thank God that I have a family that understands the things that I've been through over my thirteen-year career, and even after my fourteen or fifteen years that I've been retired. They all understand that, with my mood swings, sometimes I just can't help it."

Revealed to have a level of brain damage consistent with someone who played football for decades, Thomas added that his condition seems to be deteriorating over time, and that he expects it to continue to do so, saying, "It hasn't gotten any better. It's getting worse."

Still, as of this writing, the fifty-seven-year-old Thomas remains lucid, coherent, and capable of handling his day-to-day activities.

## BILLS CAREER HIGHLIGHTS

### Best Season

Thomas posted exceptional numbers for the Bills in 1992, earning Second-Team All-Pro honors by ranking among the league leaders with 1,487 yards rushing, 9 rushing TDs, and 12 touchdowns, and topping the circuit with a career-high 2,113 yards from scrimmage, which represents the second-highest single-season total in franchise history. But Thomas performed slightly better in 1991, earning several individual accolades, including First-Team All-Pro, NFL MVP, and *Sporting News* NFL Player of the Year honors by finishing third in the league with 1,407 yards rushing, making a career-high 62 receptions for 631 yards, scoring 12 touchdowns, and leading the NFL with 2,038 yards from scrimmage and an average of 4.9 yards per carry.

### Memorable Moments/Greatest Performances

- Excelled in his first game as a pro, rushing for 86 yards and scoring a touchdown on a 5-yard run during a 13-10 win over the Minnesota Vikings in the 1988 regular-season opener.
- Went over 100 yards rushing for the first time in his career on October 30, 1988, gaining 116 yards on 23 carries during a 28-0 victory over the Green Bay Packers.
- Turned in a tremendous all-around effort during a 31-10 win over the Patriots on October 1, 1989, rushing for 105 yards and 1 touchdown, and making 4 receptions for 99 yards and 1 TD, which came on a 74-yard catch-and-run in the fourth quarter that put the game out of reach.

- Contributed to a 31-17 victory over the Dolphins on October 29, 1989, by rushing for 148 yards and 1 touchdown, which came on a 30-yard scamper.
- Performed extremely well during a 34-30 loss to the Cleveland Browns in the divisional round of the 1989 AFC playoffs, rushing for only 27 yards, but making 13 receptions for 150 yards and 2 touchdowns.
- Earned AFC Offensive Player of the Week honors by rushing for a career-high 214 yards during a 30-7 win over the Jets on September 24, 1990.
- Led the Bills to a 27-10 victory over the Patriots on October 28, 1990, by carrying the ball 22 times for 136 yards and 1 touchdown.
- Proved to be a thorn in the side of the Patriots again a few weeks later, rushing for 165 yards and 2 touchdowns during a 14-0 Bills win on November 18, 1990, with one of his TDs coming on a career-long 80-yard run.
- Helped lead the Bills to a 24-14 win over the Dolphins on December 23, 1990, by rushing for 154 yards and 1 touchdown.
- Contributed to the Bills' 51-3 demolition of the Raiders in the 1990 AFC Championship Game by rushing for 138 yards, gaining another 61 yards on 5 pass receptions, and scoring a touchdown.
- Performed brilliantly during the Bills' 20-19 loss to the Giants in Super Bowl XXV, amassing 190 yards from scrimmage and scoring a touchdown, with 135 of his yards coming on the ground and the other 55 through the air.
- Earned AFC Offensive Player of the Week honors by rushing for 165 yards, gaining another 103 yards on 8 pass receptions, and scoring 2 touchdowns during a 35-31 win over the Dolphins in the 1991 regular-season opener, with one of his TDs coming on a 50-yard connection with Jim Kelly.
- Earned that distinction again two weeks later by rushing for 62 yards and making 13 receptions for 112 yards and 1 touchdown during a 23-20 win over the Jets on September 15, 1991, with his 15-yard TD catch in the fourth quarter providing the margin of victory.
- Led the Bills to a 41-27 win over the Dolphins on November 18, 1991, by rushing for 135 yards, gaining another 40 yards on 3 pass receptions, and scoring 2 touchdowns.
- Starred during a 40-7 manhandling of the Los Angeles Rams in the 1992 regular-season opener, rushing for 103 yards, making 3 receptions for 33 yards, and scoring 4 TDs.

- Followed that up by rushing for 85 yards, making 4 receptions for 94 yards, and scoring 2 touchdowns during a 34-31 win over the 49ers in Week 2, with his outstanding play earning him AFC Offensive Player of the Week honors.
- Contributed to a 24-20 victory over the Jets on October 26, 1992, by gaining 142 yards on the ground and catching 3 passes for 22 yards, with his 12-yard TD reception in the fourth quarter providing the winning margin.
- Earned AFC Offensive Player of the Week honors by rushing for 155 yards and 1 touchdown during a 28-20 win over the Steelers on November 8, 1992.
- Earned that distinction for the fifth and final time by amassing 159 yards from scrimmage and scoring a touchdown during a 27-17 win over the Broncos on December 12, 1992, gaining 120 of those yards on the ground.
- Proved to be too much for the Chiefs to handle in the 1993 AFC Championship Game, rushing for 186 yards and 3 touchdowns during a 30-13 Bills win.
- Led the Bills to a 23-20 victory over the Dolphins on December 17, 1995, by rushing for 148 yards and scoring 2 touchdowns, one of which came on an 11-yard reception.
- Starred during the Bills' 37-22 win over the Dolphins in the 1995 AFC Wild Card Game, scoring a touchdown and accumulating 158 yards rushing and 200 yards from scrimmage.
- Gained more than 100 yards on the ground for the final time in his career during a 20-10 win over the Jets on November 30, 1997, finishing the game with 104 yards on 18 carries.

**Notable Achievements**

- Rushed for more than 1,000 yards eight times
- Surpassed 50 receptions and 500 receiving yards four times each
- Amassed more than 1,000 yards from scrimmage nine times, topping 2,000 yards twice
- Scored more than 10 touchdowns four times
- Led NFL in rushing attempts once, yards from scrimmage four times, all-purpose yards three times, and rushing average once
- Finished second in NFL in rushing yards once, yards from scrimmage once, and all-purpose yards once

- Finished third in NFL in rushing attempts three times, rushing yards three times, all-purpose yards once, and rushing average once
- Led Bills in rushing nine times
- Holds Bills career records for most rushing attempts (2,849), yards rushing (11,938), yards from scrimmage (16,279), all-purpose yards (16,279), rushing touchdowns (65), and touchdowns (87)
- Ranks among Bills career leaders with 456 receptions (3rd), 4,341 receiving yards (6th), 522 points scored (5th), and 173 games played (tied for 9th)
- Six-time division champion (1988, 1989, 1990, 1991, 1993, and 1995)
- Four-time AFC champion (1990, 1991, 1992, and 1993)
- Five-time AFC Offensive Player of the Week
- Two-time AFC Offensive Player of the Month
- 1991 NFL MVP
- 1991 *Sporting News* NFL Player of the Year
- 1991 NFL Offensive Player of the Year
- 1991 AFC Offensive Player of the Year
- Five-time Pro Bowl selection (1989, 1990, 1991, 1992, and 1993)
- Two-time First-Team All-Pro selection (1990 and 1991)
- Three-time Second-Team All-Pro selection (1989, 1992, and 1993)
- Five-time First-Team All-AFC selection (1989, 1990, 1991, 1992, and 1993)
- 1994 Second-Team All-AFC selection
- Pro Football Reference All-1990s Second Team
- NFL 1990s All-Decade Second Team
- No. 34 retired by Bills
- Inducted into Bills Wall of Fame in 2005
- Inducted into Pro Football Hall of Fame in 2007

# 4

## JIM KELLY

**P**erhaps the most beloved player in franchise history, Jim Kelly led a resurgence in Buffalo that resulted in the Bills winning six division titles and four AFC championships over an eight-year stretch. The unquestioned leader of one of the NFL's most potent offenses, Kelly started behind center for the Bills from 1986 to 1996, a period during which he completed more passes for more yards and touchdowns than any other signal-caller in team annals. One of only three players to have his number retired by the organization, Kelly received the additional honors of being named to five Pro Bowls, two All-Pro teams, the Bills Wall of Fame, and the Pro Football Hall of Fame, accomplishing all he did in western New York after spending the first two years of his career playing in the short-lived United States Football League (USFL).

Born in Pittsburgh, Pennsylvania, on February 14, 1960, James Edward Kelly grew up some sixty miles northeast, in the Clarion County borough of East Brady, where he starred in football and basketball at East Brady High School. A prolific scorer on the court, Brady tallied more than 1,000 points during his career, leading the Bulldogs to the Pennsylvania Class A basketball state quarterfinals his senior year by averaging 23 points and 20 rebounds per game. Even more outstanding on the gridiron, Kelly excelled at both quarterback and linebacker, passing for a total of 3,915 yards and 44 touchdowns, with his exceptional play on both sides of the ball earning him All-State honors in his final season.

Heavily recruited as a linebacker by legendary Penn State head coach Joe Paterno, Kelly instead chose to accept a football scholarship to the University of Miami, where, over the course of the next four seasons, he threw for 5,228 yards and 33 touchdowns. One of several highly touted quarterbacks that subsequently entered the 1983 NFL Draft, Kelly expressed to his agent a desire not to play for the Minnesota Vikings, Green Bay Packers, or Buffalo Bills, since he disliked cold weather. But, while the reluctance of that year's first overall pick, John Elway, to play for the Baltimore Colts

Jim Kelly led the Bills to six division titles and four AFC championships.
Courtesy of George A. Kitrinos.

ultimately landed him in Denver, Kelly found himself bound to the Bills
when they selected him in the first round, with the 14th overall pick.

Although Kelly said at the time that he had expected the Bills to choose
him, he later admitted, "You have to say those things. . . . I cried. I didn't
really literally cry. I just had tears. I'm like, 'You've got to be kidding me.'"

After initially accepting his plight, Kelly began to seriously consider the
USFL as another option when the upstart league offered him his choice of
teams. Ultimately electing to play his home games in the climate-controlled
Houston Astrodome, Kelly signed with the Houston Gamblers, saying at
the time, "Would you rather be in Houston or Buffalo?"

Establishing himself as the USFL's top quarterback over the course of the next two seasons, Kelly did an expert job of directing Houston's run-and-shoot offense, passing for 9,842 yards and 83 touchdowns. Particularly outstanding in 1984, Kelly earned league MVP honors by throwing for 5,219 yards and 44 TDs. However, when the USFL folded following the conclusion of the 1985 season, Kelly had no choice but to sign with the Bills, who still retained his NFL rights.

Arriving in Buffalo amid much fanfare shortly after he inked a five-year, $8 million deal with the Bills on August 18, 1986, Kelly joined a team that had won a total of just four games the previous two seasons. Faring little better in 1986, the Bills finished just 4-12. Nevertheless, Kelly performed well his first year in western New York, placing in the league's top 10 in passing yards (3,593), TD passes (22), pass completion percentage (59.4%), and passer rating (83.3). Posting solid numbers again during the strike-shortened 1987 campaign, Kelly earned Pro Bowl honors for the first time by throwing for 2,798 yards and 19 touchdowns, completing 59.7 percent of his passes, and compiling a passer rating of 83.8. Although Kelly subsequently passed for 3,380 yards in 1988, he threw just 15 TD passes and tossed 17 interceptions. But, with the Bills finishing first in the AFC East with a record of 12-4, Kelly once again gained Pro Bowl recognition. Establishing himself as one of the league's most proficient passers after the Bills implemented their vaunted "no-huddle" offense the following season, Kelly began an excellent four-year run during which he posted the following numbers:

1989: 3,130 Yds Passing, 25 TD Passes, 18 INTS, 58.3 Comp. Pct., 86.2 QBR

1990: 2,829 Yds Passing, 24 TD Passes, 9 INTS, **63.3** Comp. Pct., **101.2** QBR

1991: 3,844 Yds Passing, **33** TD Passes, 17 INTS, 64.1 Comp. Pct., 97.6 QBR

1992: 3,457 Yds Passing, 23 TD Passes, **19** INTS, 58.2 Comp. Pct., 81.2 QBR

Consistently ranking among the NFL leaders in passing yards, TD passes, completion percentage, and passer rating, Kelly earned three Pro Bowl selections, two All-Pro nominations, and one runner-up finish in the league MVP voting. More importantly, the Bills won three division titles and three AFC championships, advancing to the Super Bowl in all but the first of those campaigns.

Blessed with good size and a strong throwing arm, the 6'3", 220-pound Kelly also possessed outstanding pocket presence and good mobility, although he rarely took off with the football. When he did, though, Kelly ran with a linebacker's mentality, hardly ever shying away from contact. Extremely decisive, Kelly did a superb job of lining up his team, recognizing the opposing team's coverage schemes, and getting the ball out quickly.

Perhaps Kelly's greatest strengths, though, lay in his leadership abilities and tremendous determination, which enabled him to inspire confidence in his teammates. In discussing the impact that Kelly had on the other players around him, longtime Bills offensive lineman Jim Ritcher said, "Jim came in with a different attitude than what we had had. Even though I thought we had a good team, we could go out and compete, but we had this attitude that when things started going bad, we'd say, 'Oh no, here it comes again for us.' We expected bad things to happen. But Jim, if something went bad, he'd be like, 'Guys, just give me a little more time. We're gonna connect on this, and we're gonna score, believe me. Just give me a bit more time.' And he would do it, he'd get the ball moving."

Ritcher continued, "All of a sudden, guys started looking at him and thinking, 'We are gonna win.' He did it over and over again. We thought if we were anywhere close in the fourth quarter, we were gonna win the game. Jim wasn't the only reason, but it was the attitude that he brought that helped change the team."

Andre Reed expressed similar sentiments when he stated during his own Hall of Fame induction speech: "I was known for my toughness going across the middle, making that catch, breaking tackles, but the toughest individual I've ever met in my life is Jim Kelly, No. 12. You're the reason why I'm standing here today. Every time I looked into your eyes in the huddle, I knew we could get it done, I knew we had a chance to win. Leadership beyond reasonable doubt, and those around you gravitated toward your leadership and what you said. You taught us not to quit. You know what we used to say, '12 plus 83 always equals six.'"

Revealing the mental fortitude that allowed him to excel in pressure situations, Kelly said, "I thrive on having everything put in my hands. I love being the guy who has to get it done. I've always been that way. . . . If I made the big play, we were usually very successful; if I didn't, we usually lost."

Although Kelly failed to earn Pro Bowl honors in 1993, he led the Bills to their fifth division title in six seasons and their fourth straight trip to the Super Bowl by throwing for 3,382 yards and 18 touchdowns, completing 61.3 percent of his passes, and posting a passer rating of 79.9. Continuing to perform well the next three years, Kelly twice passed for more than 3,000 yards and 20 touchdowns in leading the Bills to two more playoff appearances and another division title. But, with the thirty-six-year-old Kelly having missed playing time in each of those seasons due to injury, he decided to announce his retirement following the conclusion of the 1996 campaign.

In his eleven years with the Bills, Kelly passed for 35,467 yards, threw 237 touchdown passes and 175 interceptions, completed 60.1 percent of his passes, posted a passer rating of 84.4, and ran for 1,049 yards and 7 touchdowns. Including his time in the USFL, Kelly threw for more than 45,000 yards and 320 TDs. At the time of his retirement, only Fran Tarkenton, Dan Fouts, and Johnny Unitas among Hall of Fame quarterbacks had passed for more yards, and only Tarkenton and Fouts had completed more passes. An outstanding postseason performer as well, Kelly passed for 3,863 yards and 21 touchdowns in seventeen playoff games, including four Super Bowls. Meanwhile, in Kelly's 160 regular-season starts with them, the Bills compiled a record of 101-59.

Following his playing days, Kelly devoted the early years of his retirement to his young son, Hunter, who, shortly after entering the world on February 14, 1997, received a diagnosis of globoid cell leukodystrophy (Krabbe disease), a severe and progressive neurological condition that robs its victims of their motor skills. Forced to rely on a feeding tube and forced oxygen at all times, Hunter lived until August 5, 2005, when he died at the age of eight. Recalling the anxiety that he experienced throughout the ordeal, Kelly said, "That was probably one of the toughest times in my life. Those times were very hard on all of us."

To honor his son, Kelly and his wife, Jill, established the nonprofit organization Hunter's Hope and founded the annual Hunter's Day of Hope, which is held on February 14, the birthdays of both Jim and Hunter Kelly. Kelly also dedicated his 2002 Pro Football Hall of Fame induction speech to his son, saying as he choked back tears, "It's been written that the trademark of my career was toughness. The toughest person I ever met in my life was my hero, my soldier, my son, Hunter. I love you, buddy."

Reestablishing his priorities after his son died, Kelly set about forging a closer relationship with his wife and two young daughters, who he frequently neglected during his playing days and son's illness, later saying, "We had our nuptials redone, which is awesome. My two beautiful daughters, we just raised them."

Some years later, Kelly, himself, faced a near-death experience when, in June 2013, he was found to have squamous cell carcinoma, a form of cancer, in his upper jaw. Eventually forced to undergo forty-five rounds of radiation and chemotherapy, Kelly had his upper jaw removed after doctors discovered that the cancer had spread. But even though Kelly at one point received a diagnosis of stage IV cancer that gave him less than a 10 percent chance of survival, he ultimately overcame his illness and is now cancer-free.

Currently living with his wife in East Aurora, New York, the sixty-three-year-old Kelly is involved in several business ventures, including Hall of Fame Life Promotions, which donates a percentage of all its proceeds to the Hunter's Hope Foundation. He also hosts the annual Jim Kelly Celebrity Golf Classic to benefit his Kelly for Kids Foundation and is committed to other children's charities, such as the Cystic Fibrosis Foundation.

## BILLS CAREER HIGHLIGHTS

### Best Season

Although Kelly performed brilliantly in 1990, winning twelve of his fourteen starts behind center, throwing for 2,829 yards and 24 touchdowns, and leading the league with a pass-completion percentage of 63.3 and a passer rating of 101.2, he posted slightly better overall numbers the following year. En route to earning his lone First-Team All-Pro nomination and a runner-up finish to teammate Thurman Thomas in the league MVP voting in 1991, Kelly finished third in the NFL with 3,844 yards passing and threw a league-leading 33 touchdown passes, which set a single-season franchise record that stood for nearly three decades. Kelly also completed a career-best 64.1 percent of his passes and compiled a passer rating of 97.6 that ranked as the third highest in the league.

### Memorable Moments/Greatest Performances

- Excelled in his first game with the Bills, passing for 292 yards and three touchdowns during a 28-24 loss to the Jets in the opening game of the 1986 regular season.
- Again starred in defeat on November 2, 1986, throwing for 342 yards and 3 touchdowns during a 34-28 loss to the Tampa Bay Buccaneers.
- Earned AFC Offensive Player of the Week honors for the first of ten times by passing for 293 yards and 3 TDs during a 34-30 win over the Houston Oilers on September 20, 1987.

- Excelled in his first game back following the players' strike in 1987, completing 29 of 39 pass attempts for 359 yards and 2 touchdowns during a 34-31 overtime win over the Dolphins on October 25.
- Led the Bills to a 34-23 victory over the Colts on October 9, 1988, by throwing for 315 yards and 3 touchdowns, with one of his TD tosses going to Ronnie Harmon and the other two to Andre Reed.
- Gave the Bills a dramatic 27-24 victory over the Dolphins in the 1989 regular-season opener by scoring the game-winning touchdown on a 2-yard run on the game's final play.
- Earned AFC Offensive Player of the Week honors by passing for 363 yards and 5 touchdowns during a 47-41 victory over the Houston Oilers on September 24, 1989, giving the Bills the win with a 28-yard TD pass to Andre Reed in overtime.
- Performed brilliantly against the Cleveland Browns in the divisional round of the 1989 AFC playoffs (though losing 34-30), throwing for 405 yards and 4 touchdowns, the longest of which went 72 yards to Andre Reed.
- Led the Bills to a 30-27 win over the Jets on October 21, 1990, by passing for 297 yards and 4 touchdowns, one of which went 60 yards to James Lofton.
- Starred during a 30-23 win over the Eagles on December 2, 1990, throwing for 334 yards and 3 touchdowns, the longest of which went 63 yards to Lofton.
- Led the Bills to a 44-34 victory over the Dolphins in the divisional round of the 1990 AFC playoffs by passing for 339 yards and 3 touchdowns, connecting with James Lofton once and Andre Reed twice.
- Followed that up by throwing for 300 yards and 2 touchdowns during the Bills' 51-3 massacre of the Raiders in the 1990 AFC Championship Game, completing both his TD passes to Lofton.
- Continued to torch Miami's defensive secondary in the 1991 regular-season opener, passing for 381 yards and 2 touchdowns during a 35-31 Bills win, with one of his TD tosses going 54 yards to Andre Reed.
- Earned AFC Offensive Player of the Week honors by throwing for 363 yards and a career-high 6 touchdowns during a 52-34 win over the Steelers on September 8, 1991, with four of his TD passes going to Don Beebe and the other two to Andre Reed and James Lofton.
- Led the Bills to a 35-16 win over the Cincinnati Bengals on October 21, 1991, by passing for 392 yards and 5 touchdowns, the longest of which went to James Lofton for 74 yards.

- Performed magnificently during the latter stages of a 30-27 overtime victory over the Raiders on December 8, 1991, bringing the Bills back from a 13-point fourth-quarter deficit by leading them on two late scoring drives. Kelly finished the game with 347 yards passing and 2 touchdown passes, earning in the process AFC Offensive Player of the Week honors.
- Earned that distinction again by throwing for 308 yards and 3 touchdowns during a 41-7 blowout of the Patriots on September 27, 1992, with his longest TD pass of the day being a 45-yard connection with Andre Reed.
- Kelly and Reed proved to be lethal to the Packers on November 20, 1994, with Kelly throwing for 365 yards and hitting his favorite receiver with a pair of touchdown passes during a 29-20 Bills win.
- Led the Bills to a 42-31 victory over the Dolphins on December 4, 1994, by throwing for 299 yards and 4 touchdowns, which included a 72-yard strike to Don Beebe and an 83-yard connection with Reed.
- Earned AFC Offensive Player of the Week honors by passing for 237 yards and 4 touchdowns during a 45-27 win over the St. Louis Rams on December 10, 1995, with the longest of his TD tosses going 28 yards to Steve Tasker.
- Earned AFC Offensive Player of the Week honors again by throwing for 279 yards and 2 touchdowns during a 20-9 win over the Chiefs in the final game of the 1996 regular season, completing both his TD passes in the fourth quarter.

**Notable Achievements**

- Passed for more than 3,000 yards eight times, topping 3,500 yards twice
- Threw more than 30 touchdown passes once (33 in 1991)
- Completed more than 60 percent of passes four times
- Posted touchdown-to-interception ratio of better than 2-1 once
- Posted passer rating above 90.0 twice, finishing with mark above 100.0 once
- Led NFL in touchdown passes once, pass completion percentage once, and passer rating once
- Finished third in NFL in passing yards twice, touchdown passes once, and passer rating once
- Holds Bills career records for most pass attempts (4,779), pass completions (2,874), passing yards (35,467), and touchdown passes (237)

- Six-time division champion (1988, 1989, 1990, 1991, 1993, and 1995)
- Four-time AFC champion (1990, 1991, 1992, and 1993)
- Ten-time AFC Offensive Player of the Week
- Three-time AFC Offensive Player of the Month
- Five-time Pro Bowl selection (1987, 1988, 1990, 1991, and 1992)
- 1991 First-Team All-Pro selection
- 1992 Second-Team All-Pro selection
- 1991 First-Team All-AFC selection
- 1990 Second-Team All-AFC selection
- No. 12 retired by Bills
- Inducted into Bills Wall of Fame in 2001
- Inducted into Pro Football Hall of Fame in 2002

# 5

# BILLY SHAW

The only member of the Pro Football Hall of Fame who spent his entire career playing in the AFL, Billy Shaw starred for the Bills at left guard throughout the 1960s, establishing himself over the course of the decade as the league's finest player at his position. A dominant run-blocker and exceptional pass-protector, Shaw helped lead the Bills to three division titles and two league championships, earning in the process eight AFL All-Star (Pro Bowl) nominations and seven All-AFL (All-Pro) selections. Also named to the AFL All-Time First Team and Pro Football Reference's All-1960s First Team, Shaw accomplished all he did as an offensive lineman for the Bills after turning down an offer to play linebacker for the Dallas Cowboys.

Born in Natchez, Mississippi, on December 15, 1938, William Lewis Shaw grew up some seventy miles northeast, in the town of Vicksburg, where he began competing in football at the age of ten. Getting his start in organized sports at Carr Central High School, Shaw started at both offensive and defensive tackle his senior year, with his strong play on both sides of the ball earning him an athletic scholarship to the Georgia Institute of Technology.

Shaw, who stood 6'2" but weighed only 188 pounds when he first arrived in Atlanta, continued to excel on both offense and defense while at Georgia Tech, earning All-America honors as a two-way tackle his senior year, by which time he had increased his weight to 220 pounds. Looking back on his college career, Shaw said, "Actually, I thought I played defense much better than offense, and I still believe most of the honors I received were for my defensive play."

Believing that Shaw's future lay on the defensive side of the ball, the Dallas Cowboys selected him in the 14th round of the 1961 NFL Draft, with the 184th overall pick, in the hope of converting him into a linebacker, with Shaw recalling, "I had been in contact with the Cowboys mostly prior

After gaining All-America recognition at Georgia Tech, Billy Shaw earned eight AFL All-Star and seven All-AFL nominations as a member of the Bills.

to the Bills getting involved. The Cowboys wanted me to play at linebacker. We had lengthy conversations at that point in time."

However, prior to being selected by the Cowboys, Shaw faced a difficult decision when the Bills claimed him in the 2nd round of that year's AFL Draft, with the 9th overall pick, remembering, "The Bills wanted to play me at either defensive end or an offensive line position. I really wanted to play on the defensive side of the ball as a defensive end. So, that triggered a real interest for me."

Seeking guidance from the man whose opinion he valued most, Shaw recalled, "I went to my mentor, and that was coach Bobby Dodd at Georgia Tech. And I just presented to him what my options were. Coach Dodd told

BILLY SHAW **39**

me straight up, 'Billy, there is room for another pro league. The timing is right. I think that your potential is either on the offensive or defensive side of the ball as a lineman, not a linebacker. You have an opportunity to go to a new league, play early, and be a part of history.'"

Heeding the advice of his former coach, Shaw signed with the Bills, later saying, "I had never ever played linebacker before. I didn't want to learn a new position. I thoroughly enjoyed playing on both sides of the ball, but I didn't have a preference. So, I signed with the Bills prior to the NFL Draft, thinking at that point in time that I would be a defensive end."

However, a few weeks after signing with the Bills, Shaw realized that his path to success lay at offensive guard, recalling how he came to that conclusion: "We went to the College All-Star game, and I was playing on the defensive side of the ball behind Bob Lilly. I saw very quickly that I didn't match up on the defensive side of the ball like I thought I would. . . . Houston Antwine was the best defensive tackle I ever played against in the AFL, but, at the All-Star game, he was playing guard for our team, and he was stinking it up, probably more than I was stinking it up on the defensive side. So, coach [Otto] Graham changed us. He put me at offensive guard and Houston at defensive tackle. And our careers kind of took off from there. . . . That's where my career changed, at the College All-Star game."

Inserted at left guard immediately upon his arrival in Buffalo, Shaw ended up starting every game at that post as a rookie, displaying a considerable amount of potential, although he vastly improved his performance the following year under new head coach Lou Saban, who remembered, "We studied the films of his play after we took over that winter. He needed additional polishing to become a good player. That's when we decided to put him up against Tom Sestak every day in practice. He had to get better if he wanted to survive in that matchup. I told him, 'If you want to be the best, you have to go up against the best.'"

Claiming that his daily confrontations with Sestak helped make both men better players, Shaw said, "Those were some battles. I like to think that I had some influence in the way Tom progressed as a player, and he certainly was instrumental in my becoming a better player."

Developing into an elite blocker his second year in the league, Shaw gained AFL All-Star recognition for the first of eight straight times and received the first of his five consecutive First-Team All-AFL nominations. Playing between center Al Bemiller and left tackle Stew Barber, Shaw fit perfectly into Buffalo's offense, which, unlike most others in the pass-happy AFL, predicated much of its success on its powerful running game. A classic "pulling guard" who possessed good strength and outstanding speed, the 6'2", 258-pound Shaw proved to be particularly effective at leading Bills running backs downfield after creating holes for them at the line of scrimmage.

In discussing how the Bills' style of play suited him perfectly, Shaw stated, "Going to Buffalo was a blessing. We were one of the few AFL teams that looked like an NFL team. We didn't throw much; we ran. We had a fullback and a halfback, Cookie Gilchrist and Wray Carlton, who were pounders. Buffalo was the perfect fit."

Outstanding in pass-protection as well, Shaw held his own against some of the league's most physically imposing players, preventing giants such as Buck Buchanan, Ernie Ladd, and Earl Faison from getting to quarterback Jack Kemp, who later said, "Of all the offensive linemen I played with in my ten years, other than Ron Mix, my old roommate with the Chargers, Billy Shaw is the greatest lineman in the history of the American Football League. He ranked right there, parallel with Mix."

Referred to as "the driving force of the offensive unit" by former Bills offensive line coach Jerry Smith, Shaw also earned the respect and admiration of his teammates with the intensity, enthusiasm, and intelligence he displayed on the playing field, with Wray Carlton, who spent seven seasons running behind him, saying, "Billy was a hard-nosed competitor who didn't like to get beat. To me, he was a fullback playing guard. I think the greatest moment I'll always remember about Billy was the hole he blew open for me in a 1965 game against the Houston Oilers. I ran through it for 80 yards and a touchdown. And Billy was leading the way for me all the way. I was even having a problem keeping up with him the final 10 yards or so. That's how good of an athlete Billy was."

Shaw, who served as offensive captain of the Bills for six years, also proved to be an exceptional leader, although he led by example rather than by making speeches. In discussing his former teammate's leadership ability, Paul Maguire stated, "He was a great leader on and off the field. Everyone had respect for Billy."

Meanwhile, Ernie Warlick, one of the team's few Black players, said, "Off the field, Billy was one of the most genuine people you would ever want to meet. He got along with everyone. It set the example for the rest of the team. It didn't matter if you were Black or white. We all got along. The Bills of that era were a very close-knit team."

After starting every game that the Bills played his first six years in the league, Shaw underwent surgery for a torn knee ligament in July 1967 that forced him to miss the first five games of the regular season. However, after reclaiming his starting job upon his return to action, Shaw performed well enough from 1967 to 1969 to earn three more AFL All-Star selections and a pair of Second-Team All-AFL nominations. Choosing to announce his retirement following the conclusion of the 1969 campaign, just prior to the NFL/AFL merger, Shaw ended his career having appeared in 119 out of a possible 126 contests.

Following his playing days, Shaw became involved in the precast concrete business, first working as a manual laborer, before opening his own business in the mid-1970s. Eighty-four years old at the time of this writing, Shaw feels lucky to have experienced so much good fortune in life, saying, "I got a supporter or two and built a plant. That plant ended up being seven plants, and I sold my company in 2005 and retired. My string of fortunate opportunities existed after playing ball and kind of paralleled my playing career. Not many balls bounced the wrong way. . . . That was my life in football, that was my life in the business world. I made some of my own opportunities, but the good Lord put his arms around me."

## CAREER HIGHLIGHTS

**Best Season**

Shaw gained First-Team All-AFL recognition five straight times from 1962 to 1966, with the Bills annually placing near the top of the league rankings in total offense. A strong argument could certainly be made for identifying the 1964 campaign as Shaw's finest season since Buffalo finished first in the AFL in points scored (400), total yards gained, and rushing average (4.1 yards per carry). But the Bills also surrendered 50 sacks to the opposition. Meanwhile, even though the Bills tallied just 309 points two years earlier, they allowed far fewer sacks (32) and ran the ball much better, averaging a league-leading 5.0 yards per carry. Furthermore, they did so with a different quarterback starting for them behind center, with Warren Rabb serving as their primary signal-caller in 1962 and Jack Kemp directing the team in 1964. All things considered, it seems that Shaw and his line-mates performed their best in 1962.

**Memorable Moments/Greatest Performances**

- Starred during a 45-38 victory over the Denver Broncos on October 28, 1962, helping the Bills gain 199 yards on the ground and another 253 yards through the air.

- Helped the Bills rush for 306 yards and amass 405 yards of total offense during a 10-6 win over the Oakland Raiders on November 18, 1962.
- With his line-mates, dominated the Jets at the point of attack on December 8, 1963, helping the Bills amass 370 yards of total offense during a lopsided 45-14 victory, with 285 of those yards coming on the ground.
- Along with the rest of the offensive line, controlled the line of scrimmage against the Jets once again on October 24, 1964, with the Bills rushing for 180 yards and amassing 527 yards of total offense during a 34-24 win.
- Followed that up by helping the Bills gain a season-high total of 290 yards on the ground during a 24-10 victory over the Houston Oilers on November 1, 1964.
- With his line-mates, dominated the Oilers at the line of scrimmage once again on November 20, 1966, with the Bills amassing 508 yards of total offense during a 42-20 win.

### Notable Achievements

- Started eighty-four consecutive games from 1961 to 1966
- Three-time division champion (1964, 1965, and 1966)
- Two-time AFL champion (1964 and 1965)
- Eight-time AFL All-Star selection (1962, 1963, 1964, 1965, 1966, 1967, 1968, and 1969)
- Five-time First-Team All-AFL selection (1962, 1963, 1964, 1965, and 1966)
- Two-time Second-Team All-AFL selection (1968 and 1969)
- Pro Football Reference All-1960s First Team
- AFL All-Time First Team
- Inducted into Bills Wall of Fame in 1988
- Inducted into Pro Football Hall of Fame in 1999

# 6

# ANDRE REED

The most prolific receiver in franchise history, Andre Reed spent fifteen years in Buffalo, amassing more receptions, receiving yards, and touchdown catches than any other player to ever don the red, white, and blue. Known for his toughness and ability to run after the catch, Reed, who also ranks extremely high in team annals in yards from scrimmage, all-purpose yards, and points scored, proved to be a key weapon in the Bills vaunted no-huddle offense of the 1990s, making more than 80 receptions three times and accumulating more than 1,000 receiving yards on four separate occasions. A member of Bills teams that won six division titles and four AFC championships, Reed gained Pro Bowl recognition seven times and earned two All-Pro selections, before being further honored by gaining induction into both the Bills Wall of Fame and the Pro Football Hall of Fame.

Born in Allentown, Pennsylvania, on January 29, 1964, Andre Darnell Reed grew up with his three siblings in a strict household, learning the value of hard work from his father, Calvin, a construction worker, and mother, Joyce, who worked twelve-hour days sewing at the local garment factory. Unfortunately, Reed's dad suffered from alcoholism, with Andre saying years later that he "saw things growing up no child should see."

Turning to sports as a way of escaping his troubles, Reed played baseball, football, and basketball at the local Boys & Girls Club of America, before beginning his athletic career in earnest as a quarterback at Dieruff High School. Later crediting his high school football experience for much of the success he enjoyed as a pro, Reed claimed that evading the opposing team's pass rush helped him develop the agility and nimbleness he needed to play wide receiver.

After graduating from Dieruff High, Reed enrolled at nearby Division II Kutztown University, where he ended up setting nine school records at wide receiver, including most receptions (142), receiving yards (2,020), and touchdowns (14), en route to earning First-Team Eastern College Athletic

Andre Reed holds franchise records for most receptions, receiving yards, and touchdown catches.
Courtesy of George A. Kitrinos.

Conference honors twice. Nevertheless, Reed's small college background scared off many pro scouts, causing him to fall to the 4th round of the 1985 NFL Draft, where the Bills finally selected him with the 86th overall pick.

Despite being the thirteenth wide receiver taken in the draft, Reed made more of an impact than most of the other wideouts selected before him his first year in the league, finishing second on the Bills with 48 receptions and 637 receiving yards, while also making a team-high 4 TD catches. Continuing to perform well the next two seasons for mediocre Bills teams,

Reed totaled 110 receptions, 1,491 receiving yards, and 12 touchdowns, establishing himself in the process as the favorite target of new Buffalo quarterback Jim Kelly. With the Bills subsequently emerging as perennial Super Bowl contenders in 1988, Reed began an exceptional seven-year run during which he posted the following numbers:

1988: 71 Receptions, 968 Receiving Yards, 6 Touchdown Receptions
1989: 88 Receptions, 1,312 Receiving Yards, 9 Touchdown Receptions
1990: 71 Receptions, 945 Receiving Yards, 8 Touchdown Receptions
1991: 81 Receptions, 1,113 Receiving Yards, 10 Touchdown Receptions
1992: 65 Receptions, 913 Receiving Yards, 3 Touchdown Receptions
1993: 52 Receptions, 854 Receiving Yards, 6 Touchdown Receptions
1994: 90 Receptions, 1,303 Receiving Yards, 8 Touchdown Receptions

Consistently ranking among the NFL leaders in receptions, Reed finished as high as second in 1989, when he also placed near the top of the league rankings in receiving yards and TD catches. Named to the Pro Bowl all seven years, Reed also earned two Second-Team All-Pro nominations and four First-Team All-AFC selections. More importantly, the Bills advanced to the playoffs six times, won five division titles, and captured four AFC championships.

Although the 6'2", 200-pound Reed lacked elite speed, he possessed superior strength and exceptional quickness, making him extremely difficult to bring down once he gathered in the football. A master at gaining extra yards after the catch, Reed did most of his best work in the middle of the field, where he used his size, strength, and elusiveness to turn short gains into big plays.

In discussing Reed's proficiency in that area, Jim Kelly said, "I think he was one of the greatest ever to play the inside position at wide receiver. I knew throwing him a 5- or 6-yard pass, he could turn it into a 30-, 40-, 50-yard touchdown or a big run. . . . One-on-one, his strength, his run-after-catch ability was unmatched. I think he's definitely in the top three or four with run after catch ever. . . . The thing about Andre was when he was inside, it didn't matter if it was an 8-yard pass or a 12-yard pass; it was his effectiveness running after the catch. He was so good inside nobody could ever bump him; nobody could ever touch him."

Steve Tasker also addressed Reed's ability to gain huge chunks of yardage, saying, "He was really good at running the short route and turning it into a long gain. Jim [Kelly] loved it because it was an easy throw for a lot of yards. We all loved it because he could turn a nothing 5-yard completion into a 65-yard touchdown. That's what Andre's gift was."

Well-respected by the opposition, Reed drew praise from Hall of Fame defensive back Rod Woodson, who said, "He had the body, he had the strength. He was tough. He was elusive. He was hard to bring down, and you better bring him down or he was gone."

Meanwhile, four-time Pro Bowl cornerback Albert Lewis stated, "He helped define what we all know now as that slot position. And, in my opinion, the only guy who played that position better was Jerry Rice."

After being limited by a serious hamstring injury to just six games, 24 receptions, and 312 receiving yards in 1995, Reed returned to top form the following year, making 66 receptions for 1,036 yards and 6 touchdowns. However, although Reed remained one of the league's better receivers the next few seasons, his production declined steadily, bottoming out in 1999, when he caught just 52 passes, amassed only 536 receiving yards, and scored just 1 touchdown. Informed by the Bills at season's end that they planned to use him more as a backup moving forward, Reed asked for his release, after which he signed with the Denver Broncos.

Reed, who left Buffalo with career totals of 941 receptions, 13,095 receiving yards, 13,595 yards from scrimmage, 13,609 all-purpose yards, 86 TD catches, and 87 touchdowns, subsequently found himself buried on the depth chart in Denver, causing him to ask for his release once again. Signing with Washington shortly thereafter, Reed spent one season playing in the nation's capital, making just 10 receptions for 103 yards and 1 touchdown, before announcing his retirement. In addition to leaving the game as the NFL's third all-time leading receiver, Reed combined with Jim Kelly for 663 pass completions, which represented the highest total compiled by any quarterback/receiver tandem in league history at the time.

Following his playing days, Reed established his own line of food products he appropriately named "Over the Middle" and created the Andre Reed Foundation, which strives to help underprivileged youth reach their full potential and become responsible members of their community. Currently a Boys & Girls Clubs of America ambassador, Reed also occasionally appears as a guest analyst on ESPN or FOX Sports.

Looking back on the time he spent in Buffalo, Reed, whom Marv Levy called "maybe one of the most underrated receivers that ever played the game," says, "Yeah, we didn't win any Super Bowls. But you know what? That was the ride of my life. You couldn't get me off that ride. There will never be an assembly of players like that here again. Never. It will never be duplicated. I don't know if it will ever be duplicated in the NFL again."

# BILLS CAREER HIGHLIGHTS

## Best Season

Although Reed posted extremely comparable numbers in 1994 and caught one more touchdown pass in 1991, he had his finest all-around season in 1989, when he earned Second-Team All-Pro honors by ranking among the league leaders with 88 receptions, 1,312 receiving yards, and 9 touchdown catches.

## Memorable Moments/Greatest Performances

- Scored the first touchdown of his career when he gathered in an 18-yard pass from Vince Ferragamo during a 17-14 loss to the Patriots on September 22, 1985.
- Contributed to a 34-23 win over the Colts on October 9, 1988, by making 7 receptions for 124 yards and 2 TDs, which came on passes from Jim Kelly that covered 16 and 12 yards, respectively.
- Followed that up by making 7 receptions for 132 yards and 2 touchdowns during a 37-14 win over the Jets on October 17, 1988, with one of his scoring plays covering 65 yards.
- After collaborating with Jim Kelly on a 78-yard scoring play earlier in the contest, gave the Bills a 47-41 win over the Houston Oilers on September 24, 1989, when he hauled in a 28-yard touchdown pass from Kelly in overtime.
- Provided further heroics on October 16, 1989, when he gathered in an 8-yard TD pass from Frank Reich in the closing moments to give the Bills a 23-20 win over the Rams.
- Earned AFC Offensive Player of the Week honors by making 8 receptions for 116 yards and 2 touchdowns during a 30-27 win over the Jets on October 21, 1990.
- Helped lead the Bills to a 35-31 win over Miami in the 1991 regular-season opener by making 11 receptions for 154 yards and 1 TD, which came on a 54-yard pass from Jim Kelly.
- Helped the Bills build a 14-0 lead against Kansas City in a 1991 divisional round playoff game they went on to win by a score of 37-14 by collaborating with Jim Kelly on scoring plays that covered 25 and 53 yards.

- Contributed to a 41-7 blowout of the Patriots on September 27, 1992, by making 9 receptions for 168 yards and 1 touchdown, which came on a 45-yard pass from Jim Kelly.
- Played a huge role in the Bills' miraculous comeback against Houston in the 1992 AFC Wild Card Game that saw them overcome a 35-3 third-quarter deficit, making 8 receptions for 136 yards and 3 touchdowns.
- Proved to be too much for the Patriots to handle in the 1993 regular-season opener, making 6 receptions for 110 yards and 3 touchdowns during a 38-14 Bills win, with his longest scoring play covering 41 yards.
- Torched the Washington defensive secondary for 7 receptions, 159 yards, and 1 touchdown during a 24-10 Bills win on November 1, 1993, with his TD coming on a 65-yard connection with Jim Kelly.
- Earned AFC Offensive Player of the Week honors by scoring 2 touchdowns and establishing career-high marks with 15 receptions and 191 receiving yards during a 29-20 win over the Packers on November 20, 1994.
- Contributed to a 42-31 win over Miami on December 4, 1994, by making 3 receptions for 106 yards and 2 touchdowns, one of which came on a career-long 83-yard catch-and-run.
- Helped lead the Bills to a 23-20 overtime win over the Giants in the 1996 regular-season opener by making 5 receptions for 138 yards and 1 TD, which came on a 60-yard hookup with Jim Kelly.

**Notable Achievements**

- Surpassed 70 receptions five times, topping 80 catches on three occasions
- Surpassed 1,000 receiving yards four times
- Surpassed 1,000 yards from scrimmage five times
- Scored 10 touchdowns in 1991
- Finished second in NFL with 88 receptions in 1989
- Led Bills in receptions ten times and receiving yards nine times
- Holds Bills career records for most receptions (941), receiving yards (13,095), touchdown receptions (86), touchdowns (87), and games played (221)
- Ranks among Bills career leaders with 13,595 yards from scrimmage (2nd), 13,607 all-purpose yards (2nd), and 522 points scored (4th)
- Six-time division champion (1988, 1989, 1990, 1991, 1993, and 1995)

- Four-time AFC champion (1990, 1991, 1992, and 1993)
- Two-time AFC Offensive Player of the Week
- Seven-time Pro Bowl selection (1988, 1989, 1990, 1991, 1992, 1993, and 1994)
- Two-time Second-Team All-Pro selection (1989 and 1990)
- Four-time First-Team All-AFC selection (1989, 1990, 1991, and 1994)
- Inducted into Bills Wall of Fame in 2006
- Inducted into Pro Football Hall of Fame in 2014

# 7

## JOE DELAMIELLEURE

The cornerstone of Buffalo's famed "Electric Company" offensive line that helped O. J. Simpson establish himself as the NFL's premier running back during the 1970s, Joe DeLamielleure performed brilliantly for the Bills at right guard while starting every game they played from 1973 to 1979. A five-time Pro Bowler and five-time All-Pro, DeLamielleure received several other individual accolades during his time in Buffalo, before spending five years in Cleveland, where he earned one more Pro Bowl nomination and another two All-Pro selections. Later rejoining the Bills for one final season, DeLamielleure ended his thirteen-year playing career with a legacy that landed him a spot on the NFL 1970s All-Decade First Team and a place in the Pro Football Hall of Fame.

Born in Detroit, Michigan, on March 16, 1951, Joseph Michael DeLamielleure grew up with his nine siblings in nearby Warren, where his father, Alphonse, owned and operated the Victory Inn. Claiming that he acquired his strong work ethic from his father, DeLamielleure recalled, "Dad had a bar. I think it was 43 years that he worked it—from 7 in the morning to 2:30 at night, open seven days a week, except Thanksgiving, Christmas, and Easter. He taught me the meaning of work and what it meant. He was a dedicated dad who cared about his kids."

A fan of Detroit sports teams growing up, DeLamielleure emerged as a standout athlete at St. Clement High School, where he excelled in baseball, basketball, and football. Performing especially well as a fullback on the gridiron, DeLamielleure helped his team win the Detroit Catholic League's East Division championship, with St. Clement head coach Al Baumgart later saying, "Joe never gave up at anything. He always gave his best. An East Detroit coach once even called him an animal—but in a good way."

Recruited by several major colleges, DeLamielleure eventually narrowed his choices down to Michigan, Notre Dame, and Michigan State. Ultimately deciding to attend Michigan State on the advice of his father, DeLamielleure recalled, "I said, 'Dad, I want to go to Michigan,' and he

Joe DeLamielleure earned Pro Bowl and All-Pro honors five times each during his time in Buffalo.
Courtesy of RMYAuctions.com.

said, 'No, I don't want you to go there because I can't pronounce that guy's name [Michigan head coach Bo Schembechler].' Then I said, 'Ok, I'm going to Notre Dame.' He says, 'No that coach [Ara Parseghian] is a phony, a Protestant coaching at a Catholic school. You go to Michigan State—Duffy [Daugherty] is a Catholic.' That's how I ended up at Michigan State. True story."

A three-year starter for the Spartans, DeLamielleure earned All-Big Ten honors at guard three straight times and garnered All-America recognition his senior year, prompting both the Pittsburgh Steelers and Buffalo Bills to express interest in him heading into the 1973 NFL Draft, with DeLamielleure remembering, "The Steelers told me they were going to take me in the first round unless J. T. Thomas was available, and he was a cornerback. They said, 'If we don't do that, we're taking you with the first pick in the second round.' And that Steelers staff had three former Michigan State coaches on it at the time, including George Perles and Woody Widenhofer. So, I thought for sure I'd be going to Pittsburgh."

However, Bills owner Ralph Wilson, head coach Lou Saban, and offensive line coach Jim Ringo also held DeLamielleure in high esteem, especially after Saban and Ringo coached him at the Senior Bowl. Recalling his first experience with Saban and Ringo, DeLamielleure said, "I played guard the whole week in practice and then the day before the game coach Ringo came up to me and told me he was going to play me at right tackle for the game. I wasn't too happy about that, but Ringo said to me, 'Come on, you've played it before.' I told him, 'Yeah, for one week against Purdue.'"

DeLamielleure continued, "I wondered why the heck he was moving me to tackle. It kind of made me think that they didn't believe I could play and that they were moving me to tackle for the heck of it. Now looking back, I think they wanted to see how I would adjust and if I was versatile at all. . . . The guy I was going against in the game wound up being Wally Chambers. He was the eighth pick in the draft for the Bears that year, but he was also from Detroit, and I knew him my whole life. Fortunately, I had a pretty good game against him."

Ultimately selected by the Bills in the first round, with the 26th overall pick, DeLamielleure described the initial confusion surrounding his selection, saying, "Back then, the draft wasn't on TV, and it wouldn't have mattered anyway because on draft day I had a test. I had a five-credit class that I needed to pass to graduate in four years. I went to take my test, and it was a long one."

Revealing that he received a phone call shortly after he arrived home, DeLamielleure continued, "There's a voice on the other end that says, 'Hello, this is Mr. Wilson, and we took you in the first round.' So, I'm thinking everything is great, and the conversation was really brief, and I hung up the phone. Everything was such a blur, and I was so excited that I called my dad, and I told him, 'Hey, I just got drafted by the Steelers in the first round.' And my dad was going nuts. So, I hang up the phone again and the next call I get is from [*Buffalo News* columnist] Larry Felser."

Learning from Felser that he had actually been selected by the Bills, DeLamielleure, who did not know at the time that Ralph Wilson owned the team, later said, "Mr. Wilson didn't say Buffalo Bills, he just said they took me in the first round. Mr. Wilson always told me that I was his pick.

He had some inside knowledge on me because he was good friends with my college coach Jim Russell under [head coach] Duffy Daugherty."

Despite being hailed by Lou Saban as "the next Billy Shaw" after being drafted by the Bills, DeLamielleure nearly never made it to Buffalo after doctors determined two months later that an irregular heartbeat would likely prevent him from ever playing pro football. Refusing to accept their prognosis, DeLamielleure traveled to the renowned Cleveland Clinic, where he underwent corrective procedures that enabled him to embark on an extremely successful career during which he never missed a game until his final season.

Even though the immensely talented DeLamielleure laid claim to the starting right guard job as soon as he joined the Bills in 1973, he had to overcome further obstacles before he became a member of the NFL's elite, recalling, "I think Lou [Saban] liked me just because I played hard, but I was a basket case. I was too aggressive all the time when I played. If it wasn't for Coach Ringo coaching me, I'd have been getting too many personal fouls. He cooled me down. I just thank God that the Bills drafted me because Coach Ringo and Lou were good for me."

Flanked by center Mike Montler and right tackle Donnie Green most of his time in Buffalo, DeLamielleure soon became the most prominent member of an outstanding offensive line that also included left tackle Dave Foley and left guard Reggie McKenzie. Using his strength, quickness, and exceptional balance to outmaneuver defensive linemen, who often outweighed him by twenty or thirty pounds, the 6'3", 254-pound DeLamielleure excelled as both a straight-ahead and downfield blocker for the Bills' primary offensive weapon, O. J. Simpson, who experienced his greatest success running behind the Hall of Fame guard. Recognized for his contributions to Buffalo's offense, DeLamielleure received five consecutive Pro Bowl, All-Pro, and First-Team All-AFC nominations from 1975 to 1979, making him one of the decade's most decorated offensive linemen. Greatly respected by his opponents, DeLamielleure received high praise from Pittsburgh Steelers Hall of Fame defensive tackle "Mean" Joe Greene, who stated, "No one ever blocked me better than Joe DeLamielleure."

Nevertheless, with the Bills having posted a losing record in each of the previous four seasons, they traded DeLamielleure to the Cleveland Browns for a pair of high draft picks just prior to the start of the 1980 campaign. After developing a reputation with the Bills as arguably the league's best run-blocker, DeLamielleure displayed the totality of his game in Cleveland, with Larry Felser saying during his Hall of Fame induction ceremony, "By the end of his rookie season, Joe D had opened the holes through which

Simpson ran to set the NFL's then all-time seasonal rushing record. He was stuck with the great run blocker label for a number of years. But then he was traded to the Browns, was just brought up and joined the 'Kardiac Kids,' and became known as more than just a run blocker, as Brian Sipe and Cleveland led the NFL in passing. That didn't surprise Hall of Famer Jim Ringo, his offensive line coach in Buffalo. 'He's the best pass blocker I ever coached,' says Jim."

Continuing his string of consecutive starts in Cleveland, DeLamielleure appeared in seventy-three straight games with the Browns from 1980 to 1984, earning All-Pro and All-AFC honors twice each along the way. Released by the Browns in September 1985, DeLamielleure signed with the Bills, with whom he spent one final season assuming a backup role, before announcing his retirement at the end of the year.

In 1992, DeLamielleure returned to the game as community relations director for the Charlotte Rage of the Arena Football League. He later spent two seasons serving as offensive line coach at Liberty College and another five seasons coaching offensive linemen at Duke University. DeLamielleure also took a job as head football coach and head of athletic facilities at Providence Day School in Charlotte, North Carolina. He and his son started a moving company, while he also began another company, "Joe D Bands," which markets exercise stretch bands and other fitness products. A philanthropist at heart, DeLamielleure has also been involved in several charitable activities, including taking part in a two-thousand-mile bicycle ride from East Lansing, Michigan, to Mexico in 2009 to help raise money for an orphanage there. Four years later, DeLamielleure walked 213 miles from Orchard Park, New York, to the Pro Football Hall of Fame in Canton, Ohio, to raise awareness for Grace's Lamp, a Charlotte, North Carolina, organization that helps children afford the cost of new adult prosthetic legs once they grow out of their youth prosthetics.

Unfortunately, the seventy-two-year-old DeLamielleure, who now lives with his wife in Charlotte, North Carolina, has begun to display symptoms and has been diagnosed with chronic traumatic encephalopathy (CTE). The dreaded disease has been linked to depression, dementia, and memory loss. DeLamielleure received an estimated 225,000 blows to his head during his playing career, according to doctors at UCLA, causing him to suffer mood swings, sleeplessness, hearing loss in his left ear, and buzzing in his head for the last thirty years.

In discussing his condition, DeLamielleure says, "I know I have brain damage. You know you have some issues when you can't get it out of your head."

# BILLS CAREER HIGHLIGHTS

### Best Season

DeLamielleure performed exceptionally well in both 1973 and 1977, earning Co-Offensive Lineman of the Year honors from the 1,000-Yard Rusher Club in Columbus, Ohio, in the first of those campaigns, before being named the winner of the Forrest Gregg Award as the NFL's Top Offensive Lineman four years later. But DeLamielleure had the finest season of his career in 1975, when, in addition to being accorded Pro Bowl, All-Pro, and First-Team All-AFC honors for the first of five straight times, he gained recognition from the NFLPA as Offensive Lineman of the Year by helping the Bills lead the league in points scored (420), offensive yards (5,467), and rushing yards (2,974), with Buffalo running backs averaging a robust 5.1 yards per carry.

### Memorable Moments/Greatest Performances

- Helped the Bills rush for 259 yards during a convincing 31-13 victory over the Baltimore Colts on October 14, 1973.
- With he and his line-mates creating huge holes all day, the Bills threw the ball just twice during a 16-12 win over the Jets on September 29, 1973, gaining all of their 223 yards on the ground.
- His superior blocking at the point of attack helped the Bills rush for 349 yards and amass 468 yards of total offense during a 34-14 victory over the Patriots on December 14, 1975.
- He and the rest of Buffalo's offensive line enabled the Bills to rush for 266 yards and amass 446 yards of total offense during a 50-17 rout of the Chiefs on October 3, 1976.
- He and his cohorts turned in another dominant performance on November 26, 1978, with the Bills gaining 366 yards on the ground and amassing 465 yards of total offense during a lopsided 41-17 victory over the Giants.

### Notable Achievements

- Started 102 consecutive games from 1973 to 1979
- 1973 1,000-Yard Rusher Club NFL Co-Offensive Lineman of the Year
- 1975 NFL Players Association Offensive Lineman of the Year
- 1977 Forrest Gregg Award winner as NFL's Top Offensive Lineman

- Five-time Pro Bowl selection (1975, 1976, 1977, 1978, and 1979)
- Three-time First-Team All-Pro selection (1975, 1976, and 1977)
- Two-time Second-Team All-Pro selection (1978 and 1979)
- Five-time First-Team All-AFC selection (1975, 1976, 1977, 1978, and 1979)
- NFL 1970s All-Decade First Team
- Inducted into Bills Wall of Fame in 1997
- Inducted into Pro Football Hall of Fame in 2003

# 8

# JOSH ALLEN

mong the very best quarterbacks in the game today, Josh Allen has given the Bills the kind of play they have not seen since the days of Jim Kelly. An excellent passer, outstanding runner, and superb leader, Allen has started behind center for the Bills since he first arrived in Buffalo in 2018, serving as the central figure on teams that have made four playoff appearances and won three division titles. Along the way, Allen has garnered Pro Bowl recognition twice and All-Pro honors once and has earned one runner-up finish in the league MVP voting.

Born in the small San Joaquin Valley farming community of Firebaugh, California, on May 21, 1996, Joshua Patrick Allen grew up on a three-thousand-acre cotton farm located some forty miles west of Fresno, California. The descendant of Swedish immigrants who first settled in the United States during the Great Depression, Allen spent much of his youth working with his younger brother, Jason, on the family farm, hacking away weeds, digging ditches, and moving irrigation pipes.

Although Allen realized at an early age that his future lay in something other than farming, he drew inspiration from his father, saying years later, "I had, in my opinion, the greatest role model in the world in my dad. The things he did for our family to keep food on the table, he's a smart businessman and a hard worker. It's something that I look up to, how hard he works to support our family. Having to see your dad wake up before sunrise, coming home after sunset, and helping him in the 105-, 110-degree weather . . . there's no days off. It's something that's special to me, something that I believe has helped me get to where I am today."

Hoping to avoid working on the farm as much as possible, Allen, his brother, and two sisters remained active in sports, with Allen remembering, "Our out was sports and that's what we did. We stayed competitive year-round to try to stay off the farm as much as we could, though we did help out quite a bit."

Josh Allen has led the Bills to three straight division titles.
Courtesy of Keith Allison and All-Pro Reels Photography.

Although Allen competed in baseball, basketball, and soccer as well, he developed a particularly strong affinity for football, recalling, "Sitting there in our living room watching Monday Night Football, running around the living room table. Me and my brother made tracks around that. We'd run around it and my dad would throw us the ball while he was watching the game. There were a few dents in the walls, some broken cases, stuff like that."

After getting his start on the gridiron in the local youth leagues, Allen began to make a name for himself at Firebaugh High School, where, in his two seasons as starting quarterback, he threw for 5,269 yards and 59 touchdowns. Excelling in baseball and basketball as well, Allen featured a 90-mph fastball on the diamond and led the team in scoring on the hardwood.

Despite his athletic prowess, Allen garnered little interest from college recruiters, stating, "I had no offers because no one had ever come out of Firebaugh for football. It's not what we're known for, so coaches didn't get around to seeing much film, coaches didn't get out to see me in person."

Left with no other options, Allen enrolled at Reedley College, where he spent one year starting at quarterback, before an aggressive email campaign, waged by himself, resulted in him finally receiving a scholarship offer from the University of Wyoming. Looking back at the lack of interest he generated with his play on the field, Allen stated, "I couldn't believe it. I definitely had a chip on my shoulder any time I went to practice or worked out or stepped on the field. It was definitely a big motivating piece of why I played the game."

After missing most of his first season with a broken clavicle, Allen started behind center for the Wyoming Cowboys the next two years, compiling rather pedestrian numbers. But even though Allen completed just 56.2 percent of his passes, threw for 5,066 yards, and tossed 44 TD passes and 21 interceptions, he impressed pro scouts with his powerful throwing arm, superior athletic ability, and tremendous determination. Considered a top prospect by most teams for his "raw potential," Allen ended up being selected by the Bills with the seventh overall pick of the 2018 NFL Draft after they completed a trade with the Tampa Bay Buccaneers that allowed them to move up five spots in the first round.

Following his arrival in Buffalo, Allen spent most of training camp and the 2018 preseason competing for playing time with A. J. McCarron and Nathan Peterman, before laying claim to the starting job in Week 2 of the regular season. Experiencing the usual growing pains of most rookie quarterbacks, Allen finished his first NFL season with 2,074 passing yards, 10 touchdown passes, 12 interceptions, a 52.8 pass completion percentage, and a 67.9 passer rating, although he also ran for 631 yards and 8 TDs. Far more accurate in 2019, Allen completed 58.8 percent of his passes, posted a passer rating of 85.3, and threw for 3,089 yards and 20 touchdowns, while also running for 510 yards and 9 TDs, with his solid play leading the Bills to a record of 10-6 that earned them a wild card playoff berth.

Often praised his first two years in the league for his superior arm strength, exceptional athleticism, and mental toughness, Allen also drew occasional criticism for his gunslinger's mentality, which caused him to take unnecessary risks at times. But, with the help of former Bills offensive coordinator Brian Daboll and quarterback coach Ken Dorsey, Allen displayed tremendous maturity and greater awareness as a passer in 2020, earning a runner-up finish in the NFL MVP voting and garnering Pro Bowl, Second-Team All-Pro, and NFL Most Improved Player honors by placing near the top of the league rankings with 4,544 passing yards, 37 touchdown passes, a pass completion percentage of 69.2, and a passer rating of 107.2, with the first two figures both establishing new single-season franchise records.

Signed to a six-year contract extension worth up to $258 million prior to the start of the ensuing campaign, Allen proved his worth in 2021 by throwing for 4,407 yards and 36 touchdowns, completing 63.3 percent of his passes, posting a passer rating of 92.2, and running for 763 yards and 6 touchdowns, becoming in the process the first quarterback in NFL history to amass more than 100 touchdowns passes and 30 rushing TDs his first four years in the league. Although the Bills failed to advance to the Super Bowl, losing to Kansas City in overtime by a score of 42-36 in the divisional round of the playoffs after routing New England, 47-17, in the opening round, Allen performed magnificently in both contests, posting a composite passer rating of 149.0 that represents the highest mark ever compiled in a single postseason.

Blessed with tremendous physical ability, the 6'5", 240-pound Allen possesses great size, strength, and mobility, all of which make him extremely difficult to bring down whenever he decides to run with the football. A gifted runner who is not afraid to take on would-be tacklers in the open field, Allen drew comparisons to longtime Pittsburgh Steelers quarterback Ben Roethlisberger from Aaron Donald, who said, "He's a big guy. He's a tough guy. He's athletic. In my opinion, he's like a futuristic Big Ben. A little bit more athletic, can move a little bit better. But he's a guy that ain't gonna go down easy, so you gotta come with your big boy pads when you get to wrap him up."

Also known for his arm strength, mental fortitude, leadership skills, and ability to overcome adversity, Allen has been likened to Hall of Fame quarterbacks John Elway and Brett Favre for his excellence in those areas, with NBC's Chris Simms stating during a March 2022 interview with WKBW-TV in Indianapolis, "You can win without a great quarterback, I think that gets overblown, at times. But when the team doesn't play as well, or you're playing a team that's a mismatch against you, or you've got a few injuries, when you've got a guy like Josh Allen, he can cover those holes. That's what he does, let alone gives the team confidence every time they step on the field. . . . That's why I love him. I've said this a few times, he's the best player in football."

Simms continued, "To me, the last two years, he's outplayed Patrick Mahomes. I think those are the two best players in the game right now, and if you made me choose one, I'd go Josh Allen, and there's nobody better in the league right now. He's the best player in the NFL."

Meanwhile, former NFL quarterback and coach Jordan Palmer said of Allen, "I think he's the most physically talented player to play the position . . . ever."

A quality person as well, Allen is involved in several charitable causes, including the Fresno, California, chapter of the Leukemia & Lymphoma Society, where his sister works in fund-raising, and the Jessie Rees Foundation, which assists children fighting cancer. Allen is also a huge supporter of the John R. Oishei Children's Hospital in Buffalo, frequently visiting patients at the facility, making donations, and serving as a spokesperson to help fund-raising efforts.

Extremely committed to the western New York community, Allen expressed his love for the city of Buffalo and its fans during a 2022 interview with Colin Cowherd on his radio show, *The Herd*, saying, "I love this place. It's my home now. I love playing for Bills Mafia. I think it is the greatest football city in America. People just love football here, and they love their Bills. I am honored and proud to be in Buffalo."

Although Allen struggled somewhat at times during the 2022 season, ranking among the league leaders with 14 interceptions and committing far too many red-zone turnovers, he ended up posting excellent numbers once again, leading the Bills to their third straight division title by throwing for 4,283 yards and 35 touchdowns, while also running for 762 yards and 7 TDs. Unfortunately, the season once again ended in disappointing fashion for Allen and the Bills, who subsequently lost to the Cincinnati Bengals, 27-10, in the divisional round of the playoffs. Yet with Allen, who currently boasts career totals of 18,397 yards passing, 138 touchdown passes, 3,087 yards rushing, and 39 touchdowns scored, a pass-completion percentage of 62.5, and a passer rating of 92.2, running their offense, the Bills seem poised to capture their fifth AFC championship at some point in the near future.

## BILLS CAREER HIGHLIGHTS

### Best Season

Although Allen also compiled excellent numbers in each of the last two seasons, he proved to be a bit more consistent in 2020, when, in addition to setting single-season franchise records by passing for 4,544 yards and 37 touchdowns, he established career-best marks with a 69.2 pass-completion percentage and a 107.2 passer rating, threw only 9 interceptions, gained 421 yards on the ground, and ran for 8 touchdowns, earning in the process a runner-up finish to Aaron Rodgers in the NFL MVP balloting.

### Memorable Moments/Greatest Performances

- Performed well in his first start as a pro, running for two scores and completing 15 of 22 pass attempts for 196 yards and 1 touchdown during a 27-6 win over the Minnesota Vikings on September 23, 2018.
- Earned AFC Offensive Player of the Week honors for the first time by throwing for three touchdowns and running for two more during a lopsided 42-17 victory over the Miami Dolphins in the final game of the 2018 regular season.
- Earned that distinction again by throwing for 256 yards and 3 touchdowns, carrying the ball seven times for 56 yards, and scoring a TD on an 8-yard run during a 37-20 win over the Dolphins on November 17, 2019.
- Threw for more than 300 yards for the first time in his career in the opening game of the 2020 regular season, when he led the Bills to a 27-17 victory over the Jets by passing for 312 yards and 2 touchdowns, while also running for 57 yards and 1 TD.
- Topped that performance one week later, earning AFC Offensive Player of the Week honors for the third time by throwing for 415 yards and 4 touchdowns during a 31-28 win over the Dolphins on September 20, 2020, with his longest TD pass of the day coming on a 46-yard connection with John Brown.
- After the Bills blew a 25-point third-quarter lead, he gave them a 35-32 victory over the Los Angeles Rams on September 27, 2020, by hitting Tyler Kroft with his fourth touchdown pass of the day from 3 yards out with only 15 seconds remaining in regulation.
- Despite being sacked seven times, he led the Bills to a 44-34 win over the Seattle Seahawks on November 8, 2020, by running for 1

touchdown and completing 31 of 38 pass attempts for 415 yards and 3 TDs, with his strong performance gaining him recognition as AFC Offensive Player of the Week.

- Earned that distinction again by completing 32 of 40 pass attempts for 375 yards and 4 touchdowns during a 34-24 win over the San Francisco 49ers on December 7, 2020.
- Led the Bills to a convincing 48-19 victory over the Denver Broncos on December 19, 2020, by running for 2 scores and throwing for 359 yards and 2 touchdowns, earning in the process AFC Offensive Player of the Week honors once again.
- Helped the Bills earn their first postseason victory in twenty-five years by running for 1 touchdown and throwing for 324 yards and 2 TDs during a 27-24 win over the Indianapolis Colts in the 2020 AFC Wild Card game.
- Gained recognition as AFC Offensive Player of the Week by running for 1 score and throwing for 358 yards and 4 touchdowns during a 43-21 victory over the Washington Football Team on September 26, 2021.
- Led the Bills to a 45-17 win over the Jets on November 14, 2021, by passing for 366 yards and 2 touchdowns.
- Helped lead the Bills to a lopsided 47-17 victory over the Patriots in the wild card round of the 2021 AFC playoffs by rushing for 66 yards and completing 21 of 25 pass attempts for 308 yards and 5 TDs, the longest of which came on a 34-yard hookup with Emmanuel Sanders.
- Although the Bills subsequently suffered a heartbreaking 42-36 overtime loss to the Kansas City Chiefs in the divisional round of the 2021 postseason tournament, he turned in one of the finest performances of his young career. In a memorable contest that featured three lead changes in the final two minutes of regulation, Allen, who finished the game with 329 passing yards, 4 touchdown passes, and 68 yards rushing, led the Bills on two long scoring drives during the latter stages of the fourth quarter, giving them a 36-33 lead with just thirteen seconds left by tossing his second TD pass to Gabriel Davis in less than two minutes. However, after needing only two plays to get the Chiefs in field goal range, Patrick Mahomes led his team on a 75-yard scoring drive on the first possession of overtime that culminated with a game-winning 8-yard touchdown pass to Travis Kelce.
- Led the Bills to a 41-7 rout of the Tennessee Titans on September 19, 2022, by throwing for 317 yards and 4 touchdowns, tossing three of his TD passes to Stefon Diggs and the other to Reggie Gilliam.

- Earned AFC Offensive Player of the Week honors by throwing for 424 yards and 4 touchdowns during a convincing 38-3 win over the Pittsburgh Steelers on October 9, 2022, with his 98-yard TD strike to Gabriel Davis in the first quarter representing the longest pass play in franchise history.
- Earned that distinction again the following week by passing for 329 yards and 3 touchdowns during a 24-20 win over the Chiefs in Kansas City, giving the Bills the victory with a 14-yard TD pass to Dawson Knox with just 1:04 left in the final period.
- Garnered AFC Offensive Player of the Week honors for the third time in 2022 by throwing for 304 yards and 4 touchdowns, carrying the ball 10 times for 77 yards, and leading the Bills on two fourth-quarter scoring drives during their 32-29 win over Miami in Week 15.

**Notable Achievements**

- Has passed for more than 4,000 yards three times
- Has thrown more than 30 touchdown passes three times
- Has completed more than 60 percent of passes three times
- Has posted touchdown-to-interception ratio of better than 2-1 four times
- Has posted passer rating above 90.0 three times, finishing with mark above 100.0 once
- Has rushed for more than 500 yards four times
- Has scored 9 touchdowns twice
- Holds NFL record for highest passer rating in a single postseason (149.0 in 2022)
- Holds Bills single-season records for most passing yards (4,544 in 2020), TD passes (37 in 2020), rushing yards by a quarterback (763 in 2021), and rushing TDs by a quarterback (9 in 2019)
- Ranks among Bills career leaders with 2,566 pass attempts (3rd), 1,604 pass completions (3rd), 18,397 passing yards (3rd), 138 touchdown passes (3rd), 38 rushing touchdowns (3rd), and 39 touchdowns (tied for 6th)
- Three-time division champion (2020, 2021, and 2022)
- Ten-time AFC Offensive Player of the Week
- Two-time AFC Offensive Player of the Month
- 2020 NFL Most Improved Player

- Finished second in 2020 NFL MVP voting
- Two-time Pro Bowl selection (2020 and 2022)
- 2020 Second-Team All-Pro selection

# 9
# CORNELIUS BENNETT

Acquired by the Bills in one of the most famous trades in franchise history, Cornelius Bennett spent parts of nine seasons in Buffalo, proving to be a huge contributor to teams that won six division titles and four AFC championships. An exceptional all-around linebacker who earned AFC Defensive Player of the Year honors twice, Bennett not only holds the franchise record for most fumble recoveries, but also ranks extremely high in team annals in tackles, sacks, and forced fumbles. A five-time Pro Bowler, one-time All-Pro, and six-time All-AFC selection, Bennett later received the additional honor of being named to the NFL 1990s All-Decade Second Team, after splitting his final five seasons between the Atlanta Falcons and Indianapolis Colts.

Born in Birmingham, Alabama, on August 25, 1965, Cornelius O'Landa Bennett grew up in the city's crime-ridden Ensley neighborhood, where his strong mind-set helped him to remain focused on his studies in school. Always big for his age, Bennett, who acquired the nickname "Biscuit" because of his fondness for baked bread, said his mother, "was 11 pounds, 4 ounces at birth, and he just kept getting bigger and bigger."

Unable to compete in the local youth leagues because of his size, Bennett had to settle for watching the games from the sidelines, with his mother recalling, "He was so hurt when they told him he couldn't play. He loved football. He was always talking about it or watching in on TV. But when the other kids went to play, he had to tag along with his brother and be the water boy."

Revealing the hurt he felt at the time, Bennett said, "I remember being very disappointed. The other kids brought home their uniforms at the beginning of the season and their trophies at the end. I remember being the only kid on the block who didn't get to go to a banquet at the end of the year. I was left out."

Nevertheless, Bennett learned how to play the game from his older brother, Curtis, a standout high school player in Birmingham who later

Cornelius Bennett earned AFC Defensive Player of the Year honors twice.
Courtesy of RMYAuctions.com.

played quarterback at Alabama A&M. Crediting much of the success he experienced later in life to his brother, Bennett stated, "I owe at least half of what I have to my brother. He always had time for me. He always encouraged me. When the other kids were playing [in the youth league], he would always take me out in the street and teach me how to throw and how to tackle and how to block."

Eventually emerging as a star on the gridiron at Ensley High School, which first began integrating in September 1964, Bennett played running back on offense and linebacker, end, and cornerback on defense, typically lining up across from the opposing team's best player. But, while Bennett excelled in football, he failed to display the same skill in other sports, with former Ensley High School football coach Steve Savarese saying of his one-time protégé, "He was at both ends of the spectrum as a high school athlete. He was the best football player in the state, a role player on the basketball team, and a benchwarmer on the baseball team. But it never seemed to matter to him. He just wanted to be part of the game."

Offered a football scholarship to the University of Alabama after rushing for 1,099 yards and catching 12 touchdown passes as a senior at Ensley, Bennett signed with the Crimson Tide a month after Ray Perkins replaced the recently retired Paul "Bear" Bryant as head coach. Performing exceptionally well under Perkins the next four years, Bennett gained All-America recognition three straight times by recording 287 tackles and 21.5 sacks. Particularly outstanding his senior year, Bennett registered 10 sacks and 9 other tackles for loss, earning in the process SEC Player of the Year honors and a seventh-place finish in the Heisman Trophy voting. Also named the winner of the Lombardi Award as the nation's top college lineman or linebacker, Bennett later received high praise from Perkins, who said, "He was the Lawrence Taylor of college football and the most dominating defender I've ever coached."

Meanwhile, Steve Savarese commented, "There's no question in my mind that if Alabama would have played him on offense, he would be as good a runner as Bo Jackson. He had the same speed, the same power, the same moves."

Selected by the Indianapolis Colts with the second overall pick of the 1987 NFL Draft, Bennett balked at the idea of going to Indianapolis, making it extremely difficult for the two sides to come to terms on a contract. With negotiations continuing well into October and Eric Dickerson also in the middle of a contract dispute with the Rams, Bills general manager Bill Polian spearheaded a massive three-team trade that sent the future Hall of Fame running back from Los Angeles to Indianapolis, Bennett from Indianapolis to Buffalo, and running back Greg Bell and three high draft picks from Buffalo to Los Angeles.

Joining the Bills midway through the 1987 campaign, just two weeks after the players' strike ended, Bennett said upon his arrival in Buffalo, "The strike helped me. The players lost three weeks, so I'm not as far behind in football shape. . . . I've been playing serious basketball at Alabama, so I'm ready."

Acquitting himself extremely well the final two months of the season after being inserted at left-outside linebacker, Bennett recorded 69 tackles, forced 5 fumbles, and finished second on the team with 8.5 sacks, earning in the process a spot on the NFL All-Rookie team.

His confidence buoyed by his strong performance, Bennett said prior to the start of the 1988 season, "I think I'll be able to do a lot more than I did last year. I'm just beginning to figure out how the pro game is played. I didn't get a chance to learn last year. By learning the system and not thinking so much on the field, I'll probably be a step faster than I was last year."

Bills defensive coordinator Walt Corey also looked forward to even bigger things from Bennett, stating in an article that appeared in the September 2, 1988, edition of the *Chicago Tribune*, "He has the height and weight, the strength and quickness, the intelligence and intensity to do more than any linebacker who has ever played. It will be interesting to see how far he goes."

Corey continued, "I've worked with a lot of linebackers over the years. I coached two Hall of Famers (Bobby Bell and Willie Lanier). I worked with Jack Ham and Ted Hendricks and Jack Reynolds at the College All-Star Game. They will be Hall of Famers, too, but Cornelius is a different breed from those guys. Lawrence Taylor is, too, but he's not as fast."

Living up to the hype, Bennett helped lead the Bills to their first division title in eight years by recording 103 tackles, 9.5 sacks, 2 interceptions, 3 forced fumbles, and 3 fumble recoveries, with his superb play earning him Pro Bowl, First-Team All-AFC, First-Team All-Pro, and AFC Defensive Player of the Year honors. Also named NFL Defensive Player of the Year by United Press International (UPI), Bennett received high praise during the season from New York Jets fullback Roger Vick, who, when asked to rank the league's best pass rushers, said, "I'll put L. T. [Lawrence Taylor] first, then [Andre] Tippett, and Bennett behind him."

Continuing to perform at an elite level the next seven seasons, Bennett earned four more trips to the Pro Bowl and another three First-Team All-AFC nominations, in helping the Bills win five more division titles and four AFC championships. Particularly outstanding in 1991, Bennett once again gained recognition as AFC Defensive Player of the Year by registering 107 tackles, 9 sacks, and 4 forced fumbles.

Blessed with tremendous natural ability, the 6'2", 237-pound Bennett possessed the strength to defend against the run at the line of scrimmage and the speed to pursue ball carriers from sideline to sideline and cover backs coming out of the backfield. Meanwhile, Bennett's quickness, power, and tenacity made him an extremely effective edge rusher. Commenting on the manner with which Bennett contributed to the success the Bills experienced during his time in Buffalo, Bruce Smith said, "We wouldn't have been able to accomplish our incredible run and pretty much having a foothold in the history books without Cornelius Bennett."

After recording a team-high 104 tackles in 1995, Bennett chose to leave Buffalo and sign with the Atlanta Falcons as a free agent. Bennett, who, in his nine years with the Bills, registered 52.5 sacks, 793 tackles, 6 interceptions, forced 22 fumbles, recovered 19 others, and scored 3 touchdowns, spent the next three seasons in Atlanta, never quite attaining the same level of success, before ironically spending his final two seasons with the Indianapolis Colts. Announcing his retirement following the conclusion of the 2000 campaign, Bennett ended his career with 1,190 tackles, 71.5 sacks, 31 forced fumbles, 27 fumble recoveries, 7 interceptions, and 3 TDs.

Unfortunately, Bennett ran afoul of the law shortly after he left the Bills. He was accused of sexually abusing a woman he had previously dated while in town to attend an event honoring Jim Kelly. Accused of committing "rape, sodomy, sexual abuse, and unlawful imprisonment" in his room at the Hyatt Regency in downtown Buffalo, Bennett pleaded guilty to a misdemeanor charge of sexual misconduct and received a sentence of sixty days in jail, a $1,000 fine, a $617.26 hospital bill, one hundred hours of community service, and anger management and substance abuse counseling.

Expressing his regrets at his sentencing hearing in February 1998, Bennett apologized to the victim, telling her he "didn't intend to put us in the situation that we're in now."

Bennett also told the judge, "This is the first time in my life I've ever had to go through anything like this. I just wish I could take back that evening altogether."

Although the NFL did not fine or suspend Bennett for his horrific behavior, the Bills have chosen not to be as lenient, to this point excluding him from their Wall of Fame.

Since committing his crime, Bennett, who now lives in Hollywood, Florida, with his second wife, Kimberly, seems to have turned his life around. As a member of the NFL Players Association for nearly fifteen years, Bennett has helped secure $620 million in funding for the league's Legacy Fund, which is paid to former athletes who played before 1993. He also runs charity golf tournaments in South Florida and his hometown of Birmingham, Alabama.

In recent years, Bennett has also become an ordained deacon with the First Baptist Church Piney Grove, in Lauderdale Lakes, Florida. Prior to accepting Bennett, the church ran a background check on him that led to a one-on-one conversation with Pastor Derrick Hughes about his guilty plea. In discussing their meeting, Hughes told the *Buffalo News*, "I came away convinced he is not that person. He convinced me of that in multiple ways. I watched his consistency. I watched him in worship. He has focused his life to be useful in the lives of others. Christianity is about how God can turn things around and give us another opportunity. He has seized that opportunity."

## BILLS CAREER HIGHLIGHTS

### Best Season

Bennett performed magnificently for the Bills in 1991, earning AFC Defensive Player of the Year honors by recording a career-high 107 tackles, registering 9 sacks, forcing 4 fumbles, and recovering two others, one of which he returned for a touchdown. But, in addition to also being named AFC Defensive Player of the Year in 1988, Bennett earned his lone First-Team All-Pro nomination by making 103 tackles, recording a career-high 9.5 sacks, picking off 2 passes, forcing 3 fumbles, and recovering 3 others, with his exceptional play helping the Bills capture the division title for the first of four straight times.

### Memorable Moments/Greatest Performances

- Recorded the first sack of his career when he brought down John Elway behind the line of scrimmage during a 21-14 win over the Denver Broncos on November 8, 1987.
- Earned AFC Defensive Player of the Week honors for the first of seven times by recording 17 tackles, forcing 3 fumbles, and sacking Randall Cunningham four times during a 17-7 loss to the Philadelphia Eagles in the final game of the 1987 regular season, prompting Bills defensive coordinator Walt Corey to tell reporters afterward, "They ought to put a film of that in a time capsule."
- Contributed to a 13-10 win over the Minnesota Vikings in the 1988 regular-season opener by recording a sack and an interception.
- Earned AFC Defensive Player of the Week honors after registering 2.5 sacks during a 28-0 shutout of the Green Bay Packers on October 30, 1988.

- Turned in another outstanding effort almost exactly one year later, recording a sack and intercepting a Dan Marino pass during a 31-7 win over the Dolphins on October 29, 1989.
- Helped lead the Bills to a 37-0 rout of the Jets in the final game of the 1989 regular season by recording an interception and 2 sacks.
- Scored the first points of his career when he returned a blocked field goal attempt 80 yards for a touchdown during a 29-28 win over the Broncos on September 30, 1990.
- Earned AFC Defensive Player of the Week honors by recording 2 sacks during a 34-28 victory over the Los Angeles Raiders in the Bills' next game on October 7, 1990.
- Earned that distinction again by registering 2 sacks during a 17-10 win over the Tampa Bay Buccaneers on September 22, 1991.
- Contributed to a 41-27 victory over the Dolphins on November 18, 1991, by recording a sack and returning a fumble 6 yards for a touchdown.
- Helped lead the Bills to a 16-7 win over the Patriots on November 1, 1992, by recording 2.5 sacks.
- Sacked John Elway twice during a 27-20 victory over the Broncos on September 26, 1994, earning in the process AFC Defensive Player of the Week honors.
- Scored the last of his three career touchdowns when he ran 69 yards to paydirt after intercepting a Drew Bledsoe pass during a 35-26 loss to the Patriots on November 26, 1995.

**Notable Achievements**

- Scored 3 touchdowns
- Recorded more than 100 tackles four times
- Recorded more than 8 sacks three times
- Finished second in NFL with 5 forced fumbles in 1987
- Led Bills in tackles twice and sacks once
- Holds Bills career record for most fumble recoveries (19)
- Ranks among Bills career leaders with 22 forced fumbles (2nd), 793 tackles (4th), and 52.5 sacks (5th)
- Six-time division champion (1988, 1989, 1990, 1991, 1993, and 1995)
- Four-time AFC champion (1990, 1991, 1992, and 1993)
- Member of 1987 NFL All-Rookie team
- Seven-time AFC Defensive Player of the Week
- October 1988 AFC Defensive Player of the Month

- Two-time AFC Defensive Player of the Year (1988 and 1991)
- Two-time United Press International NFL Defensive Player of the Year (1988 and 1991)
- Five-time Pro Bowl selection (1988, 1990, 1991, 1992, and 1993)
- 1988 First-Team All-Pro selection
- Four-time First-Team All-AFC selection (1988, 1990, 1991, and 1992)
- Two-time Second-Team All-AFC selection (1989 and 1994)
- NFL 1990s All-Decade Second Team

# 10

# KENT HULL

dentified by longtime teammate Steve Tasker as "the greatest center in Bills history," Kent Hull served as one of the key figures in the no-huddle offense the Bills ran during their Super Bowl years of the early 1990s. A huge contributor to teams that won six division titles and four AFC championships, Hull missed just two nonstrike games his eleven years in Buffalo, earning three Pro Bowl selections and four All-Pro nominations. Later accorded the additional honor of being inducted into the Bills Wall of Fame, Hull accomplished all he did as a member of the team after spending his first three professional seasons playing in the short-lived United States Football League (USFL).

Born in Pontotoc, Mississippi, on January 13, 1961, James Kent Hull grew up some one hundred miles southwest, in Greenwood, Mississippi, where he and his younger brother, Maury, helped their father manage the family farm, with Hull recalling, "We'd spend all day getting worn out chasing those cows."

Forced to assume numerous odd jobs to help support his family after his parents separated, Hull bagged groceries, worked at a tire store, and managed the Army Corps of Engineers' local flood levee, while also attending Greenwood High School, where he starred in football and basketball. Offered a basketball scholarship to LSU, Hull, who played quarterback, inside linebacker, and tight end at Greenwood High before finally moving to the offensive line his senior year, instead accepted a football scholarship to Mississippi State University. Explaining years later why he chose football over basketball, his favorite sport, Hull told former *Buffalo News* sportswriter Vic Carucci in 1990, "I grew up thinking I was going to be in the NBA. Then the game got so tall, and I got so slow."

Hull subsequently spent four years anchoring the Bulldogs offensive line from his center position, before signing with the New Jersey Generals after they selected him in the 7th round of the 1983 USFL Draft. Performing at an extremely high level the next three years, Hull helped Herschel

Kent Hull helped the Bills run their famed "no-huddle" offense to perfection.

Walker gain more than 1,000 yards on the ground each season, with Walker's 2,411 rushing yards in 1985 setting a single-season professional record that still stands.

Despite his outstanding play for the Generals, Hull, who had originally been ranked as a 7th- to 10th-round prospect by most NFL scouts, remained uncertain about his ability to compete at a higher level, stating, "I look at my career—even in the USFL they were very skeptical about me, coming out of a wishbone offense [in college]. . . . When I was with the Generals, people told me I could play in the NFL. But still, there was that question in my mind because I had never played in the NFL."

However, when the USFL folded at the end of the 1985 season, Hull received offers from nine different NFL teams. Choosing to sign with the Bills, whose new head coach, Marv Levy, had seen him play while coaching in the USFL, Hull joined the team the same day as Jim Kelly, whom the Bills welcomed to Buffalo by parading him around the city on a motorcade.

Meanwhile, Hull witnessed the festivities from the back of an equipment truck.

An immediate starter upon his arrival in Buffalo, Hull performed well his first year in Orchard Park, recalling, "I was doing a lot of right things the first year. But I noticed real quick I needed some more strength to stay with those blocks longer."

Adding some twenty pounds of muscle onto his 6'5" frame over the course of the next two seasons, Hull, who spent most of his career playing at close to 280 pounds, became known before long as one of the league's strongest players, with teammate Will Wolford stating, "He may be the only center in the league strong enough to handle any nose tackle one on one."

Having established himself as an elite performer, Hull earned All-Pro honors four straight times from 1988 to 1991, a period during which he displayed his intelligence and tremendous versatility by adapting extraordinarily well to the no-huddle offense the Bills adopted in 1990. Forced to assume a whole new set of responsibilities, Hull had to call out the blocking assignments from the shotgun formation and work in tandem with Jim Kelly, who called the plays at the line of scrimmage.

In discussing the integral role that Hull played in the operation of the no-huddle, Steve Tasker said, "The no-huddle would not have worked had we not had Kent at center. He was brilliant at quickly diagnosing defensive fronts and making blocking calls that put us in matchups that would enable a play to succeed. . . . He was so intelligent, there were times when he would look back and have Jim alter a play call. Jim trusted him implicitly."

Revealing the extent to which he depended on Hull, Kelly stated, "His impact was huge. He put guys in the right places. He was so smart in how he did things and set up his blocks. Thurman got used to seeing his blocks, reading his blocks, and how Kent engineered the running game."

Meanwhile, Marv Levy expressed his appreciation for everything Hull brought to the team by saying, "He was as bright as can be. The responsibility of seeing that our difficult-to-run-but-vaunted no-huddle offense ran smoothly rested just as heavily upon the physical and mental abilities of Kent Hull as it did upon those of our quarterbacks. . . . Kent was the ultimate teammate, and I loved coaching him. He could block 300 pounds of dynamite. Consistency was his long suit, and he was as dependable a guy as you can imagine. He was always prepared. He had no ego and his teammates liked him. He was the best center in the league for quite a while."

An outstanding team leader who spent his final seven seasons in Buffalo serving as an offensive captain, Hull also drew praise for his leadership ability from Steve Tasker, who stated, "He became the quarterback of our offensive line and one of the smartest and most respected guys in the locker room. When he spoke in that thick-as-Mississippi-mud drawl of his, guys listened. . . . I think guys respected him not only for his brains and toughness, but also for his honesty and humility. He wasn't afraid to point a finger at himself and say he had screwed up, and neither was he afraid to call out someone who wasn't doing his job."

Darryl Talley added, "He didn't yell or scream. But when he spoke, people listened. . . . He'd just shake his head, look at you, and sit down to talk. And you damn well listened. He was a very old soul who was really calming in a storm. . . . You can't hide what you are in the locker room. You can't be a phony. I remember a bunch of times thinking to myself, 'What Kent said is what I should think.' I adopted his opinions as my own."

Talley also spoke of Hull's toughness and ability to play through pain, saying, "I called him 'Tough' because he was one of the toughest guys I ever saw. He dealt with pain on a consistent basis. But it didn't matter. He knew he had a job to do, and he was going to do it. He'd get hurt and say, 'I can't come out of the damn game.' He instilled that mentality in the rest of the O-linemen. He held them to that standard."

Hull continued to start at center for the Bills until the end of 1996, when he announced his retirement. Making his decision known to the public on December 30, 1996, just two days after the Bills suffered a 30-27 loss to the Jacksonville Jaguars in the wild card round of the AFC playoffs, Hull told the assembled media, "It's been a great ride. I had an opportunity to play with Hall of Fame players, and for Hall of Fame coaches. And, without a doubt, for the greatest fans in the world."

After retiring from football, Hull, who started 170 of the 172 contests the Bills played during his time in Buffalo, returned to Mississippi, where he worked extensively on his cattle ranch. He also became heavily involved in the United Negro College Fund and the Make-A-Wish Foundation, giving much of himself to both causes, before sadly passing away at only fifty years of age from gastrointestinal bleeding, on October 18, 2011.

Upon learning of his former teammate's passing, Andre Reed said, "He was bigger than life, and I don't think he really got his just due, even though he went to some Pro Bowls. He was one of the best. . . . Kent was a soft-spoken guy, and he was one of the smartest guys I ever met too. I'm sad for his family, and all the people who knew him. He's going to be missed as a friend."

Thurman Thomas also spoke fondly of his former teammate, saying, "I owe a lot of that stitching in my Hall of Fame jacket to Kent Hull. Our hearts are broken. Myself, my wife Patti and our four children send our love and prayers to his wonderful family. He was my teammate, a brother, and a best friend. He will be in my heart forever."

## BILLS CAREER HIGHLIGHTS

### Best Season

Hull played his best ball for the Bills from 1988 to 1991, earning All-Pro honors all four years. With the Bills scoring a franchise-record 458 points in 1991, Buffalo running backs averaging a robust 4.7 yards per carry, and Hull being named First-Team All-Pro for the second straight time, we'll identify the 1991 campaign as the finest of his career.

### Memorable Moments/Greatest Performances

- Helped the Bills rush for 292 yards and amass 451 yards of total offense during a 30-7 win over the Jets on September 24, 1990.
- His exceptional play at the point of attack helped the Bills amass 493 yards of total offense during a 44-34 victory over the Miami Dolphins in the divisional round of the 1990 playoffs.
- Helped the Bills gain a total of 502 yards on offense during a 51-3 blowout of the Los Angeles Raiders with his dominant play up front in the 1990 AFC Championship Game.
- Allowed the Bills, along with his cohorts, to rush for 262 yards and amass 433 yards of total offense during a 41-27 victory over the Dolphins on November 18, 1991.
- Helped the Bills amass 490 yards of total offense during a lopsided 41-7 victory over the Patriots on September 27, 1992, with 182 of those yards coming on the ground and the other 308 through the air.

### Notable Achievements

- Missed just two nonstrike games his entire career, starting 170 out of 172 contests
- Six-time division champion (1988, 1989, 1990, 1991, 1993, and 1995)
- Four-time AFC champion (1990, 1991, 1992, and 1993)
- Three-time Pro Bowl selection (1988, 1989, and 1990)
- Two-time First-Team All-Pro selection (1990 and 1991)
- Two-time Second-Team All-Pro selection (1988 and 1989)

- Four-time First-Team All-AFC selection (1988, 1989, 1990, and 1991)
- 1995 Second-Team All-AFC selection
- Inducted into Bills Wall of Fame in 2002

# 11
# FRED SMERLAS

One of the more colorful characters ever to wear the red, white, and blue, Fred Smerlas helped anchor the Bills defense from his nose tackle position for more than a decade, combining with linebackers Shane Nelson and Jim Haslett much of that time to form the famed and feared "Bermuda Triangle" that became known for swallowing up opposing ball carriers. A member of the Bills for eleven seasons, Smerlas started every nonstrike game they played in the last ten of those, with this strong play up front making him a huge contributor to teams that won three division titles and made four playoff appearances. A five-time Pro Bowler and two-time All-Pro, Smerlas also earned six All-AFC nominations and a place on Pro Football Reference's All-1980s First Team, before being further honored by being inducted into the Bills Wall of Fame.

Born in Waltham, Massachusetts, on April 8, 1957, Frederic Charles Smerlas got his start in organized football at Waltham High School, where, in addition to starring as a two-way lineman on the gridiron, he won the New England heavyweight wrestling championship his last two years. Offered an athletic scholarship to Boston College after earning All-American honors in both sports twice at Waltham, Smerlas subsequently spent his college career playing for mostly mediocre teams, with the Eagles failing to win a single game his senior year.

Nevertheless, Smerlas performed extremely well at defensive tackle for Boston College, prompting both the Bills and the Tampa Bay Buccaneers to express serious interest in him during the early stages of the 1979 NFL Draft. Ultimately selected by the Bills in the 2nd round, with the 32nd overall pick, Smerlas recalled being told by the Buccaneers that they planned to bring him to Florida when the Bills claimed him for themselves, remembering, "They [Tampa Bay] told me, 'We can't believe you're still here,' and then they say, 'Oh, Buffalo took you!'—and slam down the phone."

Fred Smerlas served as the central figure in the Bills' feared "Bermuda Triangle" defense.

Smerlas revealed that he then received a phone call from Buffalo head coach Chuck Knox, who told him, "I hear you're a mean (expletive). I want you to come up here and kick some (expletive) ass."

Later explaining the reasoning behind his selection of Smerlas, Knox stated, "We had a guy coming to the Bills that we knew would never quit on us. Norm Pollum [Buffalo's chief scout at the time] had told me that he had never seen a player like Fred before."

Knox continued, "You have to remember that Fred came from a college team that had not won a game in his senior year. Yet the scouts that saw Fred play all had the same report. And that was that, despite how bad his team might be losing in the fourth quarter, Fred would still be coming on with every play. With that kind of play on such a poor team, we knew that we had a guy that wouldn't give up on anything when we got him."

After spending the first several weeks of the 1979 campaign assuming a backup role in Buffalo's new 3-4 defensive scheme, Smerlas replaced Mike Kadish as the starting nose tackle during the season's second half. Performing well the rest of the year, Smerlas earned a spot on the NFL All-Rookie team by recording 57 tackles, registering 2 sacks, and recovering 3 fumbles, one of which he returned 13 yards for a touchdown. Taking his game up a notch the following year, Smerlas helped the Bills win their first division title since 1966 by excelling against the run, while also recording 6.5 sacks for the league's top ranked defense, with his stellar all-around play gaining him Pro Bowl and All AFC-recognition for the first of four straight times.

Although the Bills posted just one winning record over the course of the next seven seasons, they consistently fielded one of the league's better defenses, largely because of Smerlas, whose ability to occupy multiple blockers improved the play of others around him. Doing most of the dirty work inside, Smerlas faced double-team blocking on almost every play, freeing up the linebackers to make tackles and the ends to record sacks. Standing 6'3" and weighing close to 300 pounds, Smerlas proved to be a master of leverage, a trait he acquired while wrestling in high school and college. Making good use of his knowledge and strength to overpower centers and control the heart of the Bills defense, Smerlas received high praise from former teammate, Steve Tasker, who wrote in his book *Steve Tasker's Tales from the Buffalo Bills*, "Fred was an unmovable object up front—an incredibly powerful 300-pounder who would tie up blockers so others could make tackles. He made it to the Pro Bowl five times doing the grunt work on the defensive line that often goes overlooked. Centers hated seeing him lined across from them."

Helping to revolutionize the position of nose tackle with his unusual combination of size, strength, and athleticism, Smerlas served as the blueprint for players who manned his post, with rival coaches often using game film of his technique to train their own nose tackles. Extremely durable as well, Smerlas started 149 consecutive nonstrike games from 1980 to 1989, making him one of the league's true iron men.

In addition to his many contributions on the playing field, Smerlas entertained fans and motivated teammates with his outgoing persona that made him the Bills' most quotable player, with longtime *Buffalo News* sportswriter Vic Carucci, who collaborated with him on the 1990 book *By A Nose: The Off-Center Life of Football's Funniest Lineman*, saying, "He was the go-to-quote for everyone."

Meanwhile, Steve Tasker stated, "Fred was/is the most outspoken teammate I ever had. But he was also a great leader. He loved his team, his town, and the game like no one else, and we all knew it. He had the ability to listen and learn from everyone, and he wasn't afraid to admit that, while he was sometimes wrong, he was never in doubt."

Persevering through the dark days of the mid-1980s, Smerlas helped the Bills win consecutive division titles in 1988 and 1989, earning the last of his five Pro Bowl nominations in the first of those campaigns and All-AFC honors both years. But, after Smerlas experienced differences with head coach Marv Levy, the latter left him unprotected on the Plan B free-agent list at the end of 1989. Electing to sign with the San Francisco 49ers, Smerlas unfortunately left Buffalo just before the Bills began their extraordinary four-year run as AFC champions.

Smerlas ended up spending just one injury-marred season in San Francisco, appearing in only six games for the 49ers in 1990, before serving the New England Patriots as a part-time player the next two years. Choosing to announce his retirement following the conclusion of the 1992 campaign, Smerlas ended his career with 29 sacks, 10 fumble recoveries, 2 interceptions, and 1 touchdown, compiling all those numbers during his time in Buffalo.

Since retiring from football, Smerlas, who currently resides in Massachusetts, has been involved in various business ventures, stating during a 2019 interview, "When I retired, I knew no one was going to give me handouts, so I started my own business—I do telemarketing, I do entertainment, I own a television show and market that, I do a postgame show for the Patriots on WEEI, and I'm in real estate. You know, I do a little bit of everything."

Sixty-six years of age at the time of this writing, Smerlas admits to feeling the painful side effects of two hundred games played and twenty-seven surgeries, saying, "I was at my doctor's, and he said, 'You're the only player that I've ever known who's been through what you've been through and doesn't take any medication, and is still alive.' I don't sleep. I stay up until two or three in the morning and then I go to bed for a couple of hours. Then I watch some TV some more until I get out of bed. So, that's a little difficult."

Nevertheless, Smerlas says that he has no regrets over pursuing a career in football, stating, "I look at the gifts that I have because of it. I wouldn't have met my wife. It gave me so much, and it gives a lot of these guys so much. The thing I remember most is the camaraderie in the locker room. I was captain for like six or seven years, so I really got to know some phenomenal people. I still talk to the guys all the time—Fat Benny, (Jim) Richter, (Mark) Kelso, Shane (Conlan), Tasker. Kent Hull was a sweetheart. Kelly, of course, all the time. Thurm the Germ. Talley and I are very close. . . . And I never would have met those guys if I didn't end up in Buffalo."

## BILLS CAREER HIGHLIGHTS

### Best Season

Although Smerlas gained First-Team All-Pro recognition for the only time in 1982, he had the finest season of his career in 1980, when he recorded a career-high 6.5 sacks en route to earning First-Team All-AFC honors for the first of four times and a top-five finish in the NFL Defensive Player of the Year voting.

### Memorable Moments/Greatest Performances

- Scored the only points of his career when he returned a fumble 13 yards for a touchdown during a 46-31 win over the Jets on September 23, 1979.
- Anchored a Bills defense that allowed just 39 yards rushing and 148 yards of total offense during a 31-13 victory over the Patriots on October 26, 1980.
- Contributed to a 31-27 win over the Jets in the 1981 AFC wild card game by sacking Richard Todd twice.
- Led a smothering Bills defense that surrendered just 36 yards rushing and 88 yards of total offense during a 20-0 shutout of the Colts on November 28, 1982.
- Proved to be a tremendous force up front during a 13-0 win over the Steelers on December 12, 1982, recording 2 sacks and anchoring a defense that allowed just 94 yards of total offense.
- Helped lead the Bills to a 30-13 victory over the Houston Oilers on September 25, 1983, by recording a career-high 3 sacks.
- Helped the Bills begin the 1988 campaign on a positive note by sacking Wade Wilson twice during a 13-10 win over the Minnesota Vikings in the regular-season opener.
- Earned AFC Defensive Player of the Week honors by recording a sack, blocking a potential game-winning field goal attempt, and doing an outstanding job of clogging up the middle against the run during a 9-6

overtime victory over the Jets on November 20, 1988, that clinched the division title for the Bills.

### Notable Achievements

- Missed just three nonstrike games in eleven seasons, starting 149 consecutive contests
- Scored one defensive touchdown
- Ranks among Bills career leaders with 10 fumble recoveries (tied for 6th)
- Three-time division champion (1980, 1988, and 1989)
- Member of 1979 NFL All-Rookie team
- 1988 Week 12 AFC Defensive Player of the Week
- Finished second in 1980 NFL Defensive Player of the Year voting
- Five-time Pro Bowl selection (1980, 1981, 1982, 1983, and 1988)
- 1982 First-Team All-Pro selection
- 1983 Second-Team All-Pro selection
- Four-time First-Team All-AFC selection (1980, 1981, 1983, and 1988)
- Two-time Second-Team All-AFC selection (1982 and 1989)
- Pro Football Reference All-1980s First Team
- Inducted into Bills Wall of Fame in 2001

# 12
## ERIC MOULDS

A victim of bad timing, Eric Moulds joined the Bills in 1996, three years after their extraordinary Super Bowl run of the early 1990s ended. Moulds also had the misfortune of playing with Jim Kelly for just one season, spending his other nine years in Buffalo catching passes from far less accomplished quarterbacks. Nevertheless, Moulds established himself as one of the most potent offensive weapons in franchise history during his ten years in Orchard Park, helping the Bills advance to the playoffs three times by amassing the second-most receptions, receiving yards, and touchdown catches in team annals. A three-time Pro Bowler and two-time All-Pro, Moulds surpassed 80 receptions and 1,000 receiving yards four times each, setting along the way single-season franchise records in both categories that stood for close to two decades.

Born in Lucedale, Mississippi, on July 17, 1973, Eric Shannon Moulds displayed an affinity for basketball as a youngster, before he began focusing on football during his teenage years at the suggestion of his grandfather. Recalling how he got his start on the gridiron, Moulds said, "As an eighth grader, I played on the high school basketball team and I was like, 'Grand-daddy, I'm pretty good in basketball, and I'm going into my sophomore year.' He said, 'I don't want to watch basketball. I'm a football guy.' That's how I got into football."

A McDonald's All-American in basketball at Lucedale's George County High School, Moulds received scholarship offers from hardwood power-houses Duke, Kentucky, and Georgetown. However, with Moulds also having developed into a standout wide receiver in his final three seasons at George County, virtually every school in the SEC recruited him for his skills on the gridiron. Ultimately choosing to accept a football scholarship to Mississippi State University, Moulds based his decision on a number of factors, saying years later, "I fell in love with how close all the players were at Mississippi State, so I wanted to be a part of that. . . . I could've gone to one of those places that got a lot of national exposure, but I always saw a

Eric Moulds ranks second in franchise history in every major pass-receiving category.

lot of Mississippi guys leave the state. I've always said, if we can keep our guys in-state, we could build something special."

Adding that he never expected to become such a highly sought-after commodity when he first took up the sport, Moulds stated, "I wanted to be a high school player and wind up doing that. I started getting all these offers and thought to myself, 'What can I really do if I apply myself?' It was one of those things that I felt like, 'If I go to Mississippi State or go to college and just be a pretty good player, I'll be happy and get a degree.' Once I got the opportunity, I wanted to make the most of it."

Making the most of his opportunity, Moulds spent three seasons starting for the Bulldogs at wide receiver, earning First-Team All-SEC honors twice by making 118 receptions for 2,022 yards and 17 touchdowns. Excelling on special teams as well, Moulds, who also ran track in college, returned 29 kickoffs for 828 yards, averaging in the process almost 29 yards per return.

Singing the praises of Moulds years later, former Mississippi State head coach Jackie Sherrill said, "Size, speed, maturity, and football knowledge, Eric Moulds had it all. I was fortunate to have some great ones who had many years in the NFL, but Eric was the best overall. He won so many games for his teams, first at State, and then at Buffalo in the NFL."

Selected by the Bills in the 1st round of the 1996 NFL Draft, with the 24th overall pick, Moulds spent his first year in Buffalo returning kickoffs and serving as a backup wide receiver, earning a spot on the NFL All-Rookie Team by amassing 1,528 all-purpose yards and scoring 3 touchdowns, one of which came on a 97-yard kickoff return. After assuming a similar role the following season, Moulds displaced Quinn Early as the full-time starter opposite Andre Reed in 1998, beginning in the process an outstanding five-year run during which he posted the following numbers:

1998: 67 Receptions, 1,368 Receiving Yards, 9 Touchdown Receptions
1999: 65 Receptions, 994 Receiving Yards, 7 Touchdown Receptions
2000: 94 Receptions, 1,326 Receiving Yards, 5 Touchdown Receptions
2001: 67 Receptions, 904 Receiving Yards, 5 Touchdown Receptions
2002: 100 Receptions, 1,292 Receiving Yards, 10 Touchdown Receptions

A Pro Bowler in three of those five seasons, Moulds also received two Second-Team All-Pro nominations and earned First-Team All-AFC honors in 1998, when his 1,368 receiving yards set a new single-season franchise record that stood until Stefon Diggs established a new mark in 2020. Four years later, Moulds became the first Bills player to make 100 receptions in a season, setting in the process another franchise record that Diggs eventually broke.

Although Moulds excelled throughout the period, he took special pride in his 1998 performance, saying, "I averaged 20 yards a catch, and it's only a handful of guys that have done it in NFL history. It was extremely difficult to do, and you got to make a lot of people miss and make plays. It was exciting because Doug Flutie was a small version of Josh Allen and kept plays alive. He could make every throw, and if he was 6'2", he would be in the Hall of Fame."

Blessed with good size, excellent speed, and soft hands, the 6'2", 220-pound Moulds possessed all the physical tools necessary to succeed in the NFL. But he also proved to be an extremely hard worker who managed to reach elite status despite playing with eight different starting quarterbacks during his time in Buffalo. In comparing his situation to that of Indianapolis Colts wide receiver Marvin Harrison, Moulds, whose signal-callers included Jim Kelly, Todd Collins, Doug Flutie, Rob Johnson, Alex Van Pelt, Drew Bledsoe, Kelly Holcomb, and J. P. Losman, stated, "Marvin knows what to expect every week. . . . He knows Peyton [Manning] is going to look for him. He knows Peyton is probably the best in the game at making adjustments during games. I'm in a situation that's a little different. I've had different quarterbacks and had to adjust to their style. It's a little tough, a little frustrating."

Appearing in only thirteen games in 2003 due to injury, Moulds made 64 catches for just 780 yards and 1 touchdown. However, he rebounded the following year to catch 88 passes, amass 1,043 receiving yards, and score 5 touchdowns. Although Moulds posted solid numbers again in 2005, concluding the campaign with 81 catches, 816 receiving yards, and 4 TDs, the Bills traded him to the Houston Texans for a 5th-round draft pick in April 2006 after he refused to restructure his $10 million contract.

Revealing that he never wanted to leave Buffalo, Moulds recalled, "I always said I wanted to finish what I started. I saw a lot of turnaround. I saw a lot of young players come in. I saw them draft Peerless Price. I saw them draft Lee Evans. Even when the trade happened, people were like, 'Oh, you wanted to leave Buffalo.' It wasn't that situation at all. I didn't really want to leave Buffalo. I was asked to go make a decision and I said, 'If you guys don't want me, just trade me.' Even at that point, I was still going to other teams and looking around, but I said if Buffalo wants me back, that's where I want to go first. That's what I told my agent. It didn't work out that way."

Moulds, who, in his ten years with the Bills, caught 675 passes, scored 49 touchdowns, and amassed 9,096 receiving yards, 9,253 yards from scrimmage, and 11,405 all-purpose yards, ended up spending just one season in Houston, making 57 receptions for 557 yards and 1 touchdown in 2006, before being released at the end of the year. Moulds subsequently signed with the Tennessee Titans, for whom caught 32 passes and accumulated 342 receiving yards in a part-time role in his final NFL season. Released by the Titans following the conclusion of the 2007 campaign, Moulds announced his retirement, ending his career with 764 receptions, 9,995 receiving yards, 10,158 yards from scrimmage, 12,310 all-purpose yards, and 50 touchdowns.

Following his playing days, Moulds moved to Charlotte, North Carolina, where he opened a training facility to work with athletes from high school and the NFL. He claims that doing so helps him to remain close to the game. Moulds said, "There's a lot about football I don't miss, but I miss the camaraderie of the locker room and the relationships you have with your teammates. My business still connects me to that. I enjoy it."

Moulds added, "You can show a kid that doesn't know how to be fundamentally sound how to play the game, be smart, and become a better player. You're doing yourself a discredit if you don't really get involved in young kids' lives because they are the future of the game."

Still holding the city of Buffalo close to his heart, Moulds stated during a 2018 interview, "Buffalo's my second home. It's one of those things where you get addicted to the city, the people, the culture. That's why I like Buffalo so much. It has so much culture, so many different personalities. Obviously, the main reason is it's a football city. Bills fans are football crazy."

Moulds continued, "I played in a lot of cities, I played against a lot of players, and I've been to cities where I've gone around with players in their cities where they're famous and they're friends of mine and I'm like, 'This is not like Buffalo.' The fans are sitting on their hands and drinking wine. Buffalo fans are not like that—they feel like they're a part of the game, they have passion for the game. It was an attractive thing for me as a player. I played in the SEC and it's like that in the Southeastern Conference because football is religion. It's like that in Buffalo, too. . . . Buffalo is still in my heart, and I'm still a Buffalo Bills fan. That's the way it will always be."

## BILLS CAREER HIGHLIGHTS

### Best Season

Moulds earned Pro Bowl and Second-Team All-Pro honors for the first time in 1998 by catching 67 passes, scoring 9 touchdowns, and finishing second in the league with 1,368 receiving yards. He had another huge year in 2000, earning his second trip to the Pro Bowl by making 94 receptions for 1,326 yards and 5 TDs. But Moulds posted slightly better overall numbers in 2002, when he gained All-Pro recognition for the second time by accumulating 1,292 receiving yards and establishing career-high marks with 100 receptions and 10 touchdowns.

## Memorable Moments/Greatest Performances

- Scored the first TD of his career when he returned a kickoff 97 yards during a 35-10 win over the Jets on November 24, 1996.
- Went over 100 receiving yards for the first time as a pro when he made 5 receptions for 145 yards and 2 touchdowns during a 30-14 victory over the Carolina Panthers on October 25, 1998, collaborating with Doug Flutie on scoring plays that covered 20 and 82 yards.
- Starred in defeat during a 25-21 loss to the Patriots on November 29, 1998, making 8 receptions for 177 yards and 1 TD, which came on a career-long 84-yard catch and run.
- Helped lead the Bills to a 33-20 win over Cincinnati on December 6, 1998, by making 6 receptions for 196 yards and 2 TDs, the longest of which covered 70 yards.
- Performed brilliantly in the 1998 AFC wild card game, catching 9 passes for 240 yards and 1 TD during a 24-17 loss to the Miami Dolphins, with his 240 receiving yards setting an NFL single-game playoff record that still stands.
- Contributed to a 27-24 overtime victory over the San Diego Chargers on October 15, 2000, by making 11 receptions for 170 yards.
- Starred in defeat again on November 25, 2001, catching 6 passes for 196 yards and 2 touchdowns during a 34-27 loss to the Dolphins, with his TDs coming on a pair of long connections with Alex Van Pelt that covered 80 and 54 yards.
- Although the Bills ended up losing their 2002 regular-season opener to the Jets in OT by a score of 37-31 on a 96-yard kickoff return by Chad Morton, Moulds sent the game into overtime by gathering in a 29-yard TD pass from Drew Bledsoe with just 26 seconds left in regulation.
- Contributed to a 38-31 win over Miami on December 1, 2002, by catching 6 passes for 130 yards and 1 TD, which came on a 57-yard connection with Drew Bledsoe.

## Notable Achievements

- Surpassed 80 receptions four times, catching 100 passes in 2002
- Surpassed 1,000 receiving yards four times
- Surpassed 1,000 all-purpose yards six times
- Scored 10 touchdowns in 2002
- Returned 1 kickoff for a touchdown
- Averaged more than 20 yards per reception once

- Finished second in NFL in receiving yards once and yards per reception once
- Led Bills in receptions seven times and receiving yards eight times
- Ranks among Bills career leaders with 675 receptions (2nd), 9,096 receiving yards (2nd), 9,253 yards from scrimmage (4th), 2,128 kickoff-return yards (4th), 11,401 all-purpose yards (4th), 48 touchdown receptions (2nd), 49 touchdowns (4th), and 298 points scored (11th)
- Member of 1996 NFL All-Rookie Team
- Three-time Pro Bowl selection (1998, 2000, and 2002)
- Two-time Second-Team All-Pro selection (1998 and 2002)
- 1998 First-Team All-AFC selection

## 13
# DARRYL TALLEY

The heart and soul of Bills teams that won five division titles and four AFC championships, Darryl Talley spent twelve years in Buffalo, recording more tackles during that time than any other player in franchise history. Known for his toughness and tremendous work ethic, Talley appeared in every nonstrike game the Bills played from 1983 to 1994, starting most of those at right-outside linebacker. Among the team's all-time leaders in forced fumbles, fumble recoveries, and sacks as well, Talley gained Pro Bowl and First-Team All-AFC recognition twice each, before being further honored by being inducted into the Bills Wall of Fame.

Born in Cleveland, Ohio, on July 10, 1960, Darryl Victor Talley attended Shaw High School in East Cleveland, where he starred on the gridiron at fullback and linebacker. Lightly recruited since he missed the last seven games of his senior year with a broken ankle, Talley ultimately accepted a football scholarship to West Virginia University. A four-year starter at linebacker for the Mountaineers, Talley registered 484 tackles and 19 sacks during his college career, performing especially well his senior year, when he earned consensus First-Team All-America honors.

Selected by the Bills in the 2nd round of the 1983 NFL Draft, with the 39th overall pick, Talley spent his first year in Buffalo playing on special teams and assuming a part-time role on defense, initially experiencing difficulties on that side of the ball, with longtime Bills athletic trainer Eddie Abramoski recalling, "He was a second-round draft pick, but not playing like it. In one game in particular he was struggling, and at halftime the defensive coaches were getting on him pretty good. We had Talley fitted out for contact lenses when he took his physical after the draft. When the coaches stopped yelling at him, I asked Darryl if he was wearing his contact lenses."

When Talley replied he wasn't, Abramoski ordered him to put them in, adding, "Things got better for him right after that."

Darryl Talley registered more tackles than anyone else in team annals.

Starting at left-outside linebacker the next three seasons, Talley performed well for losing Bills teams, playing some of the best ball of his career in 1986, when he recorded 116 tackles, 3 sacks, and 1 interception. Shifted to right-outside linebacker in 1987, Talley remained at that post for the next eight years, a period during which he established himself as an indispensable member of one of the league's better defenses. In addition to continuing his streak of consecutive starts that eventually reached 140 games, Talley led the Bills in tackles five times from 1989 and 1994, registered 6 sacks once, and once recorded a team-high 5 interceptions.

Noted for his speed and intensity, the 6'4", 235-pound Talley, whose nicknames included "The Duke of Awesome," "Spider-Man," and "The Hammer," excelled in all phases of linebacker play. A stout run-defender who led the Bills in tackles a total of seven times, Talley also did an out-standing job of covering backs downfield and applying pressure to opposing quarterbacks.

More than anything, though, Talley became known for his toughness and tremendous leadership ability, with Bruce Smith, who credited his close friend for helping him improve his work habits during the early stages of his career, calling him, "the greatest teammate a person could ever have."

Meanwhile, longtime teammate Steve Tasker spoke of Talley's tough-ness, saying, "I played with and against a lot of tough guys in the NFL, but nobody had a higher pain threshold than Darryl Talley. He'd be out there with broken bones and torn muscles and strained ligaments, and you wouldn't hear a peep from the guy. You could count on him every Sunday."

Tasker continued, "I'd be on the sideline, watching him play at his usual high level, and our trainer, Eddie Abramoski, would come up to me and say, 'I can't believe Darryl's even in uniform today.' When Abe said something like that, you took heed because nobody had a better read on tough Bills through the years than he."

And, as for Talley's leadership skills, Tasker said, "Everybody—and I mean everybody—on the team respected Darryl, and they feared him too. Nobody wanted to mess with him. He clearly was one of our leaders, and he was not afraid to speak his piece when he believed it was necessary. He'd tell Bruce Smith to shut up and sit down, and he'd pull Jim [Kelly] aside and say, 'Jim, you can't do that. You've got to knock it off.' And Jim and Bruce and all the other stars would listen to him and take his words to heart."

In discussing the attitude that he took with him to the playing field, Talley told WVNews, "I just figured I was going to play as hard as I could play for as long as I could play. I was going to leave my legacy on the field. I wasn't going to talk a whole lot; I was just going to do a lot. . . . You take your hard hat and your lunch bucket, and you go to work. You try to out-work everybody on the field, and you hold everybody on your team to that same standard. That's the way I played."

Earning the respect of his opponents as well with the no-nonsense approach he took to his craft, Talley received praise from Jerry Rice, who stated, "I like the fact that he's about winning. He's not about showboating, or who's getting the glory, or who's making the plays. To me, that's a person giving of himself."

After registering more than 100 tackles in each of the previous five seasons, Talley signed with the Atlanta Falcons as a free agent following the conclusion of the 1994 campaign. Before leaving Buffalo, though, Talley placed an ad in the sports section of a local newspaper, thanking the city's fans for their support by saying: "In leaving Buffalo, I want to express my sincerest thanks to everyone who has made my 12 years here the most memorable time of my life. I will go away only with fond memories. I realize that not all players have the privilege to play for such a successful franchise in such a great city. Those four Super Bowls will live on in my memories and in my family's memories forever. . . . To the people of Buffalo, thanks for making me feel like one of your own. I hope that Atlanta is as welcoming. Finally, to the Buffalo Bills organization and to my teammates, what can I say? You were simply the best. On behalf of my family, thanks for the memories. It was my honor. Darryl Talley."

Talley, who left Buffalo with career totals of 1,137 tackles, 38.5 sacks, 11 interceptions, 179 interception-return yards, 14 forced fumbles, 12 fumble recoveries, and 2 touchdowns, ended up spending just one season in Atlanta, recording 73 tackles for the Falcons in 1995, before retiring one year later after making another 51 stops for the Minnesota Vikings in 1996.

Settling in Central Florida following his playing days, Talley initially experienced financial success, establishing a thriving barricades business, before a series of bad decisions left him broke and dejected. With Talley having lost his business and home, a story appeared in the *Buffalo News* in November 2014 that shed light on his sad situation, with Tim Graham writing, "He's often depressed beyond the point of tears. He's bitter at the National Football League for discarding him and denying that he's too disabled to work anymore. He says the Bills have jilted him, too. He learned after he retired that he'd played with a broken neck. He had a heart attack in his 40s. He lost his business. The bank foreclosed on the Talleys' home of 17 years. Against her husband's pride, Janine Talley has accepted money from friends to pay the bills. He contemplates killing himself."

Graham continued, "'I've thought about it,' Darryl Talley flatly said last month on the patio of the house he and Janine rent. 'When you go through the shit that I've gone through, you start to wonder: Is this really worth it? Is it worth being here, worth being tortured anymore.'"

However, Talley could not bring himself to abandon his wife and two daughters, saying, "I was not willing to check out and leave them here to fend for themselves."

Ultimately choosing to accept the help of others, Talley overcame his depression and financial woes after lifelong Bills fan Frank Thomas Croisdale set up a GoFundMe page called "Circle the Wagons for Darryl Talley." The fund raised $153,479 for the Talley family, which remained together through all the adversity. Expressing his appreciation to his wife, Janine, for sticking with him through thick and thin, Talley told the *Orlando Sentinel* in 2018, "I honor and cherish her because a lot of folks would have walked away. That let me know I did do one thing right: I picked a good woman, and I will never forget her for that."

Talley, who now lives with his wife in Dallas, Texas, has spent the last several years serving as an ambassador for the NFL legends community of players, which strives to help former players by making them aware of the different programs that are available to them from the league.

## BILLS CAREER HIGHLIGHTS

**Best Season**

Talley gained First-Team All-AFC recognition for one of two times in 1993 by recording a career-high 136 tackles, forcing 4 fumbles, recovering 2 others, and registering 3 interceptions, which he returned for a total of 74 yards and 1 touchdown. But he had his finest all-around season in 1991, earning one of his two trips to the Pro Bowl by recording 117 tackles, picking off 5 passes, registering 4 sacks, and forcing 4 fumbles.

**Memorable Moments/Greatest Performances**

- Starred during a 42-0 shutout of the Cleveland Browns on November 4, 1990, recording 2 interceptions, one of which he returned 60 yards for a touchdown.
- Contributed to a 30-23 victory over the Philadelphia Eagles on December 2, 1990, by sacking the elusive Randall Cunningham twice.
- Recorded two interceptions during the Bills' 51-3 manhandling of the Los Angeles Raiders in the 1990 AFC Championship Game, returning one of his picks 27 yards for a touchdown.
- Helped lead the Bills to a 19-10 win over the Jets on October 24, 1993, by recording a sack and an interception, which he returned 61 yards for a touchdown.

**Notable Achievements**

- Scored 2 defensive touchdowns
- Intercepted 5 passes in 1991
- Recorded more than 100 tackles six times.
- Led Bills in tackles seven times and interceptions once

- Holds Bills career record for most tackles (1,137)
- Ranks among Bills career leaders with 14 forced fumbles (5th), 12 fumble recoveries (4th), 38.5 sacks (10th), and 188 games played (6th)
- Five-time division champion (1988, 1989, 1990, 1991, and 1993)
- Four-time AFC champion (1990, 1991, 1992, and 1993)
- 1990 Week 16 AFC Defensive Player of the Week
- Two-time Pro Bowl selection (1990 and 1991)
- Two-time First-Team All-AFC selection (1990 and 1993)
- Inducted into Bills Wall of Fame in 2003

# 14

## — TOM SESTAK —

A tremendous force on the interior of the Bills defensive line for seven seasons, Tom Sestak proved to be one of the AFL's premier players at his position his entire career, earning four All-Star selections and five consecutive All-AFL nominations with his stellar play at right-defensive tackle. Combining great size and strength with exceptional speed and quickness, Sestak established himself as arguably the most important member of an outstanding defense that led the Bills to three straight division titles and two league championships. Named to the AFL All-Time First Team and inducted into the Bills Wall of Fame, Sestak accomplished all he did after being selected in the 17th round of the 1962 AFL Draft and beginning his pro career at the rather advanced age of twenty-six.

Born in Gonzales, Texas, on March 9, 1936, Thomas Joseph Sestak grew up in a tottering little house located in an area known at the time as "the chicken capital of the world." After competing in several sports as a child, Sestak concentrated primarily on football and track at Gonzales High School, where he excelled on the gridiron on both sides of the ball. Offered an athletic scholarship to Baylor University, Sestak spent two years playing tight end for the Bears, before dropping out of school entirely and joining the army, recalling years later, "I was very low and discouraged. I didn't know what to do with myself, so I volunteered and served two years in the army. That convinced me I should finish my education."

Following his discharge, Sestak enrolled at McNeese State University in Lake Charles, Louisiana, the same institution that his older brother attended. Starting at tight end and defensive end for the Cowboys the next two seasons, Sestak did an outstanding job at both positions, gaining Little All-America recognition from United Press International his senior year.

An impressive physical specimen, the muscular Sestak, who stood 6'5" and weighed 240 pounds when he first arrived at McNeese State, earned the attention of his new teammates immediately, with former Cowboys fullback Ted Brevelle recalling, "The first days, he looked like a mountain

Tom Sestak (left), seen here with Cookie Gilchrist at the 1963 AFL All-Star Game, earned five straight All-AFL nominations as a member of the Bills.

out there to me. I remember he had the biggest calves and the biggest legs I had ever seen."

Brevelle added, "He was a great defensive player. He could literally close that side of the field down for running. He couldn't hardly be blocked. . . . You couldn't get into his legs like a lot of defensive ends. You couldn't get there on him."

Brevelle also claimed that Sestak had tremendous speed for someone his size, stating, "In the offseason, we would get out and run and try to stay in shape, and he was hard to keep up with on a 30–40-yard sprint. I'm sure that led to him getting to the pros. It didn't surprise me that he got in."

McNeese State offensive tackle Huey Simoneaux also stood in awe of Sestak, recalling, "When Tom came in before our first practice, I thought he was one of the coaches, he was so big. Then we started putting on the uniforms and I said, 'Lord have mercy, that's not a coach.'"

Simoneaux, who had the misfortune of going up against Sestak every day in practice, continued, "He had arms like an octopus. Plus, he'd hit you. Back then, you used forearms and shoulder blocking. He was tough. He'd get in that hole—to block him, you had to hit him below the knee. I remember one time in practice, I got in on his knee to block him and he literally picked me up and said, 'Stay off my knee.'"

Simoneaux added, "As big and tough and mean as he could have been, he wasn't bad. Now, you didn't want to get on his bad side. But he was a great guy. Easygoing, anything goes."

Ultimately selected by the Bills in the 17th round of the 1962 AFL Draft, with the 132nd overall pick, and by the Detroit Lions in the 16th round of that year's NFL Draft, with the 220th overall pick, Sestak chose to sign with the Bills, whose scout, Harvey Johnson, later said, "He stuck out because he was a big kid and could move. But there was no way to evaluate him because he wasn't playing against top competition."

Arriving at his first pro training camp weighing a svelte 270 pounds, Sestak, with his magnificent physique, surprised even the man who dis-covered him when he walked into the team hotel, with longtime Bills beat reporter Larry Felser remembering, "I was sitting there one evening and this guy gets out of the cab, and the guy would make Superman look like a ballet dancer. It was Sestak. Harvey Johnson, the chief scout, was sitting next to me and I said, 'Who the hell is this guy?' He says, 'I drafted him, but I don't remember who he is.' Then he says, 'My God, that's Sestak, the tight end from McNeese State.'"

After toying with the idea of using him on offense, Bills head coach Lou Saban decided to move Sestak to right-defensive tackle, where he had to face second-year guard Billy Shaw each day in practice. Explaining his reasoning at the time, Saban told the two men, "You're either going to beat the hell out of each other and be out of football, or you'll be the best line-men in pro football."

Shaw and Sestak ended up bringing out the best in one another, with both men soon emerging as the league's finest players at their respective posi-tions. While Shaw went on to earn eight straight trips to the AFL All-Star game and five consecutive First-Team All-AFL nominations, Sestak gained All-League recognition in each of his first five seasons. Later crediting Shaw for much of his success, Sestak said, "I asked Shaw what the hardest moves to block were, and he taught me. In my rookie year, I tried to get away with banging straight ahead, but I found out you can't simply overpower people. The guards are too good. You have to have a combination of power and agility. What I do depends on the guy I'm playing against. I tend to go inside quite a bit." Equally effective at rushing the passer and defending against the run, Sestak dominated his opponent at the point of attack, serving as the centerpiece of a Bills defense that annually ranked among the league's best. In addition to helping the Bills go seventeen straight games from 1964 to 1965 without allowing a rushing touchdown, Sestak did a superb job of applying pressure to opposing quarterbacks up the middle, recording a career-high and league-leading 15.5 sacks during the championship campaign of 1964.

Commenting on Sestak's brilliant all-around play, longtime Bills trainer Eddie Abramoski stated, "He was a dominant player. If you ever needed a stop or a sack, Tom got it when you needed it."

When arguing the merits of the AFL versus the NFL in 1965, New York Jets owner Sonny Werblin used Sestak as his primary example of why he believed the upstart league had the ability to compete against the more established circuit when he said that the Bills defensive tackle was "as good a football player as there is in the country."

Lou Saban also had high praise for Sestak, stating, "He's one of the best defensive tackles I've ever seen on any field, in any league. . . . Sestak is great at going after the ball to either side of the field."

In discussing Sestak's ability to manhandle his opponent, San Diego Chargers guard Pat Shea said, "What he likes to do is grab you by the shoulders and throw you someplace. He's extremely strong."

Further elaborating on his favorite maneuver, Sestak stated, "A good defensive tackle has to have strength in his arms and shoulders. You try to shove your man one way and go the other, and you never play against anybody who's little. One of my favorite defenses is what we call our 44. It's for a running situation and our front four doesn't have to worry about anything but crash, haul, and hit. We try to knock the offensive linemen off balance and just bang in there. In a passing situation, we can go either inside or outside, whichever we think is best."

Extremely tough and durable, Sestak started every game the Bills played from 1962 to 1967, despite suffering numerous injuries. In addressing Sestak's ability to play with pain, athletic trainer Eddie Abramoski said, "He's an easy fellow to take care of. Once he came to me and said he had a little pain in his side that had been bothering him for a couple of weeks, and he wanted an aspirin. We checked, and he had two broken ribs. But he played anyhow. Tom thinks a couple of aspirin will cure anything."

Former Bills punter and linebacker Paul Maguire said of his longtime roommate, "He could sit out the entire week, and, as long as he played

Sunday, we never cared. He'd walk into the locker room Sunday, you'd ask him if he was playing, and he'd give you that fucking grin."

Maguire continued, "The reason people talk about him so much is that those guys didn't miss games. The same guys, week in and week out, lined up and played. Unless they ripped your leg off, you played, or else they'd find someone else to take your job. They said, 'Can you play?' and the answer was an emphatic, 'Hell yes!' That's just the way those guys played. Those guys were so good because they knew what each other would do the whole time."

However, after appearing in every game in each of the previous six seasons, Sestak missed two contests in 1968 due to injuries to both knees that forced him to announce his retirement at the end of the year. Commenting on the determination that Sestak displayed his last two years in the league, Eddie Abramoski said, "He was probably the toughest player in my 37 years as a trainer for the Bills. He just was outstanding. He always wanted to be on the field. The last two years, he just rode the exercise bike and played the games."

After retiring as an active player, Sestak, who ended his career with 2 interceptions, 2 fumble recoveries, 3 defensive touchdowns, an unofficial total of 52 sacks, and countless unrecorded tackles, remained in the Buffalo area, where he ran a few businesses with Paul Maguire, before dying of a heart attack at the age of fifty-one on April 3, 1987, just one week after being diagnosed with amyotrophic lateral sclerosis (Lou Gehrig's Disease).

Upon learning of Sestak's passing, Maguire said, "He was absolutely superb. . . . I don't know if the Bills have ever had a better defensive tackle. . . . But the best way anybody can describe him was a great friend to all of us. The first time I ever met him, in training camp in 1964, he damn near broke my hand when I shook it. You knew you had a friend from the first time I met the guy. And it never changed. He was that kind of guy. Not one bad thing was said about this guy by anyone, ever. And, if they did, they sure as hell never said it to his face."

## CAREER HIGHLIGHTS

### Best Season

Sestak played his best ball for the Bills from 1963 to 1965, gaining consensus First-Team All-AFL recognition all three years. With Sestak recording a career-high 15.5 sacks in 1964 and the Bills capturing the AFL

Championship behind a defense that allowed the opposition just 3.0 yards per carry, we'll identify that as the finest season of his career.

## Memorable Moments/Greatest Performances

- Anchored a Bills defense that allowed just 43 yards rushing and 115 yards of total offense during a lopsided 35-10 victory over the San Diego Chargers on October 13, 1962.
- Scored the first points of his career when he returned his interception of a Frank Tripucka pass 6 yards for a touchdown during a 45-38 win over the Broncos on October 28, 1962.
- Led the defensive charge when the Bills recorded 7 sacks and allowed just 24 yards rushing and 143 yards of total offense during a 12-0 shutout of the Raiders on October 5, 1963.
- Contributed to a 34-17 win over the Kansas City Chiefs in the opening game of the 1964 regular season by returning his interception of a Len Dawson pass 15 yards for a touchdown.
- Recorded 3 of the 11 sacks the Bills registered against Denver quarterback Mickey Slaughter during a 30-19 win over the Broncos on December 13, 1964.
- Continuing his outstanding play in the postseason, recorded the lone sack the Bills registered during their 20-7 victory over the San Diego Chargers in the 1964 AFL Championship Game when he brought down Tobin Rote behind the line of scrimmage.
- Recorded another 2 sacks during the Bills' 23-0 shutout of the Chargers in the 1965 AFL Championship Game.
- Scored the last of his three career touchdowns when he recovered a fumble in the end zone during a 28-21 loss to the Raiders in the final game of the 1967 regular season.

## Notable Achievements

- Scored three defensive touchdowns
- Missed just two games in seven seasons, appearing in 96 out of 98 contests
- Led AFL with 15.5 sacks in 1964
- Tied for sixth in franchise history with 52 career sacks
- Three-time division champion (1964, 1965, and 1966)
- Two-time AFL champion (1964 and 1965)
- Four-time AFL All-Star selection (1962, 1963, 1964, and 1965)

- Three-time First-Team All-AFL selection (1963, 1964, and 1965)
- Two-time Second-Team All-AFL selection (1962 and 1966)
- Pro Football Reference All-1960s Second Team
- AFL All-Time First Team
- Inducted into Bills Wall of Fame in 1987

# 15
# MIKE STRATTON

A foundational piece upon which the Bills built their dominant defense of the mid-1960s, Mike Stratton spent eleven seasons in Buffalo, during which time he proved to be a key contributor to teams that won three division titles and two AFL championships with his exceptional all-around play at right-outside linebacker. A six-time AFL All-Star and four-time All-AFL selection, Stratton received the additional honors of being named to the AFL All-Time Second Team and the Bills' 50th Anniversary Team. Despite his many accomplishments, though, Stratton will always be remembered for one pivotal play he made during the 1964 AFL Championship Game that completely shifted the momentum of the contest in the Bills' favor.

Born in Vonore, Tennessee, on April 10, 1941, David Michael Stratton grew up in nearby Tellico Plains, a tiny town situated some fifty miles southwest of Knoxville, where he played football and basketball at Tellico Plains High School. Although Stratton displayed a considerable amount of talent on the gridiron, starring at fullback on offense and tackle on defense, he never expected to receive a college scholarship, telling *Knoxville News-Sentinel* sportswriter Marvin West years later, "If a college recruiter ever came to Tellico Plains, nobody saw him."

However, Stratton ended up attending the University of Tennessee on a full athletic scholarship, thanks to his high school coach, who brought him to the university's offices in Knoxville and practically demanded that the college offer him one. A three-year letterman at Tennessee, Stratton saw very little action as a sophomore, before spending his final two seasons starting at tight end on offense and end on defense.

Although Stratton concluded his collegiate career with just 11 receptions and 3 touchdowns, the Bills selected him in the 13th round of the 1962 AFL Draft, with the 100th overall pick, on the recommendation of their first head coach and fellow Tennessee native, Buster Ramsey, with Stratton recalling, "Ramsey was very sympathetic to people from Tennessee,

Mike Stratton is remembered most for delivering "The Hit Heard 'Round the World" in the 1964 AFL Championship Game.

and I would expect that, if it hadn't been for Buster, I would not have been drafted by Buffalo."

However, by the time Stratton joined the Bills, Ramsey had been replaced by Lou Saban, who felt far less empathetic toward him. Remembering the cold reception he received at his first practice, Stratton said, "When the coach called everybody's name and what we were going to do, he didn't call my name. I went up and asked him, 'Where do I go?' He said, 'What was your name again?' I figured I was in a little trouble at that time. He said, 'Why don't you go with the defensive ends?' So, I went out with the defensive ends. Then, apparently, they got several linebackers hurt, and they switched me to linebacker, and I couldn't have been happier."

After missing the first two games of his rookie campaign with an ankle injury, Stratton earned the starting right-outside linebacker job by Week 5. Acquitting himself extremely well at his new post the rest of the year, Stratton recorded 1 sack and 6 interceptions, which he returned a total of 99 yards. Continuing his strong play in 1963, Stratton gained AFL All-Star (Pro Bowl) recognition for the first of six straight times by registering 2.5 sacks and picking off 3 passes, one of which he returned for a touchdown. Stratton followed that up by earning the first of his four consecutive All-AFL (All-Pro) nominations in 1964, a season in which he helped lead the Bills to their first league championship.

Playing the best ball of his career from 1962 to 1968, Stratton recorded 24.5 sacks and 17 interceptions over the course of those seven seasons, establishing himself in the process as one of the league's most versatile and finest all-around outside linebackers. Blessed with outstanding speed and quickness, the 6'3", 225-pound Stratton possessed the athleticism to drop into pass coverage, where he did an excellent job of blanketing opposing tight ends and running backs coming out of the backfield. A hard hitter who also displayed superior instincts and outstanding knowledge of his opponents' tendencies, Stratton proved to be extremely effective against the run as well, contributing greatly to the league's top rushing defense by plugging holes, bringing down runners near the line of scrimmage, and chasing ball-carriers sideline to sideline.

In discussing Stratton's varied skillset, NFL historian John Turney of *Pro Football Journal* described him as "one of those all-around linebackers . . . right up there with the Chuck Howleys and Chris Hanburgers."

AFL historian Todd Tobias from the website TalesfromtheAmerican-FootballLeague.com, also praised Stratton for the totality of his game, saying, "He was excellent. A very sound performer and solid hitter."

Meanwhile, Buffalo's Pro Football Hall of Fame guard Billy Shaw said of his longtime teammate, "Mike Stratton was a great linebacker for us. He was one of our most dedicated players. He had the physical ability, and he could run with any of the backs."

Extremely durable as well, Stratton missed just two games his first eight years in the league, starting every contest the Bills played from 1964 to 1969. Also an outstanding team leader, Stratton received praise for his excellence in that area from onetime Bills' ball boy and former Pro Football Hall of Fame director Joe Horrigan, who stated, "Mike was the player the guys rallied around. He was the one on the defensive side of the ball that pulled everybody together. And that was the most consistent defense in the AFL at the time."

Perhaps the greatest example of Stratton's ability to galvanize his team-mates occurred during the early stages of the 1964 AFL championship game, when, with the Bills trailing San Diego 7-0 in the first quarter, Chargers quarterback Tobin Rote lofted a soft swing pass to running back Keith Lincoln in the left flat. However, just as Lincoln reached for the football, a charging Stratton drove his right shoulder into his chest, driving him 2 yards backward and forcing him to leave the game with cracked ribs. Inspired by Stratton's hit, which subsequently became known as "The Hit Heard 'Round the World," the Bills went on to score 20 unanswered points, giving them the first of their two straight league championships.

Commenting on the play afterward, Stratton said, "They ran it a couple times, so when I saw it again, I turned my back to the quarterback, took a few steps to the wide receiver, and turned back to the quarterback. I went back for Lincoln and saw they were throwing to him. I just put my head down and tried to get him. I was trying to get there just as he caught it or after he caught it."

Recalling the impact that Stratton's hit had on the outcome of the game, Bills' quarterback Jack Kemp stated, "You could just see the emotions and the credibility of the Buffalo Bills come together at that point. . . . That hit and that win put Buffalo on the major-league sports map."

Former Hall of Fame executive director Joe Horrigan, who viewed Stratton's hit from the stands that day, claimed, "It's still the play that people who weren't there or weren't alive when it happened know what it is."

Although the Bills had fallen from the AFL's elite by 1967, Stratton continued to perform at an exceptional level for two more years, earning the last of his six consecutive AFL All-Star nominations in 1968, before gaining unofficial Second-Team All-AFL recognition from both the *New York Daily News* and the Newspaper Enterprise Association (NEA) the following year. But, after Stratton missed seven games due to injury in 1970 and started a total of just thirteen contests over the course of the next two seasons, the Bills traded him to the Chargers following the conclusion of the 1972 campaign.

Looking back at how his time in Buffalo ended, Stratton said, "Fortunately, I got to play 11 seasons with Buffalo, which was, at that time, longer than anyone else had played there. It didn't turn out like I would have wanted. I would have much preferred to end up with Buffalo, but they knew that they were going to have to trade me for some other things. They needed other people, and, if they could get a draft choice, or they could get something for me, better to trade me now and get something for me than to let me retire and not get anything."

Stratton, who left the Bills having recorded 31.5 sacks, 18 interceptions, 204 interception-return yards, 2 fumble recoveries, 2 touchdowns, and an unknown number of tackles as a member of the team, spent just one year in San Diego, registering another 3 interceptions, before announcing his retirement at the end of 1973.

Following his playing days, Stratton returned to Tennessee, where he became an executive with Crump Associates, an insurance company located in Knoxville. After working there for several years, Stratton retired to private life, remaining in Knoxville until March 25, 2020, when he died of heart complications at the age of seventy-eight, just a few weeks after falling and suffering a fractured hip.

Upon learning of his passing, longtime Bills fan Charlie Tracy paid his respects to one of his childhood heroes by writing a note to the Stratton family that read: "Although I never met you, the 'hit' will always be remembered. I was at War Memorial that day with my dad and brother, and, with the Bills trailing, we were all a bit 'tight.' Then the hit came, and the Bills had a complete turnaround. Thank you to Mike and his family for all those wonderful memories!!"

## BILLS CAREER HIGHLIGHTS

### Best Season

Stratton had an outstanding rookie season for the Bills in 1962, recording a career-high 6 interceptions. He also performed extremely well from 1964 through 1967, registering a career-best 7.5 sacks in the last of those campaigns and gaining First-Team All-AFL recognition the other three years. With Stratton's jarring tackle of San Diego running back Keith Lincoln in the 1964 AFL Championship Game completely shifting the momentum of the contest, the 1964 campaign stands out as the most impactful of his career.

### Memorable Moments/Greatest Performances

- Contributed to a 40-20 victory over the Chargers on November 11, 1962, by recording 2 interceptions, which he returned a total of 59 yards.
- Picked off another 2 passes during a 20-3 win over the New York Titans in the final game of the 1962 regular season.

- Scored the first touchdown of his career when he ran 26 yards to pay-dirt after intercepting a Len Dawson pass during a 27-27 tie with the Chiefs on September 22, 1963.
- Lit the scoreboard again when he combined with Harry Jacobs to tackle quarterback Tom Flores in the end zone for a safety during a 12-0 shut-out of the Raiders on October 5, 1963.
- Made the only reception of his career when he gathered in a 19-yard pass from Daryle Lamonica during a 45-14 win over the Jets on December 8, 1963.
- Recorded another safety when he brought down quarterback John Hadl in the end zone during a 27-24 win over the Chargers on November 26, 1964.
- Contributed to a 58-24 win over the Miami Dolphins on September 18, 1966, by recording a pair of interceptions, which he returned a total of 37 yards.
- Scored the final points of his career when he returned a fumble 22 yards for a touchdown during a 38-21 victory over the Denver Broncos in the final game of the 1966 regular season.
- Most remembered for the momentum-changing play he made in the 1964 AFL Championship Game, Stratton, who also recorded a key interception during the contest, said years later, "I never wanted to be known as a one-hit wonder. But when people asked about that tackle, I always smiled. . . . You can always tell when you get a good lick; I just didn't know it would have that kind of effect. Thirty-five years later, I'm proud that people remember it. They've got a better memory than I do."

## Notable Achievements

- Scored 2 defensive touchdowns
- Appeared in 110 consecutive games from 1962 to 1969
- Intercepted 6 passes in 1962
- Three-time division champion (1964, 1965, and 1966)
- Two-time AFL champion (1964 and 1965)
- 1965 Week 12 AFL Defensive Player of the Week
- Six-time AFL All-Star selection (1963, 1964, 1965, 1966, 1967, and 1968)
- Three-time First-Team All-AFL selection (1964, 1965, and 1966)
- 1967 Second-Team All-AFL selection

- Pro Football Reference All-1960s Second Team
- AFL All-Time Second Team
- Inducted into Bills Wall of Fame in 1994

# 16

## RUBEN BROWN

A stalwart on the Buffalo offensive line for nine seasons, Ruben Brown started at left guard for Bills teams that won one division title and made four playoff appearances, missing a total of just eight games from 1995 to 2003. One of only three men in franchise history to earn as many as eight Pro Bowl selections, Brown also received four All-Pro nominations, making him one of the most decorated players in team annals. A member of the Bills 50th anniversary team, Brown proved to be a high-character individual as well, being named the organization's Walter Payton Man of the Year on three separate occasions. Yet somehow, Brown has yet to gain induction into the Bills Wall of Fame or receive serious consideration for the Pro Football Hall of Fame.

Born in Englewood, New Jersey, on February 13, 1972, Ruben Pernell Brown moved with his family at a young age to Lynchburg, Virginia, where he excelled in football and wrestling at E. C. Glass High School. A *Parade* All-American on the gridiron, Brown starred as a two-way lineman, although he earned most of his acclaim for his exceptional play on defense.

Offered an athletic scholarship to the University of Pittsburgh, Brown hoped to further develop his pass-rushing and run-stopping skills as a member of the Panthers' defensive front. However, with Pittsburgh loaded on defense and thin along the offensive line, Brown moved to left tackle, where he spent four years providing superb blocking for the team's quarterbacks and running backs, earning All-Big East honors three times, and gaining First-Team All-America recognition in his final season.

Recalling how he resigned himself to accepting a position on offense, Brown said, "I was very disappointed. But I was behind two outstanding defensive linemen. I was upset, but there was a good reason for it, and I was fortunate. I wanted to get on the field, and I knew I had a good chance to start."

Impressed with Brown's outstanding play at Pittsburgh, the Bills made him the 14th overall pick of the 1995 NFL Draft when they selected him

Ruben Brown received eight Pro Bowl nominations and four All-Pro selections during his time in Buffalo.

in the 1st round. Moved inside to guard following his arrival in Buffalo, Brown adapted quickly to his new position, earning a spot on the NFL All-Rookie Team after joining the starting unit prior to the start of the regular season. Named to the Pro Bowl for the first of eight straight times the following year, Brown helped the Bills advance to the playoffs as a wild card with his strong play at left guard. Having established himself as arguably the AFC's finest player at his position by 1998, Brown earned the first of his two consecutive First-Team All-AFC selections and three straight Second-Team All-Pro nominations.

Standing 6'3" and weighing 300 pounds, Brown possessed good size and strength, making him extremely effective as a straight-ahead blocker at the line of scrimmage. Blessed with outstanding quickness as well, Brown provided superior downfield blocking for running backs Thurman Thomas, Antowain Smith, and Travis Henry, and excellent blindside pass protection for a long list of Bills quarterbacks that included Jim Kelly, Todd Collins, Doug Flutie, Rob Johnson, Alex Van Pelt, and Drew Bledsoe.

Contributing to the Bills with more than just his playing ability, Brown served as one of the team's inspirational leaders, both on and off the field, displaying his tremendous determination and commitment to his teammates by starting 136 out of 144 regular season games during his time in Buffalo. Meanwhile, Brown remained very active in the community, starting the Ruben Brown Foundation in 2001 to help children through various educational, developmental, and mentoring programs. Brown also established the Ruben Brown Motorcycle Run in Buffalo to benefit the Salvation Army. In 2003, his many philanthropic endeavors prompted *Pro Football Weekly* to name him the winner of the Arthur S. Arkush Humanitarian of the Year Award and the Salvation Army to present him with the William Booth Community Service Award.

Although Brown continued to perform at an extremely high level his entire time in Buffalo, the Bills waived him due to salary cap constraints on March 1, 2004, with three years remaining on his $32 million contract. Reacting to his release, Brown said at the time, "I feel that I still have a great deal to offer another franchise. I still enjoy the game and feel physically and mentally up to the challenge of making a worthwhile contribution to another NFL team."

Signed by the Bears one month later, Brown ended up spending four years in Chicago, appearing in Super Bowl XL and earning one more Pro Bowl nomination, before injuries forced him to officially announce his retirement after he sat out the 2008 campaign. Ending his career having started all 181 games in which he appeared, Brown played his best ball for the Bills, earning more Pro Bowl bids than any other player in team annals, excluding Bruce Smith (eleven Pro Bowl nominations) and Billy Shaw (eight AFL All-Star selections). But, while Smith and Shaw have both been inducted into the Bills Wall of Fame and the Pro Football Hall of Fame, Brown has yet to be so honored.

Following his retirement, Brown remained in the Orchard Park area, where he continues his charitable work through his foundation. He also hosts weekly sports shows on local radio and television stations, as well as a "Game Day Experience with Ruben Brown," which gives area youth the opportunity to watch a Bills game with him from a luxury suite.

## BILLS CAREER HIGHLIGHTS

### Best Season

Brown played his best ball for the Bills from 1998 to 2002, gaining All-Pro recognition in four of those five seasons. Since Brown committed just six penalties in 2002 and the Bills boasted one of the NFL's more potent offenses, scoring a total of 379 points, we'll identify that as the finest season of his career.

### Memorable Moments/Greatest Performances

- Helped the Bills rush for a season-high total of 222 yards and amass 454 yards of total offense during a 45-27 win over the St. Louis Rams on December 10, 1995.
- Performed brilliantly with the rest of Buffalo's offensive line in the 1995 AFC wild card game, with the Bills gaining 341 yards on the ground and amassing 536 yards of total offense during a 37-22 victory over the Miami Dolphins.
- Helped the Bills rush for 266 yards and accumulate a total of 476 yards on offense during a 38-13 win over Washington on November 3, 1996.
- Again dominated Washington with his line-mates at the point of attack on November 7, 1999, with the Bills rushing for 204 yards and amassing 413 yards of total offense during a 34-17 victory.
- Enabled the Bills, along with his cohorts, to gain 213 yards on the ground and amass 579 yards of total offense during a 42-23 mauling of the Seattle Seahawks in the 2000 regular-season finale.

### Notable Achievements

- Missed just eight games in nine seasons, starting 136 out of 144 contests
- 1995 division champion
- Member of 1995 NFL All-Rookie Team
- Eight-time Pro Bowl selection (1996, 1997, 1998, 1999, 2000, 2001, 2002, and 2003)
- Four-time Second-Team All-Pro selection (1998, 1999, 2000, and 2002)
- Two-time First-Team All-AFC selection (1998 and 1999)

# 17

# BUTCH BYRD

A true shutdown corner before the term became a regular part of football parlance, Butch Byrd starred in the Bills' defensive secondary for seven seasons, recording more interceptions and amassing more interception-return yards during that time than any other player in franchise history. Known for his outstanding speed and tremendous physicality, Byrd did an exceptional job of blanketing opposing wideouts and creating turnovers, picking off at least five passes on six separate occasions. A standout performer on special teams as well, Byrd also ranks extremely high in team annals in punt-return yardage, with his excellent all-around play earning him five AFL All-Star nominations and four All-AFL selections. A member of Bills teams that won three division titles and two league championships, Byrd received the additional honors of being named to the AFL All-Time Second Team and the Pro Football Reference All-1960s First Team.

Born in Watervliet, New York, on September 20, 1941, George Edward Byrd Jr. grew up just a few miles north of Albany, where he starred on the gridiron while attending LaSalle Institute in nearby Troy. Excelling for the Cadets on both sides of the ball, Byrd earned four nominations to the All-Troy High School Offensive Team and three selections to the All-Defensive Team, before accepting an athletic scholarship to Boston University, where he continued his outstanding two-way play, leading the Terriers in rushing twice, while also gaining All-East recognition as a defensive back his senior year. An exceptional all-around athlete, Byrd also ran track at Boston U, posting a personal-best time of 10 seconds in the 100-yard dash.

Subsequently selected by the Bills in the 4th round of the 1964 AFL Draft, with the 25th overall pick, Byrd made an immediate impact upon his arrival in Buffalo, earning AFL All-Star honors as a rookie by recording 7 interceptions, finishing second in the league with 178 interception-return yards, and scoring 1 touchdown on defense for the eventual AFL champions after laying claim to the starting right-cornerback job. Byrd followed that up with another outstanding season, gaining AFL All-Star and

Butch Byrd holds franchise records for most interceptions and most interception-return yards.

First-Team All-AFL recognition in 1965 by picking off 5 passes, amassing 119 interception-return yards, and ranking among the league leaders with 220 punt-return yards, in helping the Bills capture their second consecutive league championship. Continuing to perform at an elite level the next five seasons, Byrd earned three more AFL All-Star selections and another three All-AFL nominations by recording a total of 28 interceptions, four of which he returned for touchdowns, while also scoring once on special teams. Particularly outstanding in 1966 and 1969, Byrd earned First-Team All-AFL honors in the first of those campaigns by picking off 6 passes, amassing 110 interception-return yards, and scoring 2 touchdowns, before earning that distinction again three years later by recording 7 interceptions, which he returned for a total of 95 yards and 1 touchdown.

The extremely opportunistic Byrd, who recorded the sixth-most interceptions and amassed the third-most interception-return yards of any player in the ten-year history of the AFL even though he competed in that league for just six seasons, always seemed to be in the right place at the right time, with his excellent speed and ability to anticipate his opponent's next move making him one of the top cover-corners in the game. The 6', 211-pound Byrd also possessed outstanding size and strength, which he used to knock opposing receivers off course. One of the most physical corners of his era, Byrd took advantage of the rules that were in effect at the time that allowed defenders to punish pass catchers as they came off the line of scrimmage, with former Bills linebacker Harry Jacobs saying of his longtime teammate, "He was one of the first big cornerbacks. He was probably the guy that brought every other DB up on top of everyone to knock receivers around a little bit. Booker [Edgerson] was on the other side, and Book was up there strong against them, but he didn't have that same physical force about him."

Looking back on how he helped Byrd develop into one of the league's top players at his position, Booker Edgerson said, "When Butch came in, I sort of took him under my wing. I told him about how certain players, certain quarterbacks, do certain things, and how to cover certain guys. So, we had a very good rapport, and I'd like to think that I made Butch a better ballplayer than I was. . . . Butch was an outstanding ballplayer."

In discussing the difficulties that Byrd presented to opposing receivers, former Patriots wideout Gino Cappelletti stated, "Every receiver has certain defenders who really give him trouble, and he was definitely one of the toughest I had to play against."

Extremely durable as well, Byrd started every game the Bills played from 1964 to 1970, appearing in 101 consecutive contests including the postseason.

Nevertheless, with the Bills in a rebuilding mode by the late 1960s, they elected to trade Byrd to the Denver Broncos for a 5th-round draft pick following the conclusion of the 1970 campaign. Byrd, who left Buffalo with career totals of 40 interceptions, 666 interception-return yards, 600 punt-return yards, 4 fumble recoveries, 5 touchdown interceptions, and 6 total TDs, subsequently spent the 1971 season in Denver assuming a backup role, before announcing his retirement at the end of the year at just thirty years of age. Looking back on his decision to leave the game when he did, Byrd said, "I had a family and had to move on."

After retiring from football, Byrd relocated to Central Massachusetts and took a job working for Chrysler in their sales department in Farmington. He later worked for Polaroid in Waltham and Cambridge, before retiring in 2005 and moving to Westboro, Massachusetts, where he became heavily involved in community activities, serving as a member of the

Westboro Civic Club, and arranging for a donation to the Westboro Pantry and Food Foundation. Byrd, who is eighty-one years old as of this writing, also spent several years attending Buffalo's annual alumni weekend, reconnecting with many of his former teammates.

Named to the Bills' 35th Anniversary All-Time Team in 1994 and their 50th Anniversary Team in 2009, Byrd holds many fond memories of his playing days, saying, "The bottom line is that pro football allowed me to grow. I met so many people I never would have met—senators, dignitaries, celebrities. It's given me so much of what I have."

## BILLS CAREER HIGHLIGHTS

### Best Season

Byrd performed magnificently for the Bills as a rookie in 1964, earning the first of his five trips to the AFL All-Star Game by recording 7 interceptions, which he returned for a total of 178 yards and 1 touchdown. But he had his finest all-around season in 1966, when, in addition to picking off 6 passes and amassing 110 interception-return yards, he scored 2 touchdowns, scoring one of those on a 60-yard pick-six and the other on a 72-yard punt-return, with his exceptional play earning him First-Team All-AFL honors.

### Memorable Moments/Greatest Performances

- Recorded his first career interception during a 30-13 win over the Broncos on September 20, 1964, subsequently returning the ball 38 yards into Denver territory.
- Followed that up by giving the Bills a 7-0 first-quarter lead over the San Diego Chargers on September 26, 1964, by returning his interception of a Tobin Rote pass 85 yards for a touchdown in a game that Buffalo went on to win by a score of 30-3.
- Intercepted 2 passes in one game for the first time in his career during a 17-14 win over the Oakland Raiders on November 14, 1965, returning his two picks a total of 66 yards.
- Starred for the Bills during their 23-0 victory over the Chargers in the 1965 AFL Championship Game, recording an interception, returning a punt 74 yards for a touchdown, and holding San Diego wide receiver Don Norton to just 1 reception.

- Performed brilliantly during a 58-24 trouncing of the Miami Dolphins on September 18, 1966, earning AFL Defensive Player of the Week honors by returning an interception 60 yards for a touchdown and scoring again on a 72-yard punt return.
- Helped lead the Bills to a 37-35 win over the Jets on September 29, 1968, by intercepting a pair of Joe Namath passes, one of which he returned 53 yards for a touchdown.
- Lit the scoreboard again almost exactly one year later, returning his interception of a Pete Liske pass 12 yards for a touchdown during a 41-28 win over Denver on September 28, 1969.
- Scored the final touchdown of his career when he ran 23 yards to paydirt after intercepting a Bobby Douglass pass during a 31-13 loss to the Chicago Bears on November 22, 1970.

### Notable Achievements

- Never missed a game in seven seasons, appearing in 98 consecutive contests
- Scored 5 defensive touchdowns
- Returned 1 punt for a touchdown
- Recorded at least 5 interceptions six times
- Amassed more than 100 interception-return yards three times
- Finished second in AFL with 178 interception-return yards in 1964
- Led Bills in interceptions three times
- Holds Bills career records for most interceptions (40), interception-return yards (666), and touchdown interceptions (5)
- Ranks seventh in Bills history with 600 punt-return yards
- Three-time division champion (1964, 1965, and 1966)
- Two-time AFL champion (1964 and 1965)
- 1966 Week 2 AFL Defensive Player of the Week
- Five-time AFL All-Star selection (1964, 1965, 1966, 1968, and 1969)
- Three-time First-Team All-AFL selection (1965, 1966, and 1969)
- 1968 Second-Team All-AFL selection
- Pro Football Reference All-1960s First Team
- AFL All-Time Second Team

# 18
# REGGIE MCKENZIE

The emotional leader of Buffalo's exceptional offensive line called "The Electric Company" for its ability to create holes in the running game for O. J. Simpson (aka "The Juice"), Reggie McKenzie spent eleven seasons starting at left guard for the Bills, appearing in every game they played in ten of those. An outstanding pulling guard whom Simpson often referred to as his "main man," McKenzie did a superb job of leading the Hall of Fame running back downfield on his frequent end runs, playing a huge role in him becoming the NFL's first 2,000-yard rusher. A member of Bills teams that made three playoff appearances and won one division title, McKenzie earned three All-Pro selections and five All-AFC nominations, before spending the final two seasons of his playing career in Seattle.

Born in Detroit, Michigan, on July 27, 1950, Reginald McKenzie grew up in nearby Highland Park, where he starred on the gridiron while attending Highland Park High School. Heavily scouted by both major in-state colleges, McKenzie recalled, "One man from Michigan State said I wasn't a football player, and then George Mans came in and said, 'Reggie, I'm George Mans from the University of Michigan. We want you.' So, I went up there with a chip on my shoulder. I knew I could play; I did a lot of fighting growing up. And that's all football is—a little fist fight. You had to hit people in the mouth and have fun doing it."

Establishing himself as one of the nation's top offensive linemen at Michigan under legendary head coach Bo Schembechler, McKenzie earned All-Big 10 honors twice and gained consensus All-America recognition his senior year. Claiming that Schembechler prepared him for life in the NFL, McKenzie remembered, "He said, 'Do it right every time, all the time, and the first time.' He was the one who really prepared me both physically and mentally to go on and play on Sundays and take that same attitude out in life."

Schembechler also had many fond memories of McKenzie, telling MLive.com some thirty years later, "His last two years, we lost only two

Reggie McKenzie served as the emotional leader of the Bills' offensive line that became known as "The Electric Company."

games. As a pulling guard, you couldn't find a better one because the guy could run and had a very strong upper body. He would just run over people. . . . And he was a great leader. Some guys, you might say, 'He's a quiet leader,' but he wasn't quiet. He was a vocal leader, mad if you lost, but he didn't play in too many losing games."

Impressed with McKenzie's outstanding play at the collegiate level, the Bills made him the 27th overall selection of the 1972 NFL Draft when they tabbed him with the first pick of the 2nd round. Laying claim to the starting left guard job as soon as he arrived in Buffalo, McKenzie made an immediate impact, helping the Bills score 73 more points and rush for nearly 800 more yards than they did the previous season. Developing into arguably the finest player at his position the following year, McKenzie helped pave the way for O. J. Simpson to set a new single-season NFL rushing record, earning in the process First-Team All-Pro and First-Team All-AFC honors. Continuing to perform at an elite level the next seven seasons, McKenzie earned two more All-Pro selections and another four All-AFC nominations, while continuing his streak of 134 consecutive starts that established a new franchise record (since broken).

A punishing run blocker who also excelled in pass protection, the 6'4", 255-pound McKenzie possessed good strength, outstanding athleticism, and excellent foot speed that enabled him to combine with Joe DeLamielleure to give the Bills the most formidable pair of pulling guards in the league. Particularly effective as a downfield blocker, McKenzie did a magnificent job of setting the edge and leading O. J. Simpson on his frequent end sweeps.

Although the Bills' heavy reliance on Simpson and their running game often prevented McKenzie and his line-mates from displaying their ability to pass protect, the All-Pro guard completely understood his team's philosophy on offense, saying, "The best way for us to win was to give O. J. the football and to dominate the game from an offensive perspective by running the ball. As long as we had the ball, the other team's offense was on the bench."

McKenzie added, "I'm a throwback to Bo [Schembechler], Woody Hayes, Lou Saban, and Jim Ringo. When you throw the football, three things can happen, and two of them are bad. We had a guy who could run with the coconut like no other."

An outstanding team leader who served as the Bills' player representative from 1973 to 1977, McKenzie inspired confidence in his teammates, predicting prior to the start of the 1973 campaign, "O. J. Simpson will rush for 2,000 yards this season." With Simpson still needing 61 yards to break Jim Brown's single-season rushing record and 199 yards to reach the 2,000-yard plateau heading into the final game of the regular season, he asked his teammate, "Reggie, what if I only gain 40 yards tomorrow?" In response, McKenzie just grinned and replied, "Now, that ain't gonna happen."

Remaining a force up front for three more years after the Bills traded Simpson to the San Francisco 49ers prior to the start of the 1978 campaign, McKenzie helped both Terry Miller and Joe Cribbs gain more than 1,000 yards on the ground, before seeing his consecutive games-played streak come to an end in 1981, when he missed ten contests due to injury. A free agent at the end of 1982, McKenzie signed with the Seattle Seahawks, with whom he spent the next two seasons starting at left guard, before announcing his retirement.

Remaining with the Seahawks following his playing days, McKenzie spent eight years serving the team as director of player relations. After leaving the Seahawks in 1994, McKenzie returned to Michigan, where he established Reggie McKenzie Industrial Materials, an industrial products company based in the city of Livonia. McKenzie, who, during his time in Buffalo, gave back to the community through worthy causes such as the Special Olympics and the United Way, is also the founder of the Reggie McKenzie Foundation, which helps Detroit youth with athletics and academics.

## BILLS CAREER HIGHLIGHTS

### Best Season

McKenzie gained First-Team All-Pro recognition for the only time in his career in 1973, when his exceptional blocking helped O. J. Simpson become the first player in NFL history to gain more than 2,000 yards on the ground in a season. In recognition of his outstanding play, the Pro Football Writers Association named McKenzie the NFL's top blocking lineman.

### Memorable Moments/Greatest Performances

- Helped the Bills rush for 360 yards and amass 459 yards of total offense during a 31-13 win over the Patriots in the opening game of the 1973 regular season.
- Along with his line-mates, dominated the Patriots at the point of attack once again during a 37-13 victory on December 9, 1973, with the Bills gaining 293 of their 324 yards on the ground.
- Helped O. J. Simpson rush for 200 yards during a 34-14 win over the Jets in the 1973 regular-season finale, enabling "The Juice" to reach the magical 2,000-yard mark.
- With the rest of Buffalo's offensive line, turned in another dominant performance against the Jets in the opening game of the 1975 regular season, with the Bills gaining 309 yards on the ground during a lopsided 42-14 victory.

- Along with his cohorts, followed that up with another strong outing, enabling Bills' running backs to rush for 310 yards during a 30-21 win over the Steelers on September 28, 1975.
- Continuing to dominate his opponent at the line of scrimmage the following week, helped the Bills rush for 293 yards and amass 436 yards of total offense during a 38-14 victory over the Denver Broncos on October 5, 1975.

**Notable Achievements**

- Started 132 consecutive games from 1972 to 1980
- 1980 division champion
- 1973 Pro Football Writers Association NFL Offensive Lineman of the Year
- 1973 First-Team All-Pro selection
- Two-time Second-Team All-Pro selection (1974 and 1975)
- Two-time First-Team All-AFC selection (1973 and 1974)
- Three-time Second-Team All-AFC selection (1975, 1976, and 1980)

# 19
# KYLE WILLIAMS

A tremendous leader who spent his entire professional career in Buffalo, Kyle Williams overcame early doubts about his ability to compete in the pros to establish himself as one of the finest defensive linemen in team annals. The versatile Williams, who ranks among the franchise's all-time leaders in both sacks and tackles, manned virtually every position along the Bills' defensive front at one time or another, with his consistently excellent play earning him six Pro Bowl selections and one All-Pro nomination. Despite his efforts, though, the Bills posted just two winning records and made only one playoff appearance during his thirteen-year stint in Buffalo.

Born in Ruston, Louisiana, on June 10, 1983, Kyle Derrick Williams grew up in a town dedicated to its high school football team, describing it as a place that "lives and dies on Friday night, and then kids do other things or other sports through the week to get to the next Friday night."

Despite the town's obsession with its high school team, Williams received very little exposure to professional or college football during his youth, recalling, "I wasn't a huge football fan growing up. I only had three [TV] channels growing up because we lived out in the country. I just kind of played."

Eventually emerging as a star in multiple sports at Ruston High School, Williams lettered in baseball, football, and track, recording a personal-best throw of 53',3" in the shotput. Meanwhile, after beginning his career on the gridiron as a running back (he rushed for 942 yards and 14 touchdowns his freshman year), Williams gradually developed into one of the best defensive players in the state, earning Class 5A Louisiana Defensive MVP honors as a senior by registering 7 sacks and 78 tackles, 17 of which resulted in a loss. Realizing by that time that any possible future he had in professional sports lay in football, Williams remembered, "I started getting scholarship offers, and pretty soon I was getting burned out on baseball. It seemed like the way to go."

Kyle Williams spent his entire thirteen-year NFL career in Buffalo.
Courtesy of Jeffrey Beall.

Choosing to remain close to home, Williams accepted a scholarship to Louisiana State University, spurning in the process offers from Auburn, Nebraska, Florida, and Tennessee. Enjoying a fine career at LSU, Williams played for one national championship team and recorded a total of 176 tackles and 16.5 sacks in his three seasons as a starter, performing especially well his senior year, when he earned Second-Team All-America honors from three major news services.

Subsequently selected by the Bills in the 5th round of the 2006 NFL Draft, with the 134th overall pick, Williams arrived in Buffalo weighing considerably less than the 303 pounds he carried on his 6'1" frame throughout most of his career, leaving many to feel that he lacked the size to succeed at defensive tackle in the NFL. But, through much hard work and dedication, Williams soon proved his detractors wrong, with his speed, strength, and hustle prompting many experts to identify him as one of the steals of the draft.

Revealing his tremendous determination and confidence in his abilities, Williams, who ended up starting eleven games at right tackle in the Bills' 4-3 defense his first year in the league, stated, "When I got here, I wasn't supposed to be able to do this is or do that. And yet nobody ever sent me the memo that I couldn't do it. . . . I went to a big school, where the competition was top notch. I had no reason to believe that it wouldn't carry over from there. I just wanted to do the same things. I was going to play hard, practice hard, and give everything I had."

Williams continued to man the same position for the Bills for three more years, recording a total of 8 sacks and leading the team's defensive linemen with 66 tackles in 2009, before moving to nose tackle when Buffalo switched to a 3-4 defense in 2010. Excelling at his new post, Williams earned his first Pro Bowl nomination and lone All-Pro selection by recording 5.5 sacks and 76 tackles, despite being double-teamed on almost every play.

Sidelined by injuries for most of 2011, Williams appeared in only five games. However, he started every game the Bills played in four of the next seven seasons, missing significant playing time only in 2015, when a torn MCL limited him to six contests. Establishing himself as one of the league's most versatile defensive linemen, Williams spent five seasons starting at left tackle, one at right tackle, and one at left end, performing equally well at all three positions.

Named to the Pro Bowl in five of those seven seasons, Williams removed any lingering doubts about his ability to perform at an elite level. Admitting that working with Williams forced him to change his opinion of him, Giff Smith, who spent three seasons coaching Bills' defensive linemen, said, "I was lulled into the 'try hard' perception about Kyle that's out there. When I finally got to work with him, I saw a guy that could be a dominating player. He does play hard, don't get me wrong. But he's a lot more than that. That's what I noticed when I started. I hadn't given him enough credit."

Smith added, "He really puts pressure on the offensive lineman. I remember talking to our guys in Buffalo and them saying, 'He's on you so quick.'"

Anthony Weaver, who replaced Smith as d-line coach in Buffalo, found himself being similarly impressed with Williams's athleticism, saying, "The thing about Kyle is that he's not your ideal, prototype defensive tackle in terms of size. But pound for pound, I'd say he's the best athlete on this football team. I'd put him up against anybody—in any sport. The guy's a scratch golfer. He's a great swimmer. He goes and plays in some home run derby in Toronto and hits eight or nine home runs."

Former Bills assistant coach Bob Sanders also had high praise for Williams, saying, "You know what to expect from him every day. He is so instinctive, and he has a knack for playing the position. You know you are going to get a guy who is going to bring his hard hat and give you the maximum effort."

Meanwhile, Bills center Geoff Hangartner, who had to face Williams every day in practice, spoke of the way his teammate used his balance and leverage to make up for his relative lack of size, stating, "All I know is he makes training camp really difficult. Some guys, you can get away with leaning on them or being in a bad position. But if you're in a bad position with him, he's going to toss you. I've never played against a guy who's got as good an instinct."

Revered by his teammates for his leadership ability and strong work ethic, Williams proved to be one of the biggest voices in the Bills' locker room, with former head coach Chan Gailey saying, "There's no way to put in words what a guy like that means to your team. There's no way to put a value on it."

Mindful of his responsibilities as a team leader, Williams stated, "You have to set an example for young guys. You have to correct guys when correction is needed. You need to be tough on guys when they need to be gotten on to. I think all of that rolls into one. A true leader has to be able to discern the circumstances of what different guys need."

Williams continued, "I don't think it's really that much different from a coach. Players react and players adjust to certain ways that they're coached, and I think it's the same way with a leader. What do you need to do to get this guy going? How do you need to challenge that guy? Do you need to wrap your arms around that guy? Being in the locker room and getting to know each one of those guys, you get a feel for it. I really just try to impart what I've learned to the guys and hopefully they kind of take it and run with it for their individual careers, but also for our team's success."

Although Williams showed no signs of slowing down in 2018, earning his sixth Pro Bowl selection, he announced that he planned to retire at the end of the year two days before the Bills played their final game of the regular season on December 30. Saying that he wanted to spend more time with his family, Williams stated his intentions to Bills fans in a letter that read:

This isn't easy. It was never going to be. There's no perfect time to retire from a game, a franchise, and a city that means so much to me and my family. But it's time to hang up my cleats.

I had never lived outside of Louisiana when Jill and I moved here at 22 years old, but it didn't take me long to identify with this city, with its people, with their attitude and loyalty. This place celebrates grit as much as it does talent, and there's something to be said for that. Now, I'm leaving at 35 with five kids, calling Buffalo my home. It's just not like everywhere else, and it will always be a part of me.

A singular word sticks out when I look back on my NFL career. Grateful. To have spent this much time with one team. To have had the opportunity to get to know this organization, this community, and more importantly, the people. To have raised my family here. To have made countless memories and friendships, on and off the field.

Thank you to the Pegulas, to the Wilson family, to my teammates, to Sean McDermott and Brandon Beane, to my family, and to the fans. I've been at this a really long time, but it doesn't feel like it, and that's a testament to your unwavering support.

I could not be more grateful to retire as a lifelong Buffalo Bill.

One last time, I'll see you on the field on Sunday.

Expressing his respect for Williams upon learning of his decision to retire, Bills head coach Sean McDermott said, "We need more Kyle Williams, although they're hard to find. You can't replace a guy like Kyle. They come around once in a career. . . . When you look up Buffalo Bills in the dictionary, you're going to see Kyle's picture there. That's what he's all about. . . . He's just a team guy through and through, who really personifies what Buffalo is all about."

After retiring as an active player, Williams—who recorded 48.5 sacks, 609 tackles, 103 tackles for loss, 4 forced fumbles, 6 fumble recoveries, 1 interception, and 1 touchdown over the course of his career—returned to Ruston, Louisiana, where he became defensive coordinator of the Ruston High School football team.

## CAREER HIGHLIGHTS

### Best Season

Williams earned his lone All-Pro selection in 2010 by recording 5.5 sacks, a career-high 76 tackles, including 54 of the solo variety, 13 hits on opposing quarterbacks, and 2 fumble recoveries. But he performed slightly better in 2013, gaining Pro Bowl recognition for one of six times by registering a career-high 10.5 sacks and 22 quarterback hits, making 68 tackles, 14 of which resulted in a loss, forcing a fumble, and recovering another.

### Memorable Moments/Greatest Performances

- Recorded the first sack of his career when he got to Chad Pennington during a 13-3 win over the Jets on October 28, 2007.
- Contributed to a 30-7 victory over the Colts in the final game of the 2009 regular season by recording 1 sack, registering 7 tackles, 4 of which resulted in a loss, and anchoring a defense that allowed just 25 yards rushing and 157 yards of total offense.
- Starred in defeat on November 28, 2010, recording 2 sacks, 10 tackles, and 3 tackles for loss during a 19-16 overtime loss to the Pittsburgh Steelers.
- Helped lead the Bills to a 37-14 win over the Jets on November 17, 2013, by recording 2 sacks and forcing 1 fumble.
- Proved to be a huge factor in the Bills' 19-0 shutout of the Dolphins on December 22, 2013, registering 2 sacks, recording 3 tackles for loss, and anchoring a defense that surrendered just 14 yards rushing and 103 yards of total offense.
- Recorded the only interception of his career during a 23-20 overtime win over the Chicago Bears in the 2014 regular-season opener.
- Scored the only touchdown of his career when he ran the ball in from 1 yard out during a 22-16 win over Miami in the 2017 regular-season finale.
- Made his only pass reception as a pro with a little over four minutes remaining in the final game of his career when he gathered in a 9-yard pass from Josh Allen during a 42-17 win over the Dolphins in the 2018 regular-season finale.

**Notable Achievements**

- Recorded 10.5 sacks in 2013
- Led Bills in sacks once
- Led Bills defensive linemen in tackles three times
- Ranks among Bills career leaders with 48.5 sacks (8th), 609 tackles (7th), and 183 games played (7th)
- Six-time Pro Bowl selection (2010, 2012, 2013, 2014, 2016, and 2018)
- 2010 Second-Team All-Pro selection
- 2014 First-Team All-AFC selection

## 20

## COOKIE GILCHRIST

arred from playing college football or competing in the NFL after he illegally signed a professional contract with the Cleveland Browns while still in high school, Cookie Gilchrist ended up spending many of his peak seasons playing in the Canadian Football League. Yet even though Gilchrist did not make his American pro debut with the Bills until after he celebrated his twenty-seventh birthday, he ultimately established himself as the greatest all-around running back in AFL history, winning two rushing titles, while also excelling as a blocker and receiver out of the backfield. A member of the Bills from 1962 to 1964, Gilchrist earned AFL Player of the Year honors in the first of those campaigns, before leading Buffalo to its first league championship two years later. A four-time AFL All-Star and four-time All-AFL selection, Gilchrist earned each of those honors three times while playing for the Bills, before splitting his final three seasons between the Denver Broncos and Miami Dolphins.

Born in Brackenridge, Pennsylvania, on May 25, 1935, Carlton Chester Gilchrist grew up some twenty-five miles northeast of Pittsburgh, where he starred in football while attending Har-Brack Union High School in nearby Natrona Heights. A phenomenal athlete, Gilchrist led Har-Brack Union to the Western Pennsylvania Interscholastic Athletic League cochampionship in 1953, prompting legendary Cleveland Browns head coach Paul Brown to offer him $5,500 to sign with his team prior to the start of his senior year. Committing an error in judgment, Gilchrist accepted Brown's offer, preventing him from attending college on an athletic scholarship since, by signing with the Browns, he had violated his amateur status. Meanwhile, Gilchrist also found himself being shunned by the NFL, which refused to recognize the signing of underage players.

Left with no other recourse, Gilchrist traveled to Canada, where he spent two years starring in the Ontario Rugby Football League, before splitting the next six seasons between the Hamilton Tiger-Cats, Saskatchewan Roughriders, and Toronto Argonauts of the Canadian Football League.

Cookie Gilchrist earned AFL Player of the Year honors in 1962.

Excelling on both sides of the ball for all three teams, Gilchrist earned five CFL All-Star nominations by rushing for 4,911 yards and amassing 1,068 receiving yards as a running back on offense, while also recording 12 interceptions as a linebacker on defense.

Signed by the Bills in 1962 after they failed in their attempt to lure Heisman Trophy-winning running back Ernie Davis to Buffalo, Gilchrist made his return to the United States an extremely successful one, earning AFL All-Star, First-Team All-AFL, and AFL Player of the Year honors by leading the league with 1,096 yards rushing and 13 rushing touchdowns, finishing second in the circuit with 1,415 yards from scrimmage, 15 touchdowns, and 128 points scored, and ranking among the leaders with 1,565 all-purpose yards and an average of 5.1 yards per carry. Displaying his tremendous versatility, Gilchrist also assumed place-kicking duties for the Bills, successfully converting 8 of his 20 field-goal attempts and 14 of his 17 extra-point attempts. Continuing to perform at an elite level the next two seasons, Gilchrist gained AFL All-Star and All-AFL recognition in both 1963 and 1964 by rushing for 979 yards, amassing 1,190 yards from scrimmage, and scoring 14 touchdowns in the first of those campaigns, before leading the Bills to the AFL championship the following year by gaining a league-high 981 yards on the ground, amassing 1,326 yards from scrimmage, and scoring 6 touchdowns.

Blessed with extraordinary physical ability that would have allowed him to excel in any era, Gilchrist, who stood 6'2", weighed 251 pounds, and had a 52-inch chest and a 31-inch waist, possessed great size, strength, and speed, as Bills Hall of Fame guard Billy Shaw acknowledged when he said, "He was probably the best athlete that I have ever played ball with. He had tremendous strength, and he was exceptionally quick for a man who weighed 250 pounds."

Longtime Bills owner Ralph Wilson also expressed his amazement over Gilchrist's unique skillset when he stated, "He could be an All-Pro today. He had size, 250 pounds, but could run like Thurman Thomas."

Chargers perennial All-AFL offensive tackle Ron Mix offered, "Cookie represented an almost revolutionary jump in running backs because of his combination of size and speed."

Meanwhile, in discussing his former teammate's powerful physique, Booker Edgerson said, "Cookie stood out like a giant. He looked like the Greek god Zeus had chiseled him out of the Rock of Gibraltar."

Gilchrist's size and strength made him extremely effective at running between the tackles, with Billy Shaw recalling, "There was no one any better than Cookie in hitting the hole from tackle to tackle. He would punish linebackers and defensive linemen. He would hit the blocker in front of him if he didn't get out of the way. I have scars on my back from when someone would stalemate me at the line, and here comes Cookie from behind me. He didn't care what color jersey you had on—he was going forward. . . . Cookie enjoyed running the ball straight ahead so he could hit somebody."

Claiming that Gilchrist also possessed the speed to break his runs to the outside, former Bills coach Joe Collier stated, "I don't know if he had the type of quickness Jim Brown had. Jim Brown could wiggle in the open field. Cookie was not a wiggle guy. He was a straight-ahead-type guy. But, in those days, he was the perfect guy."

An exceptional blocker as well, Gilchrist received special praise from John Madden for his excellence in that area during a 1987 CBS TV

COOKIE GILCHRIST

broadcast, with the former head coach of the Oakland Raiders saying, "Cookie Gilchrist may have been the best blocking running back that ever played the game."

In addition to his natural gifts, Gilchrist possessed a fierce competitive spirit and a nasty disposition that he exhibited during the early stages of an all-or-nothing showdown between the Bills and Boston Patriots in the final game of the 1964 regular season. Recalling the events that transpired on the very first play from scrimmage, fellow Bills running back Wray Carlton told the *Buffalo News* in 1997, "We ran a slide play. Cookie broke it to the outside, and he ran straight at Patriots cornerback Chuck Shonta. Cookie ran right over him and knocked him out cold. Shonta was laying on the field, and Cookie walked back to the huddle and said to the Patriots standing around him, 'OK, which one of you (so-and-sos) is next?'"

Stating that Gilchrist's tremendous drive and determination greatly impacted every other member of the Bills, former teammate Paul Maguire stated, "Anybody from that era would never forget him. He was that kind of a guy. When you went on the field with him, you never even doubted that you were going to win because he wouldn't let you think any other way."

Maguire continued, "He was so impressive. He was the biggest fullback in the game and could run and block. When he first came to the Bills, he was the wedge buster. . . . On the football field, he was one of the nastiest sons of bitches I ever met in my life. There was absolutely no fear in that man."

Former Bills receiver Charley Ferguson added, "He had so much character, he brought out the best in all of us. If there's ever such a thing as 110 percent, that's what you got from Cookie. There was no such thing as not being ready."

Unfortunately, Gilchrist shared a somewhat contentious relationship with Bills owner Ralph Wilson and head coach Lou Saban during his time in Buffalo, with the latter placing his star running back on waivers at one point during the 1964 season after he took himself out of a contest. Reflecting back on the incident, former Bills tight end Ernie Warlick said, "The offense got the ball, and he didn't go into the game. Saban asked, 'Hey, Cookie, why aren't you out there?' He said, 'They're not giving me the ball, so why the hell should I play?' So, he sat on the bench and told his backup to go in."

After Jack Kemp brokered a reconciliation between the two men, Gilchrist ended up leading the Bills to the 1964 AFL championship. But, when Gilchrist demanded more money at the end of the year, he sealed his fate, stating years later, "I wanted a percentage of the hot dog sales, the popcorn, the parking and the ticket sales. Lou Saban, the Bills head coach, said that would make me part owner of the team. I was a marked man after that."

Subsequently traded to the Denver Broncos for running back Billy Joe prior to the start of the 1965 season, Gilchrist left Buffalo having rushed for 3,056 yards, made 78 receptions for 875 yards, amassed 3,931 yards from scrimmage and 4,081 all-purpose yards, and scored 35 touchdowns in his three years with the Bills.

Looking back on the deal that sent Gilchrist to Denver, Butch Byrd stated, "Quite honestly, I thought it was a mistake when we traded him. I think the Bills management at the time thought it was getting rid of a problem, but we got Billy Joe in a trade for Cookie, and you could see there was a vast difference; the dynamics just weren't there. Cookie did some things that were unconscionable for an athlete. Something inside of him made him think he was being maligned or mistreated and not getting his just due, and he couldn't accept that. That was his flaw, but you had to accept that and look at all the pluses, which far outweighed his minuses."

Byrd continued, "Cookie was a leader out there. Some say he was a little ahead of his time in his thinking, but when he put on the uniform, he came to play. He was an inspiration. Controversial? Absolutely. But I have high regard for him."

Continuing his outstanding play with Denver in 1965, Gilchrist earned AFL All-Star and First-Team All-AFL honors by gaining 954 yards on the ground, amassing 1,108 yards from scrimmage, and scoring 7 touchdowns. Subsequently left unprotected in the 1966 AFL expansion draft, Gilchrist joined the Miami Dolphins, with whom he spent one injury-marred season, before retiring during the early stages of the ensuing campaign with career totals of 4,293 rushing yards, 110 receptions, 1,135 receiving yards, 5,428 yards from scrimmage, 5,578 all-purpose yards, 37 rushing touchdowns, and 43 total TDs.

Following his playing days, Gilchrist remained unhappy over his treatment by the football establishment, with close friend Booker Edgerson saying, "He couldn't get that out of his craw. He felt if he had been able to go to college, he'd have been a better person for it. . . . He never got over it. He talked about it and talked about it. He didn't take advantage of so many good opportunities he could have had. The people of Buffalo and Western New York loved him."

In addition to resisting most offers to return to Buffalo for appearances due to what he believed to be unsatisfactory compensation, Gilchrist refused induction into the CFL Hall of Fame, citing exploitation by league owners as the reason. Although longtime Bills announcer Van Miller eventually convinced Gilchrist to accept enshrinement on the Bills Wall of Fame, he did not do so in time for the former running back to gain induction prior to his death from throat, prostate, and colon cancer at the age of eighty-five on January 10, 2011. Gilchrist, who passed away at an assisted living facility in Pittsburgh, Pennsylvania, was also posthumously diagnosed with stage four chronic traumatic encephalopathy.

Upon learning of Gilchrist's passing, Ralph Wilson, who settled his differences with his former star running back just one week earlier, said, "The Bills were very lucky to have procured the services of Cookie Gilchrist, who was one of the greatest fullbacks I have ever seen in all of my years in professional football."

Expressing his appreciation for Gilchrist's greatness years earlier, Billy Shaw said, "I've been in football since I was in the fourth grade. Cookie Gilchrist is the best football player I've ever seen or been associated with."

Former *Buffalo News* football writer Larry Felser, who covered Gilchrist during his days with the Bills, wrote in 2004, "Any time. Any place. Any brand of football. Cookie was, pound for pound, the greatest all-around player I ever saw. He would be a superstar in today's football."

Jack Kemp once said of his former teammate, "Cookie Gilchrist, to my way of thinking, is one of the greatest professional football players who have ever played the game, either NFL or AFL. . . . Cookie was better than Jim Brown. Jim Brown is a good friend of mine, but Cookie, in my opinion, was better all around. He could block. He could catch passes. He could tackle. He could kick field goals. He was really one of the greatest all-around football players. Jim Brown was the greatest runner."

Butch Byrd expressed similar sentiments when he stated, "Jim Brown was the great back during that era, but I have often said that I thought Cookie was every bit as good as Jim Brown. The Buffalo Bills weren't the team that the Cleveland Browns were at that time, but, taking nothing away from Jim Brown, man for man, talent for talent, Cookie was right there."

Agreeing with Byrd's assessment, Gilchrist himself once said, "I told Jim Brown to his face that, if I had stayed with the Browns, nobody would have heard of him."

# BILLS CAREER HIGHLIGHTS

### Best Season

Gilchrist had the greatest season of his relatively brief professional career in 1962, when, as a twenty-seven-year-old rookie, he earned AFL Player of the Year honors by leading the league with 1,096 yards rushing and 13 rushing touchdowns, while also finishing second in the circuit with 1,415 yards from scrimmage, 15 touchdowns, and 128 points scored.

### Memorable Moments/Greatest Performances

- Performed brilliantly during a 23-20 loss to the Denver Broncos on September 15, 1962, scoring the first 2 touchdowns of his career on a 42-yard run and an 18-yard pass reception, and amassing a total of 255 all-purpose yards, with 131 of those coming on the ground, 48 through the air, and the other 76 on special teams.
- Led the Bills to a 35-10 win over the San Diego Chargers on October 13, 1962, by rushing for 124 yards and scoring 2 touchdowns.
- Followed that up by carrying the ball 19 times for 143 yards and 1 touchdown during a 14-6 win over the Oakland Raiders on October 20, 1962, with his 7-yard TD run in the fourth quarter sealing the victory.
- Displayed his tremendous versatility during a 45-38 win over the Broncos on October 28, 1962, rushing for 89 yards and 2 touchdowns, gaining another 76 yards on 2 pass receptions, and kicking a 33-yard field goal.
- Concluded his banner year of 1962 by kicking a pair of field goals and rushing for 143 yards and 2 TDs during a 20-3 win over the New York Titans in the regular-season finale.
- Helped lead the Bills to a 30-28 win over the Broncos on November 3, 1963, by rushing for 125 yards and scoring 2 TDs, one of which came on a 35-yard pass from Daryle Lamonica.
- Earned AFL Player of the Week honors by carrying the ball thirty-six times for a career-high 243 yards and 5 TDs during a 45-14 win over the Jets on December 8, 1963, with his 243 yards gained on the ground setting a new single-game pro football rushing record (since broken).
- Accumulated 178 yards from scrimmage during a 23-20 victory over the Raiders on October 3, 1964, gaining 91 yards on the ground and another 87 on four pass receptions.

- Led the Bills to a 24-10 win over the Houston Oilers on November 1, 1964, by rushing for 139 yards and one touchdown, which came on a 60-yard run in the fourth quarter.
- Followed that up by carrying the ball nine times for 99 yards and 1 touchdown during a 20-7 win over the Jets on November 8, 1964, with his TD coming on a career-long 67-yard run.
- Contributed to the Bills' 20-7 victory over San Diego in the 1964 AFL Championship Game by carrying the ball sixteen times for 122 yards.

**Notable Achievements**

- Rushed for more than 1,000 yards once (1,096 in 1962)
- Amassed more than 1,000 yards from scrimmage three times
- Scored more than 10 touchdowns twice
- Scored more than 100 points once (128 in 1962)
- Averaged more than 5 yards per carry once
- Led AFL in rushing attempts twice, rushing yards twice, and rushing touchdowns three times
- Finished second in AFL in yards from scrimmage once, touchdowns twice, and points scored once
- Finished third in AFL in rushing attempts once and rushing yards once
- Led Bills in rushing three times
- Ranks among Bills career leaders with 3,056 yards rushing (12th), 31 rushing touchdowns (4th), and 35 touchdowns (10th)
- 1964 division champion
- 1964 AFL champion
- 1963 Week 14 AFL Player of the Week
- 1962 AFL Player of the Year
- Three-time AFL All-Star selection (1962, 1963, and 1964)
- Two-time First-Team All-AFL selection (1962 and 1964)
- 1963 Second-Team All-AFL selection
- AFL All-Time Second Team
- Inducted into Bills Wall of Fame in 2017

# 21

# JIM RITCHER

One of only three Bills players to appear in as many as two hundred games, Jim Ritcher proved to be a model of consistency and durability during his fourteen years in Buffalo, at one point going eight straight seasons without missing a start. An invaluable member of teams that won six division titles and four consecutive AFC championships, Ritcher manned the left guard position for the Bills from 1983 to 1993, a period during which he failed to start just six nonstrike games. A two-time Pro Bowler and one-time All-Pro, Ritcher later received the additional honor of being inducted into the Bills Wall of Fame after ending his career as a backup with the Atlanta Falcons.

Born in Hinckley, Ohio, on May 21, 1958, James Alexander Ritcher grew up in the Cleveland suburb of Barea, where he got his start on the gridiron in the local Pop Warner leagues. Eventually emerging as a standout two-way lineman and wrestler at Highland High School in nearby Medina, Ritcher dreamed of one day competing in both sports for his beloved Ohio State Buckeyes. However, Ritcher took a more pragmatic approach to his future when then-North Carolina State coach Lou Holtz recruited him to play defensive end for the Wolfpack, recalling years later, "Lou Holtz was the head coach of North Carolina State, and he was recruiting in the Ohio area. He was originally from that area, and he was at a sports banquet I had been at. He made North Carolina sound so wonderful that I was interested in it. Growing up in Ohio, of course everyone would love to play for Ohio State, but I wasn't really recruited there. And, you know, there were a few bigger schools, but mostly I was getting recruited by Mid-American schools. North Carolina State was one of the bigger schools, and Lou was quite the salesman on it. I just ended up really liking the area."

Before Ritcher arrived on campus, though, Holtz left Raleigh to become head coach of the New York Jets. With Bo Rein replacing Holtz at NC State, he decided to employ Ritcher as an offensive lineman in the new

Jim Ritcher started every game the Bills played for eight straight seasons at one point during his career.
Courtesy of George A. Kitrinos.

scheme he planned to implement, telling him, "At offensive line, you'll have a better chance of playing right away. Try it for a week and see if you like it."

Disappointed at the prospect of moving to the offensive side of the ball, Ritcher later explained, "I played both ways in high school. I played offensive tackle, and on defense I was a defensive end. Most of the schools were recruiting me as a defensive end. There were some schools that were interested in me as an offensive lineman, but those are the schools I didn't want to go to because I wanted to play defense, and if you're a defensive guy making tackles, you hear your name over the loudspeaker—if you're into that kind of thing, and I probably was back then. As an offensive lineman, they don't announce your name too much. Back then it was all about me wanting to get to play defense. It was freeing, and there wasn't a lot of thinking involved, because mostly you're just running after the guy with the ball."

Nevertheless, Ritcher agreed to move to center, where he went on to establish himself as the nation's top player at his position while at NC State. A three-year starter for the Wolfpack, Ritcher helped running back Ted Brown rush for an ACC record 4,602 yards, earning in the process All-America honors twice. Also named the winner of the Outland Trophy his senior year as college football's best interior lineman, Ritcher became the first center to ever win the award, with Bo Rein later saying of his protégé, "He was strong and quick. His talent enabled us to outline certain plays we wouldn't have considered with normal players. He would be a star at any position except quarterback or wide receiver."

After hearing his name linked to the up-and-coming Seattle Seahawks prior to the 1980 NFL Draft, Ritcher headed to Buffalo when the Bills selected him in the first round, with the 16th overall pick. Coming to embrace his new home before long, Ritcher stated years later, "As you get older and you can look back on things, thank God for unanswered prayers. Because I surely loved being in Buffalo a thousand times more than I ever would have been happy in Seattle. I'm so thankful for how it happened."

After spending his first NFL season serving the Bills primarily as a long snapper on special teams, Ritcher moved to left guard, where he began to see more significant playing time in 1981. Finally joining the starting unit full time in 1983, Ritcher began a string of ten seasons during which he missed just two nonstrike games, starting 154 out of 156 contests.

Gradually establishing himself as one of the league's top interior offensive linemen, Ritcher earned Pro Bowl honors in 1991 and 1992 by helping Thurman Thomas continue his string of eight straight seasons in which he rushed for more than 1,000 yards. Outstanding in pass protection as well, Ritcher did an excellent job of allowing Jim Kelly to survey the field from his preferred place in the pocket.

Although Ritcher, who is officially listed in Pro Football Reference at 6'3" and 273 pounds, became known primarily for his speed and quickness, he also possessed great strength, with Steve Tasker writing in his book *Tales from the Buffalo Bills*, "Jim Ritcher was one of those guys I would expect to find in those 'World Strongest Man' competitions. He wasn't all that tall for an offensive lineman, maybe 6 feet, 2 inches and change, and he had problems keeping his weight above 280, but you didn't want to mess with him because he was so incredibly strong."

Tasker continued, "It was funny seeing rookies line up for pass-rushing drills the first day of training camp. They'd choose to go up against Ritcher because he appeared to be the smallest offensive lineman, and they figured they could have their way with him. They quickly discovered otherwise. More times than not, Ritcher wound up manhandling them."

An extremely hard worker who entered each game well prepared for his opponent, Ritcher said, "I always pushed myself to be the best player I could be. I studied the playbook as much as I could, and that's why I was able to start all those years, because I knew the book the best. I would study it as much as possible because, if I wasn't prepared, the coaches would bench me in a second."

Always in excellent shape, Ritcher credited his longevity to his off-season conditioning program, stating, "I would usually work out four or five days a week to make sure I kept my strength up. My wife helped me keep a strict diet so I could control my weight. Without all that, I probably would have lost my job much sooner."

After sharing playing time with Glenn Parker in 1993, Ritcher signed as a free agent with the Atlanta Falcons the following offseason, leaving Buffalo with career totals of 203 games played and 167 starts. Ritcher subsequently appeared in just fifteen games with the Falcons over the course of the next two seasons, before announcing his retirement at the end of 1995.

Following his playing days, Ritcher, who took flying lessons while with the Bills, embarked on a career as a commercial pilot that led to him serving as a captain for American Airlines for more than two decades. Now sixty-five years old, Ritcher lives with his wife, Harriet, in Raleigh, North Carolina. Although his years as an NFL offensive lineman have left their mark on him, Ritcher remains in relatively good health, saying during a 2019 interview, "Well, of course my shoulders bother me—especially my left shoulder. I've had four surgeries on that. I can't get it up very high over my head. So, I'm thinking I'll probably need a shoulder replacement. But I have to wait until I retire at 65 as far as flying for the airline. It doesn't bother me when I'm flying an airplane. I can do all of that, so there's no problem there. But I'd like to be able to play golf again. I can't really swing a club too much. And playing with the grandchildren, I'd like to be able to do more. My neck, of course, always bothered me, and sleeping at night and getting in a comfortable position. So, other than that, I'm actually in pretty good shape. I still jog a little bit and get four miles in. So many of my friends can't believe I still run."

Looking back fondly on the time he spent in Buffalo, Ritcher stated, "It has so many great memories. If it weren't for the weather, I would have stayed there. But one of the reasons I went from Ohio to North Carolina State was to get away from the cold weather. . . . There just isn't anything I can say bad about Buffalo. I enjoyed the time and wish I could have ended my career there. Buffalo was wonderful."

## BILLS CAREER HIGHLIGHTS

### Best Season

Although Ritcher perhaps performed just as well in one or two other seasons, he gained All-Pro recognition for the only time in his career at the age of thirty-three in 1991, when his outstanding blocking at left guard helped the AFC champion Bills finish second in the NFL in points scored and first in yards gained.

### Memorable Moments/Greatest Performances

• Helped the Bills amass 483 yards of total offense during a 38-35 win over the Miami Dolphins on October 9, 1983.
• Outstanding blocking at the point of attack helped the Bills rush for a season-high total of 255 yards during a 37-21 victory over the Los Angeles Raiders on December 11, 1988.
• Strong play at left guard helped the Bills gain 233 yards on the ground and amass 441 yards of total offense during a 37-0 shutout of the Jets in the 1989 regular-season finale.
• Helped the Bills rush for 276 yards and amass 396 yards of total offense during a 42-6 manhandling of the Colts on October 13, 1991.
• Along with his line-mates, dominated Atlanta at the point of attack on November 22, 1992, with the Bills rushing for 315 yards and amassing 412 yards of total offense during a 41-14 win.

### Notable Achievements

• Started 124 consecutive nonstrike games from 1985 to 1992
• Ranks third in Bills history with 203 games played
• Six-time division champion (1980, 1988, 1989, 1990, 1991, and 1993)
• Four-time AFC champion (1990, 1991, 1992, and 1993)
• Two-time Pro Bowl selection (1991 and 1992)
• 1991 Second-Team All-Pro selection
• 1990 Second-Team All-AFC selection
• Inducted into Bills Wall of Fame in 2004

# 22

## GEORGE SAIMES

O ne of the finest defensive backs in the brief history of the AFL, George Saimes spent seven seasons in Buffalo, helping to lead the Bills to three division titles and two league championships. A hard-hitting safety with superior cover skills, Saimes did an excellent job of serving as the Bills' last line of defense, earning five AFL All-Star nominations and three First-Team All-AFL selections with his outstanding all-around play. Also named to the AFL All-Time First Team, Saimes later received the additional honor of being inducted into the Bills Wall of Fame.

Born in Canton, Ohio, on September 1, 1941, George Thomas Saimes received his introduction to organized football at Lincoln High School, where, in addition to excelling on the gridiron, he starred in track and field as a hurdler and pole vaulter, with one of his teammates claiming that a coach from rival McKinley High said that he "could have won the all-city meet by himself." Outstanding in basketball as well, Saimes, who lifted weights before the practice became popular among athletes, also drew praise from one of his former teammates on the court, with Jim Osborn saying he "was a tremendous athlete who never got a big head. . . . George never complained . . . never. And never once did I hear him say, 'I did this,' or 'I did that.' He was determined. We might be down in a game, and he would be saying, 'We can beat these guys.'"

After briefly attending Bowling Green State University in Bowling Green, Ohio, Saimes transferred to Michigan State University (MSU), where he went on to make a name for himself as a standout fullback and defensive back, performing well enough at both positions to earn a seventh-place finish in the Heisman Trophy voting his senior year.

Commenting on his former teammate's brilliant play at MSU, Sherman Lewis stated, "George Saimes was the best football player I played with in college. He played both ways and never came off the field. He played fullback on offense and rover-back (strong safety) on defense. George was the heart and soul of our team—on both sides of the football. He was a

George Saimes earned a spot on the AFL All-Time First Team with his outstanding play for the Bills at safety.

tough, hard-nosed player. Since he never came off the field, he'd be black and blue after every game, but he'd bounce back the next week and come back for more."

Lewis continued, "George was a guy that worked to improve his speed in college. He wore weights on both his ankles and shoulders. By the time George was a senior, he had excellent speed. . . . I really admired the way George approached the game because he didn't like to talk. In fact, he hated it whenever he was asked to address the team. George was a different person when he stepped onto the field. He left it all on the field. Again, he's the finest player I played with at Michigan State."

Saimes also received high praise from former Spartans assistant coach Henry Bullough, who recalled, "In college, he and Sherm Lewis played both ways. They often played 60-minute games. George played the rover-back position before [future consensus All-American and AFL All-Star] George Webster came along. He was a great college player but an even better pro. There are many of us who believe George should be in the Pro Football Hall of Fame. One of his defensive coaches from the Buffalo Bills once told me that George might have missed three or four tackles during his entire career. The assistant told me, 'George was like gold' as a safety."

Bullough added, "The greatest thing about George was that he treated everybody the same. It didn't make a difference if you were an All-American or a walk-on. George gave you the same respect."

And Mark Dantonio, who served as head football coach at MSU from 2007 to 2019, stated, "George Saimes is one of the greatest two-way players in the history of Michigan State football. He was a productive runner and dominant blocker from the fullback position and a consistent playmaker as a safety."

After Saimes gained consensus All-America recognition as a fullback and strong safety his senior year at Michigan State, the Los Angeles Rams selected him in the 6th round of the 1963 NFL Draft, with the 71st overall pick. However, Saimes instead chose to sign with the Kansas City Chiefs, who claimed him in the same round of that year's AFL Draft, with the 48th overall pick. Subsequently dealt to the Bills, Saimes began his professional career in Buffalo, where he had a solid rookie season, recording 4 interceptions in 1963 after moving from halfback to safety during the early stages of the campaign. Emerging as the league's finest player at his position the following year, Saimes recorded a career-high 6 interceptions, earning in the process AFL All-Star honors for the first of five straight times and the first of his three First-Team All-AFL nominations.

Continuing to perform at an elite level the next four seasons, Saimes registered another 9 interceptions, although, according to longtime teammate Booker Edgerson, he could have had many more, with the former cornerback saying, "We used to kid him about it and say, 'If you had great hands and great eyesight, you could've had at least 50 or 60 interceptions. At least he knocked the ball down."

Even though Saimes ended up picking off a total of 22 passes for the Bills, he built his reputation more on his exceptional tackling ability. Despite being only 5'11" and 186 pounds, Saimes proved to be one of the league's hardest hitters and surest tacklers, with football writer Larry Felser, who covered the Bills for *The Buffalo News*, once describing him as "the finest open-field tackler in the league."

In discussing his former teammate, Harry Jacobs said, "George Saimes was unbelievable. What speaks to his game better than anything is in one year he had a chance for 102 tackles, and he made 100. That will tell you all you need to know about George Saimes."

Meanwhile, Booker Edgerson stated, "George Saimes was one of the surest tacklers I ever saw. If he got his hands on you, more than likely, you were going to go down."

Always a threat for a safety blitz as well, Saimes once recorded 4 sacks in one game, with his ability to apply pressure to opposing quarterbacks from his safety position inspiring favorable comparisons to St. Louis Cardinals Hall of Fame safety Larry Wilson. And, like his NFL counterpart, Saimes made opposing wide receivers think twice before coming across the middle of the field.

After missing just one game his first six years in the league, Saimes suffered through an injury-riddled 1969 season in which he appeared in just eight contests. Traded to the Denver Broncos at the end of the year, Saimes started a total of thirty games over the course of the next three seasons, before announcing his retirement following the conclusion of the 1972 campaign with career totals of 22 interceptions, 238 interception-return yards, 9 sacks, 4 fumble recoveries, and 1 defensive touchdown.

After retiring as an active player, Saimes spent many years scouting for the Tampa Bay Buccaneers, Washington Redskins, and Houston Texans, before retiring to the relative peace and quiet of his home in Canton, Ohio. Saimes lived until March 9, 2013, when he passed away at seventy-one years of age following a lengthy battle with leukemia.

Upon learning of his former teammate's passing, Booker Edgerson said, "There wasn't a better safety before him, and I don't think there's been any since, especially in terms of tackling and the intelligence of playing in the secondary with the receivers. I think that there should've been some consideration for him going into the Hall of Fame. Unfortunately, a lot of defensive backs in the '60s and '70s never really got that consideration."

## BILLS CAREER HIGHLIGHTS

### Best Season

Saimes played his best ball for the Bills in 1964, when he earned one of his three First-Team All-AFL nominations by recording a career-high 6 interceptions.

### Memorable Moments/Greatest Performances

- Recorded the first interception of his career during a 27-27 tie with the Kansas City Chiefs on September 22, 1963.
- Turned in an exceptional effort during a 30-19 win over the Denver Broncos on December 13, 1964, recording 4 sacks on his safety blitz, 3 of which came in the fourth quarter.
- Picked off 2 passes in one game for the only time as a pro during a 24-7 win over the Boston Patriots in the 1965 regular-season opener.
- Scored the only touchdown of his career on the same day his first child was born, running 18 yards to paydirt after recovering a fumble he caused during a 23-7 win over the Chiefs on October 17, 1965, earning in the process AFL Defensive Player of the Week honors.

### Notable Achievements

- Appeared in seventy consecutive games from 1963 to 1967
- Scored 1 defensive touchdown
- Recorded 6 interceptions in 1964
- Tied for 11th in Bills history with 22 interceptions
- Three-time division champion (1964, 1965, and 1966)
- Two-time AFL champion (1964 and 1965)
- 1965 Week 5 AFL Defensive Player of the Week
- Five-time AFL All-Star selection (1964, 1965, 1966, 1967, and 1968)
- Three-time First-Team All-AFL selection (1964, 1965, and 1967)
- Pro Football Reference All-1960s Second Team
- AFL All-Time First Team
- Inducted into Bills Wall of Fame in 2000

# 23
## FRED JACKSON

In discussing his long and arduous journey to the NFL, Fred Jackson said, "It's a story that's like nobody else's, and that's something to be proud of." A study in perseverance, Jackson, who made his NFL debut with the Bills as a twenty-six-year-old rookie in 2007 after spending two seasons playing indoor football and another two years competing in NFL Europe, went on to establish himself as one of the finest all-around running backs in franchise history, leading the team in rushing four times and amassing more than 1,000 yards from scrimmage on five separate occasions. An outstanding performer on special teams as well, Jackson became the first player in NFL history to amass more than 1,000 yards as both a rusher and return man in the same season, setting in the process a single-season franchise record for most all-purpose yards that still stands.

Born in Fort Worth, Texas, on February 20, 1981, Frederick George Jackson grew up in nearby Arlington, where he played football and ran track while attending Lamar High School. Although Jackson's smallish 5'8", 160-pound frame relegated him to reserve duty his two years on the varsity squad, he made a name for himself as a sprinter in track, qualifying for the state finals in the 100 meters, and serving as a member of the school's 4x100-meter relay team.

Failing to receive any scholarship offers, Jackson enrolled at Coe College, a small Division III school located in Cedar Rapids, Iowa. Emerging as a standout on the gridiron at Coe, Jackson rushed for 4,054 yards and scored 47 touchdowns, with his exceptional play earning him Iowa Conference MVP honors twice and NCAA Division III All-America recognition his senior year, when he gained more than 1,700 yards on the ground. Continuing to excel in track as well, Jackson earned All-America honors twice as a member of Coe's 4x100-meter relay team, which finished fifth at the NCAA Championships in 2002 and 2003.

Subsequently spurned by all thirty-two teams in the 2003 NFL Draft due to his small-college background, Jackson tried out for the Denver

Fred Jackson holds the Bills' single-season franchise record for most all-purpose yards.
Courtesy of Mark Cromwell

Broncos, Chicago Bears, and Green Bay Packers, all of whom chose not to sign him as an undrafted free agent. Left with no other recourse, Jackson joined the Sioux City Bandits of the National Indoor Football League, with whom he spent the next two seasons, earning league MVP honors in 2004 by rushing for 1,170 yards and 53 touchdowns, while also working as a youth counselor in his spare time. From Sioux City, Jackson headed to Europe, where he starred in the backfield of the Rhein Fire for two years, before receiving an invitation to Bills camp from fellow Coe College alum and then-Buffalo GM Marv Levy in the summer of 2006.

Unable to earn a roster spot during the 2006 preseason, Jackson spent the year on the Bills' practice squad. However, he finally became a regular member of an NFL team the following year, when, appearing in eight games as a backup running back, he rushed for 300 yards and made 22 receptions for 190 yards. Assuming a far more prominent role in 2008, Jackson rushed for 571 yards and 3 touchdowns, gained another 317 yards on 37 pass receptions, and accumulated 297 yards on special teams, giving him a total of 1,185 all-purpose yards. Jackson followed that up with the most productive year of his career, concluding the 2009 campaign with 1,062 yards rushing, 1,433 yards from scrimmage, 4 touchdowns, and a league-leading 2,516 all-purpose yards.

One of the league's more difficult backs to bring down one-on-one, the 6'1", 215-pound Jackson, who added some twenty pounds of muscle onto his frame after entering the professional ranks, earned the nickname "The InFredible Hulk" for his physical style of running and aggressive blocking of opposing pass-rushers. Blessed with good speed and soft hands, Jackson also excelled as a receiver out of the backfield, surpassing 40 receptions three times and 400 receiving yards twice during his time in Buffalo. More than anything, though, Jackson became known for his leadership and strong work ethic, which made him extremely popular with his teammates and the hometown fans.

So respected by his teammates that many of them began honoring him by wearing a T-shirt that featured the phrase "FredEx Delivers." Jackson received high praise from Kyle Williams, who said, "When I looked at Fred, I identified him as a guy like, 'You know what? I really don't want to let that guy down.'. . . Those guys are, I'm not going to say rare because I feel like we've had some good guys come through these doors. But those guys are special, and Fred's one of those guys."

Bills left tackle Demetrius Bell also had kind words for Jackson, calling him "the heart and soul of this team."

Meanwhile, Marv Levy stated, "In Buffalo, you can't imagine how much people revere Fred Jackson, because of his high character, his community involvement, and coming from a Division III school."

Continuing his outstanding play after being relieved of his kickoff- and punt-return duties prior to the start of the 2010 campaign, Jackson rushed for 927 yards, amassed 1,142 yards from scrimmage, and scored 7 touchdowns, before gaining 934 yards on the ground, accumulating 1,376 yards from scrimmage, and scoring 6 TDs in 2011, despite missing the final month of the season with a broken right leg he suffered during a Week 11 loss to Miami. Sidelined for much of the 2012 season as well with a concussion and knee injury, Jackson rushed for only 437 yards and scored just 4 touchdowns. However, he rebounded the following year to gain 890 yards on the ground, amass 1,277 yards from scrimmage, and score 10 TDs.

Jackson spent one more year in Buffalo, rushing for 525 yards, accumulating 1,026 yards from scrimmage, and scoring 3 touchdowns in 2014, before the Bills stunned their fans and many NFL observers by cutting him just prior to the start of the ensuing campaign. In addressing the team's decision to release the thirty-four-year-old running back, Bills GM Doug Whaley told reporters, "We thought for us, and at this time, we had to make this decision. There are a lot of circumstances that go into that, but we will keep that in-house for competitive reasons."

Although thousands of Bills fans subsequently signed an online petition demanding that the team bring Jackson back, the front office remained steadfast in its decision, bringing his days in Buffalo to an end. In his eight years with the Bills, Jackson rushed for 5,646 yards and 30 touchdowns, made 322 receptions for 2,640 yards and 7 TDs, amassed 8,286 yards from scrimmage, accumulated 9,717 all-purpose yards, and scored 37 touchdowns.

Signing with the Seahawks just a few days later, Jackson spent the 2015 season assuming a backup role in Seattle, gaining just 100 yards on the ground, amassing only 357 yards from scrimmage, and scoring just 2 TDs, before signing a one-day contract with the Bills in April 2018 that allowed him to officially retire as a member of the team after spending the previous two years out of football. Since leaving the game, Jackson, who now lives with his family in Ankeny, Iowa, has served as an analyst on the weekly postgame series, *Bills Tonight*, that airs on MSG Western New York. He also remains busy with his four children, saying, "I help coach my son in football, I'm coaching my girls in basketball. I'm taking my son to soccer and track practice all the time. . . . So, it's busy. I'm enjoying every minute of it. It's great to make it all about them now. They used to have to not do things on the weekend because their dad was traveling here, and they wanted to come and watch the games. So, it's fun now to make it about them and see how much fun they're having in participating in all these sports."

Passing his love for the Bills on to the other members of his family, Jackson says, "We're still huge Bills fans. This is still family for us."

## BILLS CAREER HIGHLIGHTS .

**Best Season**

Although Jackson accumulated almost as many yards from scrimmage in 2011 and scored more than twice as many touchdowns in 2013, he had the greatest season of his career in 2009, when he set a Bills single-season record by amassing 2,516 all-purpose yards and became the first player ever to accumulate more than 1,000 yards as both a rusher and return man in the same year by gaining 1,062 yards on the ground and 1,083 yards on special teams.

**Memorable Moments/Greatest Performances**

- Had his breakout game on December 2, 2007, rushing for 82 yards and making 4 receptions for 69 yards during a 17-16 win over Washington.
- Followed that up by gaining more than 100 yards on the ground for the first time in his career, carrying the ball fifteen times for 115 yards during a 38-17 victory over the Dolphins on December 9, 2007.
- Scored his first touchdown as a pro when he ran the ball in from 22 yards out during a 31-14 win over the St. Louis Rams on September 28, 2008.
- Helped lead the Bills to a 33-20 victory over the Tampa Bay Buccaneers on September 20, 2009, by carrying the ball twenty-eight times for 163 yards.
- Turned in perhaps the finest all-around performance of his career in the final game of the 2009 regular season, when he amassed 241 all-purpose yards during a 30-7 win over the Colts, gaining 212 yards on the ground, 15 through the air, and another 14 on special teams.
- Led the Bills to their first win of the 2010 campaign on November 14, when he rushed for 133 yards, made 6 receptions for 37 yards, and scored both Buffalo touchdowns during a 14-12 victory over the Detroit Lions.
- Followed that up with a strong outing against Cincinnati on November 21, 2010, rushing for 116 yards and 2 touchdowns during a 49-31 Bills win.
- Although the Bills failed to post their third straight win the following week, losing to Pittsburgh in overtime by a score of 19-16 on November 28, 2010, Jackson had another big game, gaining 59 yards on the

ground, and making 5 receptions for 104 yards and 1 touchdown, which came on a 65-yard catch-and-run.

- Helped lead the Bills to a 38-35 victory over the Oakland Raiders on September 18, 2011, by rushing for 117 yards and 2 touchdowns, the longest of which came on a 43-yard run.
- Contributed to a 34-31 win over the Patriots on September 25, 2011, by scoring a touchdown and amassing 161 yards from scrimmage, gaining 74 of those on the ground and the other 87 through the air.
- Turned in a similarly impressive performance during a 31-24 victory over the Eagles on October 9, 2011, making 6 receptions for 85 yards and rushing for 111 yards and 1 TD.
- Although the Bills lost to the Giants by a score of 27-24 the following week, Jackson gained 121 yards on the ground and scored 1 touchdown on a career-long 80-yard run.
- Proved to be a huge factor when the Bills recorded a 23-0 win over Washington on October 30, 2011, rushing for 120 yards and making 3 receptions for 74 yards.

## Notable Achievements

- Rushed for more than 1,000 yards once (1,062 in 2009)
- Surpassed 60 receptions and 500 receiving yards once each
- Surpassed 1,000 yards from scrimmage five times
- Amassed more than 2,000 all-purpose yards once
- Averaged more than 5 yards per carry twice
- Scored 10 touchdowns in 2013
- Led NFL with 2,516 all-purpose yards in 2009
- Finished second in NFL with rushing average of 5.5 yards per carry in 2011
- Led Bills in rushing four times
- Holds Bills single season record for most all-purpose yards (2,516 in 2009)
- Ranks among Bills career leaders with 5,646 yards rushing (3rd), 8,286 yards from scrimmage (5th), 9,717 all-purpose yards (5th), 322 receptions, (6th), 30 rushing touchdowns (5th), and 37 touchdowns (8th)

# 24
# JACK KEMP

Although Jack Kemp is perhaps remembered more for his lengthy career in politics, he previously spent nine years starting at quarterback in the AFL for teams that won five division titles and two league championships. Having most of his finest seasons for the Bills, Kemp served as their primary signal-caller from 1963 to 1969, a period during which he led them to three playoff appearances and consecutive AFL championships. Providing outstanding leadership and solid play behind center, Kemp earned five All-Star nominations, two All-AFL selections, and one league MVP trophy during his time in Buffalo, before being further honored following the conclusion of his playing career by being inducted into the Bills Wall of Fame.

Born in Los Angeles, California, on July 13, 1935, Jack French Kemp grew up in the predominantly Jewish Wilshire district of West Los Angeles, where he and his family attended the Church of Christ, Scientist. Consumed by sports as a youngster, Kemp dreamed of one day playing football professionally, although his mother made certain that he received exposure to other aspects of life as well by arranging piano lessons for him and trips to the Hollywood Bowl.

Eventually emerging as a standout athlete at Fairfax High School, Kemp starred in multiple sports, proving to be especially proficient in football, where he excelled on both sides of the ball. Meanwhile, Kemp developed the strong work ethic for which he later became so well-known by working with his brothers at his father's trucking company in downtown Los Angeles.

Following his graduation from Fairfax High, Kemp, who stood 5'10" and weighed 175 pounds at the time, enrolled at Occidental College, a founding member of the NCAA Division III Southern California Intercollegiate Athletic Conference, where his outstanding play at quarterback and defensive back earned him Little College All-America honors one year and All-Conference honors his final two seasons. An excellent all-around

Jack Kemp led the Bills to consecutive AFL championships in 1964 and 1965.
Courtesy of RMYAuctions.com.

athlete, Kemp also starred in track and field, setting a new school record in the javelin throw.

Choosing to further his education after he graduated from Occidental with a degree in physical education, Kemp pursued postgraduate studies in economics at Long Beach State University and California Western University in San Diego, while also trying to fulfill his dream of playing in the NFL after the Lions selected him in the 17th round of the 1957 NFL Draft, with the 203rd overall pick. However, Kemp experienced little success over the course of the next two seasons, appearing in just four games as a backup with the Pittsburgh Steelers in 1957 after being cut by the Lions, before spending the ensuing campaign on the taxi squads of the San Francisco 49ers and New York Giants. Cut by the Giants at the end of 1958, Kemp subsequently served as a private in the United States Army Reserve for one year, during which time he appeared in one game as a member of the Calgary Stampeders of the Canadian Football League.

Considered too small by most NFL teams, the 6'1", 200-pound Kemp finally received his big break when the Los Angeles Chargers of the newly formed AFL signed him early in 1960. Establishing himself as the league's top signal caller his first full year as a pro, Kemp led the Chargers to the Western Division title by throwing for 3,018 yards and 20 touchdowns, earning in the process First-Team All-AFL honors. Although Kemp posted slightly less impressive numbers the following year, he earned the first of his seven trips to the AFL All-Star game by leading the Chargers to their second straight division title.

Speaking years later of the tremendous determination that Kemp displayed en route to becoming a successful pro quarterback, longtime friend and former Saints and Colts head coach Jim Mora said, "At that time, and even now, for a player from a small school like Oxy, the chances of making it in the pros are almost nil. That's just the way it is . . . but Jack always had a strong desire to play pro ball, and the drive and the confidence to do it."

Despite the success the Chargers experienced the previous two years with Kemp starting for them behind center, they cut him loose midway through the 1962 campaign after he suffered an injury to his finger that sidelined him for several weeks. Subsequently claimed-off waivers by the Bills for the paltry sum of one hundred dollars, Kemp spent the remainder of the year in Buffalo, starting three games, before joining the starting unit full time the following season.

Performing well for the Bills in 1963, Kemp earned AFL All-Star honors by finishing second in the league with 2,910 passing yards, completing 50.3 percent of his passes, throwing for 13 touchdowns, and running for 8 others. Kemp followed that up with another solid season, leading the Bills to the first of their back-to-back AFL championships by passing for 2,285 yards and 13 touchdowns, before earning a share of the AFL MVP award in 1965, even though he finished the season with just 2,368 passing yards and 10 TD passes.

Despite being blessed with a strong throwing arm and the ability to move well in and out of the pocket, Kemp never truly established himself as an elite passer, completing just 46.7 percent of his passes and throwing nearly twice as many interceptions as touchdown passes over the course of his career. But statistics do not tell the whole story when it comes to Kemp, whose intelligence, mental and physical toughness, and extraordinary leadership ability made him one of the most impactful players in the ten-year history of the AFL. The unquestioned leader of the Bills during their glory years of the mid-1960s, Kemp not only directed the team's offense on the playing field, but he also helped mediate internal conflicts, including convincing head coach Lou Saban not to cut star running back Cookie Gilchrist in 1964 due to personal differences and managing the politics of his quarterback battle with Daryle Lamonica, who went on to star for the Oakland Raiders. Kemp also cofounded the AFL Players Association and played a pivotal role in settling a dispute that threatened to cancel the 1965 AFL All-Star game when the shabby treatment the Black players received from the host city of New Orleans prompted them to vote not to participate in the contest. Praising Kemp for his efforts on their behalf, Chargers star defensive tackle Ernie Ladd identified him as "the only white player to stand with them from the beginning."

Nevertheless, after Kemp earned AFL All-Star and Second-Team All-AFL honors in 1966 by guiding the Bills to their third straight division title, the hometown fans and media made him the scapegoat when the team experienced a precipitous fall from grace the following year. Things subsequently went from bad to worse for Kemp, who, after spending the 1967 season being booed by the fans at War Memorial Stadium, missed the entire 1968 campaign due to an injury he sustained to his right knee during the preseason.

Returning to action in 1969, Kemp earned the last of his seven AFL All-Star nominations even though he posted modest numbers for a Bills team that finished just 4-10. Approached by the Erie County Republican Party about running for Congress at the end of the year, Kemp, who earlier had worked on Barry Goldwater's presidential campaign in 1964 and Ronald Reagan's gubernatorial campaign in 1966, ultimately decided to run for office, recalling, "I had a four-year no-cut contract with the Bills at the time. . . . I figured that, if I lost, I could always come back and play. But the fans had their say and I was elected to Congress."

Retiring with career totals of 21,218 passing yards, 114 touchdown passes, 183 interceptions, 1,150 rushing yards, and 40 rushing touchdowns, a passer rating of 57.3, and a pass completion percentage of 46.7 percent, Kemp passed for 15,134 yards, threw 77 TD passes and 132 interceptions, rushed for 780 yards and 25 touchdowns, compiled a passer rating of 55.8, and completed 46.4 percent of his passes while playing for the Bills.

Elected to the House of Representatives in 1971, Kemp spent the next eighteen years serving as a congressman from Buffalo, during which time he worked tirelessly to improve economic and social conditions for the needy and minorities. Often referred to as a "bleeding heart conservative," Kemp responded, when asked why Republicans should care about those less fortunate and impoverished Blacks, who typically align themselves with the Democratic party, "Because it shows compassion, concern, and kindness toward people who are less fortunate. Practically, it will result in a much-expanded Republican Party, but of greater importance, it will produce a more civil nation."

Also a champion of tax cuts, free trade, economic growth, and a return to the gold standard, Kemp helped pass the Kemp-Roth Tax Cut in the 1980s, which proved to be the first of two major tax cuts put into law under President Ronald Reagan. In addition to his work in Congress, Kemp ran unsuccessfully for his party's presidential nomination in 1988, ran with Republican presidential nominee Bob Dole in the 1996 election, and served as secretary of housing and urban development under President George H. W. Bush from 1989 to 1993.

After retiring from public office, Kemp returned to his home in Bethesda, Maryland, where he lived until May 2, 2009, when he died of cancer at the age of seventy-three. Posthumously awarded the Presidential Medal of Freedom by Barack Obama, Kemp received high praise from the former president of the United States, who said in a statement, "Jack Kemp's commitment to public service and his passion for politics influenced not only the direction of his party, but his country. From his tenure as a Buffalo congressman to his ascent in national politics, Jack Kemp was a man who could fiercely advocate his own beliefs and principles while also remembering the lessons he learned years earlier on the football field that bitter divisiveness between race and class and station only stood in the way of the common aim of a team to win."

Several of Kemp's former Bills teammates also expressed their admiration for him following his passing, with Harry Jacobs saying, "He had the ability to come back at times of adversity and make things happen. He didn't shrink away from anything. Every challenge he ever saw, he faced up to it. He just kept going."

Billy Shaw stated, "You never saw fear in his eyes. You always saw confidence. And I saw that in his political career, too. That's what made Jack the man he was. His ability to rise to the occasion—whether it was on the football field or the political field—and always come up with a solution."

And Paul Maguire offered, "When Jack was in the huddle, they knew that some way he was going to get it done. Jack may not have gotten it done for 58 minutes, but you knew the last two, if he had to, it was going to get done. But that was his whole life, if you look at all the things that he did."

## BILLS CAREER HIGHLIGHTS

**Best Season**

Although Kemp posted better overall numbers in one or two other years, he had his finest season for the Bills in 1965, when his solid play and outstanding leadership earned him AFL Player of the Year honors.

**Memorable Moments/Greatest Performances**

- Helped the Bills forge a 27-27 tie with the Kansas City Chiefs on September 22, 1963, by running for two scores and throwing for 244 yards and 1 touchdown, which came on a 20-yard pass to Bill Miller.
- Excelled against the Chiefs once again in the second meeting between the two teams on October 13, 1963, passing for 300 yards and 2 touchdowns during a 35-26 Bills win, with his 89-yard TD pass to Elbert Dubenion in the fourth quarter extending Buffalo's lead to 9 points.
- Earned AFL Offensive Player of the Week honors for the first of four times by running for three scores and throwing for 317 yards and 1 touchdown during a 28-21 win over the Patriots on October 26, 1963, with his 72-yard TD pass to Charley Ferguson late in the final period providing the margin of victory.
- Led the Bills to a 48-17 rout of the Houston Oilers on October 11, 1964, by passing for a career-high 378 yards and 3 touchdowns, the longest of which went 94 yards to Glenn Bass.
- Ran for one score and passed for 280 yards and 1 touchdown during a 30-15 win over the Denver Broncos on September 19, 1965, earning in the process AFL Offensive Player of the Week honors for the second time.
- Earned that distinction again by throwing for 280 yards and 2 touchdowns during a 31-13 win over the Broncos on October 24, 1965, with his longest toss of the day being a 78-yard TD connection with running back Billy Joe.
- Led the Bills to a 34-25 victory over the Chiefs on December 12, 1965, by passing for 295 yards and 3 touchdowns, collaborating with Bo Roberson on scoring plays of 66 and 13 yards, before delivering a 47-yard TD pass to Ed Rutkowski late in the fourth quarter.
- Received game MVP honors despite completing only 8 of 19 pass attempts for 155 yards and 1 touchdown during the Bills 23-0 victory over San Diego in the 1965 AFL title tilt.

- With the Bills trailing the Jets by 17 points heading into the final period of the 1967 regular-season opener, Kemp led them on a furious fourth-quarter comeback that resulted in a 20-17 victory, with his 2 TD passes to Art Powell proving to be the game's most pivotal plays.
- Highlighted his final season in Buffalo with a strong outing against Denver on September 28, 1969, throwing for 249 yards and 3 touchdowns during a 41-28 Bills win.

### Notable Achievements

- Finished second in AFL in pass completions twice and passing yards once
- Ranks among Bills career leaders with 2,240 pass attempts (4th), 1,039 pass completions (4th), 15,134 passing yards (4th), 77 touchdown passes (4th), and 25 rushing touchdowns (tied for 9th).
- Three-time division champion (1964, 1965, and 1966)
- Two-time AFL champion (1964 and 1965)
- Four-time AFL Offensive Player of the Week
- 1965 AFL Player of the Year
- Five-time AFL All-Star selection (1963, 1964, 1965, 1966, and 1969)
- 1965 First-Team All-AFL selection
- 1966 Second-Team All-AFL selection
- Pro Football Reference All-1960s Second Team
- Inducted into Bills Wall of Fame in 1984

# 25
## STEVE TASKER

S peaking about one of his favorite players, Hall of Fame head coach
Marv Levy said, "There has never been a special teams player like Steve
Tasker. I was once told by a renowned head coach from another team
that the man on our team for whom they had to prepare most specifically,
despite all the many stars we had on offense and defense, was Steve."
   Considered by many to be the greatest special teams performer in NFL
history, Steve Tasker spent parts of twelve seasons in Buffalo, becoming the
first player to establish himself as a star almost exclusively through special
teams play without being either a kicker or a returner. A huge contributor
to teams that won six division titles and four AFC championships, Tasker
gained Pro Bowl and First-Team All-AFC recognition seven times each,
before being further honored by being inducted into the Bills Wall of Fame.
   Born in Smith Center, Kansas, on April 10, 1962, Steven Jay Tasker
grew up in the tiny farming community of Leoti, some thirty-five miles east
of the Colorado border. The son of a United Methodist minister, Tasker led
a somewhat sheltered life as a child, recalling, "The world was very filtered
out there."
   Eventually developing into a star athlete at Wichita County High
School, Tasker excelled in football, basketball, and track, winning the state's
AAA championship in the 100- and 200-meter dashes his senior year.
Drawing very little interest from four-year colleges due to his small frame,
Tasker accepted a football scholarship to Dodge City (Kansas) Community
College, remembering, "My freshman year, I weighed in at 147 pounds.
That was fully clothed, with my wallet and comb in my pocket."
   Put on a weightlifting regimen by his coach, Tasker added enough bulk
to earn regular playing time at wide receiver and kickoff returner, perform-
ing so well at both posts that Northwestern University came calling after
his sophomore year. Playing exclusively on special teams for the Wildcats
the next two seasons, Tasker ended up setting the school record for the best
career punt-return average (10.8 yards), prompting the Houston Oilers to

Steve Tasker is generally considered to be the greatest special teams player in NFL history.

select him in the 9th round of the 1985 NFL Draft, with the 226th overall pick. Revealing the surprise that he felt upon hearing his name called, Tasker stated years later, "I never dreamed of playing in the NFL. I knew I had the ability, but I didn't know if I had the size and the strength."

Plagued by injuries early in his pro career, Tasker appeared in only nine games with the Oilers, before new Bills head coach Marv Levy claimed him off waivers midway through the 1986 campaign. Following his arrival in Buffalo, Tasker spent the next year-and-a-half returning kickoffs for the Bills, while also assuming a prominent role on the kickoff- and punt-coverage teams, with his outstanding play on both units earning him Pro Bowl and First-Team All-AFC honors in 1987.

Relieved of his kickoff-return duties in 1988 so that he might focus exclusively on further developing his skills as a cover man, Tasker developed into the league's premier "gunner," using his speed, strength, elusiveness, and tenacity to create havoc every time he took the field. A menace to opposing teams, Tasker presented problems to anyone who stood in his path—darting, ducking, and zigzagging past blockers to tackle the ball carrier.

Performing his job so well that the opposition spent a great deal of time trying to devise a strategy to contain him, Tasker drew praise from Bills special teams coach, Bruce DeHaven, who said, "He was the first guy I ever saw anybody actually use three guys to try and block him as a gunner on a punt. He forced people to do things that no one had ever done before on special teams. . . . I coached for Bill Parcells in Dallas for four years. I remember him talking about whenever we played Buffalo, telling his team, 'The first thing we've got to do is we've got to make sure that we contain Steve Tasker because, if we don't get him blocked, then we're gonna get beat.'"

A demon on special teams despite his choirboy appearance, Tasker experienced a transformation on game day, with Marv Levy stating, "Steve's very courteous and polite. He's a wide-eyed kid. On special teams, though, he turns into a terror. He plays the game the way it should be played."

Deceptively strong, Tasker became known as one of the league's hardest hitters, even though he stood just 5'9" and weighed only 185 pounds. Blessed with remarkable leg strength, Tasker had the ability to squat five hundred pounds and dunk a basketball behind his head with two hands. Extremely fast as well, Tasker drew praise for his tremendous all-around athletic ability from renowned football writer Vic Carucci, who said, "He wasn't just an okay, nice, try-hard guy. Steve Tasker was a world-class athlete."

In discussing the joy that he derived from playing on special teams, Tasker stated, "Covering kickoffs is the funnest thing there is about football. The world would be a happier place if everybody could do that once a week. I sprint down the field with an aura of total invincibility. Nobody is going to stop me. I'm going to make the play. I don't care about my wife, my kids, my dog, my house. Nothing. With 60 yards to wind up, I know it's going to be an incredible collision. It sounds absolutely barbaric to say but laying a good lick on somebody is the best feeling ever. It doesn't hurt."

After playing almost exclusively on special teams the previous ten years, Tasker finally got an opportunity to display his pass-receiving skills in 1995, when a rash of injuries left the Bills with a depleted receiving corps. Exhibiting his tremendous versatility, Tasker made 20 receptions for 255 yards and 3 touchdowns, before gathering in another 21 passes, amassing 372 receiving yards, and scoring 3 more TDs the following year. Meanwhile, Tasker's excellent work on special teams earned him Pro Bowl and First-Team All-AFC honors for the sixth straight time in 1995.

Tasker spent one more year in Buffalo, before announcing his retirement following the conclusion of the 1997 campaign with career totals of 51 receptions, 779 receiving yards, 130 rushing yards, 9 touchdowns, 7 blocked punts, and 204 special team tackles, compiling virtually all those numbers as a member of the Bills.

After Tasker retired from football, he and his wife, Sarah, chose to remain in East Aurora, with Ms. Tasker saying, "All the kids were born here, all the puppies were raised here, all the good things that happened in our young, married lives began here. We wanted to go home so badly, and then this became home. That's as simple as it gets."

Transitioning successfully to a career in sports media following his playing days, Tasker spent twenty-one years working at CBS Sports as an NFL television analyst, before accepting the position of cohost of *One Bills Live*. Tasker has also hosted a program on the Empire Sports Network and served as a spokesman for West Herr Auto Group. A strong presence in the community, Tasker and his wife give much of themselves to several charitable causes, including the Make-A-Wish Foundation and the March of Dimes.

Still revered for his extraordinary work on special teams, Tasker received the following words of praise from former Bills GM Bill Polian: "In my mind, Steve Tasker is the greatest special-teams player certainly that I've ever seen in my lifetime. . . . If you value special teams, then Steve Tasker belongs in the Hall of Fame because of his impact on the game in so many ways on special teams, whether blocking kicks, returning kicks, creating fumbles, or making open field tackles. There was nothing on special teams that he did not excel at."

## BILLS CAREER HIGHLIGHTS

### Best Season

Tasker made his greatest overall contributions to the Bills in 1995, when, in addition to his fabulous work on special teams, he made 20 receptions for 255 yards and 3 touchdowns and amassed a career-high 533 all-purpose yards.

### Memorable Moments/Greatest Performances

- Contributed to a 21-14 win over the Broncos on November 8, 1987, by blocking a punt through the end zone for a safety.
- Made a huge play during a 38-24 victory over the Raiders on October 7, 1990, when he blocked a punt that teammate James Williams subsequently returned 38 yards for a touchdown.
- Recorded the first touchdown reception of his career when he gathered in a 24-yard pass from Jim Kelly during a 45-14 victory over the Phoenix Cardinals on November 11, 1990.
- Although the Bills ended up losing to the Detroit Lions in overtime by a score of 17-14 in the final game of the 1991 regular season, Tasker sent the game into OT by making a 20-yard TD reception late in the fourth quarter.
- Earned AFC Special Teams Player of the Week honors for his exceptional play on the Bills' kickoff- and punt-coverage units during a 13-10 win over Dallas on September 12, 1993.
- Helped set up a Bills score by returning a kickoff 67 yards during their 29-23 win over the Los Angeles Raiders in the divisional round of the 1993 playoffs.
- Turned in a pair of outstanding all-around efforts in consecutive weeks in December 1995. After making 4 receptions for 47 yards, scoring a touchdown, and amassing 161 all-purpose yards during a 27-17 loss to the 49ers on December 3, Tasker returned 3 punts for 50 yards and made 4 receptions for 54 yards and 2 touchdowns during a 45-27 win over the Rams one week later, with the longest of his TDs coming on a 28-yard pass from Jim Kelly.
- Proved to be a huge factor when the Bills recorded a 37-22 victory over the Dolphins in the 1995 AFC Wild Card Game, making 5 receptions for 108 yards and 1 touchdown, which came on a 37-yard pass from Kelly.

- Had his most productive day on offense against the Jets on November 24, 1996, making 6 receptions for 160 yards and 2 touchdowns during a convincing 35-10 Bills win.
- Performed extremely well during a 20-9 victory over the Chiefs in the final game of the 1996 regular season, making 4 receptions for 87 yards.

**Notable Achievements**

- Six-time division champion (1988, 1989, 1990, 1991, 1993, and 1995)
- Four-time AFC champion (1990, 1991, 1992, and 1993)
- 1993 Week 2 AFC Special Teams Player of the Week
- Seven-time Pro Bowl selection (1987, 1990, 1991, 1992, 1993, 1994, and 1995)
- Seven-time First-Team All-AFC selection (1987, 1990, 1991, 1992, 1993, 1994, and 1995)
- Inducted into Bills Wall of Fame in 2007

# 26
## STEW BARBER

A versatile player who performed well at multiple positions for the Bills, Stew Barber spent nine seasons in Buffalo, establishing himself as one of the AFL's most durable players during that time. Anchoring the Bills' offensive line from his left tackle position, Barber missed just one game his entire career, with his toughness and consistently excellent play making him a key contributor to teams that won three division titles and two league championships. A five-time AFL All-Star and three-time All-AFL selection, Barber received the additional honor of being named to the AFL All-Time Second Team, accomplishing all he did as an offensive lineman after beginning his pro career at linebacker.

Born in Bradford, Pennsylvania, on June 14, 1939, Stewart Clair Barber received his introduction to organized football at Bradford Area High School, where he starred on the gridiron as a two-way lineman. After accepting a football scholarship from Penn State University, Barber continued to excel on both sides of the ball for the Nittany Lions, gaining All-America recognition his senior year for his exceptional work at offensive tackle.

Subsequently selected by the Bills in the 4th round of the 1961 AFL Draft, with the 25th overall pick, and by the Dallas Cowboys in the 3rd round of that year's NFL Draft, with the 30th overall pick, Barber chose to sign with the Bills, with whom he spent his first season playing right-outside linebacker—a position he had never manned before. Nevertheless, Barber performed well as a rookie, recording 2 sacks and 3 interceptions, one of which he returned for a touchdown.

Switching to the offensive line the following year, Barber spent time at both tackle and guard, starting eight games at left tackle, while also filling in for an injured Billy Shaw at left guard for six contests. Acquitting himself extremely well at both posts, Barber helped the Bills rush for more yards (2,480) than any other team in the league, with Buffalo running backs averaging 5.0 yards per carry. Settling in at left tackle full time in 1963, Barber

Stew Barber excelled for the Bills at left tackle on offense after beginning his career as a linebacker.

established himself as arguably the league's finest player at his position, earning AFL All-Star honors for the first of five straight times and the first of his three All-AFL nominations.

A huge factor in the Bills' rise to prominence during the mid-1960s, the 6'2", 250-pound Barber used his strength and quickness to help his team develop the league's most potent running attack. In addition to being an extremely effective straight-ahead blocker, Barber excelled as a downfield blocker for Buffalo running backs Cookie Gilchrist and Wray Carlton, who gained much of their yardage on end sweeps to his side of the field. Outstanding in pass protection as well, Barber did an excellent job of protecting the blindside of quarterback Jack Kemp, who, with his help, gradually emerged as one of the league's finest signal callers.

After earning the last of his five consecutive AFL All-Star selections in 1967, Barber continued to perform at an elite level for one more year, gaining unofficial Second-Team All-AFL recognition from the *New York Daily News* in 1968, before seeing his string of eight straight seasons without missing a game come to an end the following year. Choosing to announce his retirement following the conclusion of the 1969 campaign, Barber ended his career having appeared in 125 out of 126 contests, 115 of which he started.

Named to the AFL All-Time Second Team in 1970, Barber joined New York's Winston Hill on the squad, with San Diego's Ron Mix and Kansas City's Jim Tyrer earning First-Team honors at offensive tackle. While Hill, Mix, and Tyrer all eventually gained induction into the Pro Football Hall of Fame, Barber has never come close to doing so, likely because he spent virtually his entire career being overshadowed by the man that lined up immediately next to him, Billy Shaw, who most historians consider to be the greatest offensive lineman in AFL history.

After retiring as an active player, Barber spent one season serving as offensive line coach for the New York Stars/Charlotte Hornets of the World Football League, before returning to Buffalo in a front office capacity. Barber subsequently spent the next decade assuming various roles in the Bills organization, including college scout, assistant general manager, and vice president, before resigning his post as VP in 1983. After Shaw handed in his resignation, speculation arose that new head coach Kay Stephenson demanded that he do so before replacing the recently departed Chuck Knox at the helm.

## CAREER HIGHLIGHTS

### Best Season

Although Barber played well on defense as a rookie in 1961, recording 3 interceptions and scoring the only touchdown of his career, he made his greatest overall impact on the offensive side of the ball, performing especially well in 1964, when he earned one of his two First-Team All-AFL nominations by helping the AFL champion Bills score more points and gain more yards than any other team in the league.

**Memorable Moments/Greatest Performances**

- Recorded the first of his three career interceptions during a 30-20 win over the Dallas Texans on November 12, 1961.
- Clinched a 23-10 victory over the Denver Broncos the following week by returning his fourth-quarter interception of a George Herring pass 21 yards for a touchdown.
- Continued to be a thorn in the side of the Broncos after he moved to the offensive side of the ball, helping the Bills amass 459 yards of total offense during a 30-28 win over Denver on November 3, 1963.
- Outstanding pass protection helped Jack Kemp throw for a career-high 378 yards during a 48-17 thumping of the Houston Oilers on October 11, 1964.

**Notable Achievements**

- Scored 1 touchdown on defense
- Missed just one game entire career, appearing in 125 out of 126 contests
- Three-time division champion (1964, 1965, and 1966)
- Two-time AFL champion (1964 and 1965)
- Five-time AFL All-Star selection (1963, 1964, 1965, 1966, and 1967)
- Two-time First-Team All-AFL selection (1963 and 1964)
- 1966 Second-Team All-AFL selection
- Pro Football Reference All-1960s Second Team
- AFL All-Time Second Team

# 27

## RON MCDOLE

The leader of arguably the greatest defensive line in franchise history, Ron McDole spent eight years in Buffalo starring at left-defensive end. Nicknamed the "Dancing Bear" by his teammates for his nimble feet and surprising quickness, McDole proved to be an indispensable member of Bills teams that won three division titles and two AFL championships, excelling at his post as both a pass-rusher and run defender, while also serving as defensive captain for seven seasons. A two-time AFL All-Star and three-time All-AFL selection, McDole received the additional honor of being named to the AFL All-Time Second Team, before spending eight extremely productive seasons with the team now known as the Washington Commanders.

Born in Chester, Ohio, on September 9, 1939, Roland Owen McDole grew up some 240 miles northwest, in Toledo, Ohio, where he played baseball and football at Thomas DeVilbiss High School, starring on the gridiron as a fullback and defensive end. After accepting an athletic scholarship to the University of Nebraska, McDole spent his sophomore year playing fullback, before moving to defensive tackle, where he started every game the next two seasons.

Subsequently selected by the Denver Broncos in the 4th round of the 1961 AFL Draft, with the 27th overall pick, and by the St. Louis Cardinals in the 4th round of that year's NFL Draft, with the 50th overall pick, McDole chose to sign with the Cardinals, with whom he spent his rookie season serving as a backup, before joining the Houston Oilers, who had acquired his AFL rights from Denver. Plagued by health problems in 1962, McDole ended up appearing in just four games with the Oilers, before being released by the club at season's end. Claiming that the troubles he experienced in Houston nearly ended his playing career before it truly began, McDole later said, "I used to have what was called migraine seizure. It was the closest thing you could ever get to an epileptic attack. I had started getting those when I was with the Oilers. I would get really bad

Ron McDole served as defensive captain of the Bills in seven of his eight years in Buffalo.

headaches. And I would react strangely to them. But [Lou] Saban and the Bills were willing to take a chance on me when other teams wouldn't. I'll always be grateful to Lou for giving me that chance."

Signed by the Bills prior to the start of the 1963 campaign, McDole spent his first season in Buffalo assuming a backup role, before joining the starting unit the following year. Also named a team cocaptain in 1964, McDole made a huge impact on a defense that allowed the fewest points in the league for the first of three straight times, recording 5.5 sacks and 2 safeties for the eventual AFL champions. Continuing his outstanding play over the course of the next six seasons, McDole earned two trips to the AFL All-Star game and three All-AFL nominations, performing especially well from 1966 to 1968, a period during which he recorded 18.5 sacks and 4 interceptions.

Anchoring the Bills defense from his left end position, McDole combined with right end Tom Day and tackles Tom Sestak and Jim Dunaway to form the league's top front four. While Sestak and Dunaway made it virtually impossible for opposing teams to experience much success running the football between the tackles, McDole and Day did an excellent job of defending against end sweeps and applying outside pressure to opposing quarterbacks, with Day stating, "McDole and I had a saying: 'See you in the backfield.' We had a good crew back then."

Also displaying a nose for the football during his time in Buffalo, McDole, who, despite his 6'4", 275-pound-plus frame, possessed outstanding quickness and athleticism, recorded 6 interceptions, and recovered 7 fumbles as a member of the Bills, with his six picks representing the highest total by any lineman in franchise history. In fact, McDole's agility and ability to drop into pass coverage allowed the Bills to occasionally use him as an inside linebacker in their 3-4 alignment. An extremely intelligent player as well, McDole later credited his high interception total to the time he spent studying opposing quarterbacks and their tendencies, such as which ones repeatedly threw high.

Perhaps McDole's greatest asset, though, proved to be his tremendous pursuit, which he addressed when he said, "You just had to hustle, haul ass, make good pursuit. Kids don't do it today. I was getting paid to do it."

Commenting on that particular aspect of his longtime teammate's game, former Bills linebacker Harry Jacobs stated, "Ron McDole was probably the best defensive end to go to the other side of the field to make a tackle."

A strong performer on special teams as well, McDole, in his own words, had "quite a few blocked kicks," adding, "Blocking field goals was easy. It was 'rest time' for the offensive linemen."

Yet despite McDole's outstanding all-around play, the Bills traded him to the Washington Redskins for three draft picks following the conclusion of the 1970 campaign, with Buffalo head coach John Rauch telling a local radio station at the time, "He [McDole] has not played what I would call winning football for the last three years."

Recalling how he felt about being dealt to Washington, McDole said, "I was glad to be traded. Ralph Wilson and Pat McGroder did me a favor. John Rauch was not playing me. We had a lot of communication problems. The players kept getting younger and younger. I don't begrudge a young fellow a job if he earns it; that's the way the game works. But I don't think anyone should be handed a job just because he's young. One week we'd look like Superman, the next week we'd look like nothing. It seemed like all the guys around me were young kids."

However, Rauch, who ended up losing his job after the negative comments he made about one of the Bills' most popular players caused a rift between the city and the team, told a different story of the circumstances surrounding the trade, claiming: "The first time I had an inkling that McDole wanted to be traded was the early part of February. He called me at the Bills' office and said he wanted to talk with me. We met at a coffee shop close to the Bills' office and, over a beer, Ron told me he would like to move on . . . too many of his friends had retired, and he would like to make a fresh start somewhere else. As soon as he finished, I immediately suspected that someone was tampering with him. I told him I had no thought of trading him, he was under contract to the Bills, and the coaching staff would make every effort to build around him. We enjoyed our beer, and I thought the two of us got our thoughts out into the open and we would go on from there . . . rebuilding. Ralph Wilson was the one that traded Ron McDole to George Allen for three draft choices—against my wishes."

McDole, who, in addition to his 6 interceptions and 7 fumble recoveries, left Buffalo with an unofficial total of 34 sacks, subsequently spent the next eight seasons playing for George Allen's "Over the Hill Gang" in Washington, before retiring at the end of 1978 with career totals of 77.5 sacks, 14 fumble recoveries, 2 defensive touchdowns, 3 safeties, and 12 interceptions, which established a new NFL record for most picks by a defensive lineman.

Following his playing days, McDole returned to his educational roots, industrial arts, owning a company that produced office and library furniture, and "flipping" houses before that practice became popular. Eighty-four years old at the time of this writing, McDole looks back favorably on the time he spent in Buffalo, saying, "Buffalo and the fans were just super to me. I will never forget that special something that the players, especially myself, had with the fans."

## BILLS CAREER HIGHLIGHTS

### Best Season

While McDole gained All-AFL recognition on three separate occasions, he received his only First-Team nomination in 1966, when he recorded 6.5

sacks, 69 tackles, and 1 interception, deflected 10 passes, and blocked 1 field goal attempt.

## Memorable Moments/Greatest Performances

- Scored the first points of his career when he sacked quarterback Cotton Davidson in the end zone for a safety during a 23-20 win over the Oakland Raiders on October 3, 1964.
- Recorded the first of his 12 career interceptions when he picked off a George Blanda pass during a 24-10 victory over the Houston Oilers on November 1, 1964.
- Led the defensive charge when the Bills recorded 11 sacks and allowed just 117 yards of total offense during a 30-19 win over the Broncos on December 13, 1964, with his tackle of running back Billy Joe in the end zone resulting in a safety.
- Earned AFL Defensive Player of the Week honors with his outstanding all-around play during a 33-23 win over the Jets on October 30, 1966, punctuating his exceptional effort with an interception of a Joe Namath pass.
- Recorded another interception during a 14-14 tie with the Dolphins on October 12, 1968, returning his pick of a Bob Griese pass 42 yards.

## Notable Achievements

- Missed just three games in eight seasons, appearing in 109 out of 112 contests
- Led AFL with two safeties in 1964
- Finished second in AFL with five fumble recoveries in 1965
- Three-time division champion (1964, 1965, and 1966)
- Two-time AFL champion (1964 and 1965)
- 1966 Week 8 AFL Defensive Player of the Week
- Two-time AFL All-Star selection (1965 and 1967)
- 1966 First-Team All-AFL selection
- Two-time Second-Team All-AFL selection (1967 and 1968)
- AFL All-Time Second Team

# 28
## NATE ODOMES

O ne of the NFL's premier cover-corners for most of his career, Nate Odomes spent seven seasons in Buffalo starting at right cornerback for teams that won five division titles and four AFC championships. The Bills' best man-to-man defender during their Super Bowl run of the early 1990s, Odomes recorded the fifth-most interceptions in franchise history, leading the league with 9 picks in 1993. A two-time Pro Bowler and one-time All-Pro, Odomes also earned three All-AFC selections before leaving Buffalo at the end of 1993 via free agency.

Born in Columbus, Georgia, on August 25, 1965, Nathaniel Bernard Odomes grew up in a close-knit family, recalling, "Coming from Columbus, I think my family supported me and gave me a lot of love." A star wide receiver and defensive back at Carver High School, Odomes received a football scholarship to the University of Wisconsin–Madison, where, in addition to excelling on the gridiron for three seasons on both defense and special teams, he ran track. Performing especially well his senior year, Odomes earned All-America honors by leading the Big Ten Conference with 7 interceptions while also setting a single-season school record by amassing 616 kickoff-return yards.

Selected by the Bills in the 2nd round of the 1987 NFL Draft, with the 29th overall pick, Odomes became an immediate contributor on defense, earning a spot on the NFL All-Rookie Team by recording 42 tackles, 1 forced fumble, and 2 fumble recoveries, while starting all twelve nonstrike games at right cornerback alongside the three other members of Buffalo's young defensive secondary: left cornerback Derrick Burroughs, strong safety Dwight Drane, and free safety Mark Kelso. However, after performing well once again in 1988, Odomes experienced a setback the following offseason, when Eau Claire, Wisconsin, police arrested him and former college teammate Aaron Swopes on June 25, 1989, after they found two bags of marijuana in Odomes's car. Convicted of marijuana possession one

Nate Odomes started at right cornerback for Bills teams that won five division titles and four AFC championships.

week later, Odomes, who pleaded no contest, had to pay a $240 fine and serve six months' probation.

Eager to redeem himself in the eyes of Bills fans, Odomes had his finest season to date in 1989, earning Second-Team All-AFC honors by picking off 5 passes, forcing 3 fumbles, and registering 46 tackles. Continuing his strong play from 1990 to 1992, Odomes helped the Bills capture their first three AFC championships by recording a total of 11 interceptions, while also forcing 3 fumbles, recovering 5 others, registering 181 tackles, and scoring 2 touchdowns, with his 5 picks and 63 stops in the last of those campaigns gaining him Pro Bowl recognition for the first time.

Gradually emerging as one of the leaders of the Buffalo defensive secondary, Odomes gave the Bills a true No. 1 cornerback who had the ability to cover the opposing team's top wideout mano-a-mano. Fleet afoot, Odomes did an outstanding job of guarding even the league's swiftest receivers, with his quickness, superb ball-hawking skills, and excellent instincts allowing him to make several big plays that always seemed to come at the most opportune times for his team. Although somewhat undersized at 5'9" and 188 pounds, Odomes played like a much larger man, using his leaping ability to contest catches in close quarters and his strength to bring down opposing ball carriers in the open field.

Taking his game up a notch in 1993, Odomes earned Pro Bowl, First-Team All-AFC, and Second-Team All-Pro honors by leading the NFL with 9 interceptions, amassing 65 interception-return yards, and returning a fumble for a touchdown. A free agent at season's end, Odomes signed a four-year, $8.4 million contract with the Seattle Seahawks that brought his days in Buffalo to an end. In his seven seasons with the Bills, Odomes recorded 26 interceptions, amassed 224 interception-return yards, registered 360 tackles and 3 sacks, forced 9 fumbles, recovered 8 others, and scored 3 touchdowns. Extremely durable, Odomes appeared in all 108 nonstrike games the Bills played from 1987 to 1993, starting all but one of those.

Experiencing a considerable amount of misfortune after leaving Buffalo, Odomes injured his knee while competing in a charity basketball game during the 1994 offseason, causing him to miss the entire year. Odomes missed the ensuing campaign as well after hurting the same knee in training camp, prompting the Seahawks to release him. Signed by Atlanta prior to the start of the 1996 season, Odomes appeared in just seven games with the Falcons, before announcing his retirement.

## BILLS CAREER HIGHLIGHTS

### Best Season

Odomes had an outstanding year for the Bills in 1991, earning First-Team All-AFC honors by picking off 5 passes, amassing 120 interception-return yards, scoring a touchdown, and registering a career-high 76 tackles. But he performed slightly better in 1993, earning his lone All-Pro nomination by leading the NFL with 9 interceptions, forcing a fumble, and recovering another, which he returned 25 yards for a touchdown.

## Memorable Moments/Greatest Performances

- Recorded his first career interception against Steve Grogan during a 16-14 win over the Patriots on September 18, 1988.
- Picked off a pair of Dan Marino passes during a 27-24 win over the Miami Dolphins in the opening game of the 1989 regular season.
- Scored the first points of his career when he returned a fumble 49 yards for a touchdown during a 38-24 victory over the Los Angeles Raiders on October 7, 1990.
- Lit the scoreboard again when he returned his interception of a Bubby Brister pass 32 yards for a touchdown during a 52-34 win over the Steelers on September 8, 1991.
- Contributed to a lopsided 40-7 victory over the Los Angeles Rams in the opening game of the 1992 regular season by intercepting Jim Everett twice.
- Made perhaps the biggest play of his career during the Bills' miraculous 41-38 comeback victory over Houston in the 1992 AFC Wild Card Game when he picked off a Warren Moon pass in overtime to help set up Steve Christie's game-winning 32-yard field goal.
- Recorded another pair of interceptions during a 24-10 win over the Washington Redskins on November 1, 1993, this time victimizing Mark Rypien.
- Earned AFC Defensive Player of the Week honors by intercepting a pass and returning a fumble 25 yards for a touchdown during a 47-34 win over the Dolphins on December 19, 1993.

## Notable Achievements

- Appeared in 108 consecutive nonstrike games from 1987 to 1993
- Scored 3 defensive touchdowns
- Recorded at least 5 interceptions four times
- Amassed more than 100 interception-return yards once
- Led NFL with 9 interceptions in 1993
- Finished fourth in NFL with 120 interception-return yards in 1991
- Led Bills in interceptions twice
- Ranks fifth in franchise history with 26 interceptions
- Five-time division champion (1988, 1989, 1990, 1991, and 1993)

- Four-time AFC champion (1990, 1991, 1992, and 1993)
- Member of 1987 NFL All-Rookie Team
- Two-time AFC Defensive Player of the Week
- Two-time Pro Bowl selection (1992 and 1993)
- 1993 Second-Team All-Pro selection
- Two-time First-Team All-AFC selection (1991 and 1993)
- 1989 Second-Team All-AFC selection

# 29

## SHANE CONLAN

A key contributor to the Bills' first three Super Bowl teams, Shane Conlan spent six seasons in Buffalo, proving to be one of the NFL's best run-stuffing linebackers during that time. A hard-hitting inside backer who played with reckless abandon, Conlan served as one of the leaders of an outstanding defensive unit that annually ranked among the AFC's best, with his inspirational and consistently excellent play earning him Pro Bowl and All-Pro honors three times each. The 1987 NFL Defensive Rookie of the Year, Conlan also gained All-AFC recognition twice, before leaving his home state of New York and ending his career out west as a member of the Los Angeles/St. Louis Rams.

Born some seventy-three miles southeast of Buffalo, in Olean, New York, on April 3, 1964, Shane Patrick Conlan moved with his family at the age of two to the town of Frewsburg, where he starred in multiple sports while attending Frewsburg High School. A three-time all-league selection in basketball and a four-time all-league selection in baseball, Conlan performed so well as a catcher on the diamond that he garnered serious interest from the Pittsburgh Pirates, who offered him a contract following a tryout. However, with football remaining his first love, Conlan, who earned Western New York High School Player of the Year honors as a running back and linebacker his senior year, chose instead to accept a scholarship to Penn State University, where, after redshirting as a freshman due to an injury, he spent four years playing outside linebacker for legendary head coach Joe Paterno.

Establishing himself as a top pro prospect while in college, Conlan gained All-America recognition twice, with his 79 tackles and 63 solo stops his senior year helping to lead the Nittany Lions to the National Championship. Named a Butkus Award finalist and Penn State's Outstanding Senior Player at season's end, Conlan received the additional honor of being identified by Paterno as the best outside linebacker in school history.

Shane Conlan earned Pro Bowl and All-Pro honors three times each as a member of the Bills.
Courtesy of George A. Kitrinos.

Selected by the Bills with the eighth overall pick of the 1987 NFL Draft, Conlan expressed his excitement over the idea of returning to western New York after hearing his name called, saying, "I'm very happy. It's close to home. It's a great opportunity for me. I'd rather be here than anyplace."

Joining the Bills' starting defensive unit immediately upon his arrival in Buffalo, Conlan spent the first few weeks of the 1987 campaign playing outside linebacker in the team's 3-4 defense, before moving inside following the acquisition of Cornelius Bennett later in the year. Adding some much-needed toughness to the Buffalo defense, Conlan made a huge impact his first year in the league, earning Second-Team All-Pro and NFL Defensive Rookie of the Year honors by recording a team-high 114 tackles, forcing a fumble, and registering a half sack. Despite missing a total of nine games with leg injuries over the course of the next two seasons, Conlan continued his exceptional play, gaining Pro Bowl recognition each year, his second All-Pro nomination, and the first of his two All-AFC selections by registering a total of 134 tackles, while also picking off 2 passes, forcing 2 fumbles, recovering another, and recording 2.5 sacks. Starting all sixteen games for the Bills in 1990, Conlan earned Pro Bowl, All-AFC, and Second-Team All-Pro honors for the final time by recording 93 tackles and 1 sack for the AFC champions, before registering a career-high and team-leading 122 tackles the following year.

Known affectionately to his teammates as "Buckethead," "Jarhead," and "Hammerhead" due to the unusually large size of his dome, the 6'3", 235-pound Conlan possessed a rather odd physique, with Steve Tasker stating in his book, *Steve Tasker's Tales from the Buffalo Bills*, "Linebacker Shane Conlan may have boasted one of the most disproportionate bodies I've ever seen on a football player. He had a huge head, a huge torso, and legs skinnier than a pelican's. Guys in the locker room would joke that the Buffalo Jills cheerleaders had more meat on their gams than Shane did."

However, Tasker was quick to add, "But those toothpick legs didn't prevent Conlan from delivering some of the most hellacious hits you'd ever want to see. He was your classic run-stuffing linebacker. He had kind of an old-school style. He would have fit in nicely with guys like Butkus and Nitschke. There was one time against the Jets that he pancaked Roger Vick so hard that we thought he was dead. Kent Hull said after the game, 'I was looking for a priest to give the guy his last rites.'"

Conlan spent one more season in Buffalo, helping to lead the Bills to their third straight AFC championship in 1992 by recording 82 tackles, 2 sacks, and 1 interception, before signing with the Rams as a free agent when they offered him a three-year, $5.4 million contract at the end of the year. Conlan, who, during his time in Buffalo, recorded 545 tackles, 6 sacks, 3 interceptions, 4 forced fumbles, and 3 fumble recoveries, performed well for the Rams over the course of the next three seasons, registering another 238 tackles and recording two more interceptions, forced fumbles, and fumble recoveries. Plagued by leg problems throughout his career, Conlan chose to announce his retirement when his contract expired at the end of 1995, leaving the game at only thirty-one years of age.

Following his playing days, Conlan spent several years working for Esmark Inc. as the company's vice president of commercial real estate, before becoming Pittsburgh Power's vice president of corporate partnerships in 2013. A community leader, Conlan organizes the Shane Conlan Classic golf tournament, which raises money for the Heritage Valley Health System, the Shane Conlan Scholarship Fund at his old high school, and various projects at Penn State University.

## BILLS CAREER HIGHLIGHTS

### Best Season

Although Conlan recorded significantly more tackles in both 1987 and 1991, he had his finest all-around season for the Bills in 1988, when the Associated Press, *Sporting News*, Pro Football Writers, and *Pro Football Weekly* all accorded him All-Pro honors, with three of the four naming him to their First Team.

### Memorable Moments/Greatest Performances

- Contributed to a 28-0 win over the Packers on October 30, 1988, by recording a sack and anchoring a defense that allowed just 131 yards of total offense.
- Recorded the first interception of his career during a lopsided 31-6 victory over the Miami Dolphins on November 14, 1988.
- Although the Bills suffered a heartbreaking 20-19 defeat at the hands of the New York Giants in Super Bowl XXV, Conlan performed magnificently, recording a game-high 13 tackles.
- Served as the focal point of a Bills defense that allowed just 46 yards rushing and 174 yards of total offense during a 41-14 win over the Atlanta Falcons on November 22, 1992.

### Notable Achievements

- Recorded more than 100 tackles twice
- Led Bills in tackles twice
- Ranks 10th in Bills history with 545 tackles
- Four-time division champion (1988, 1989, 1990, and 1991)
- Three-time AFC champion (1990, 1991, and 1992)

- Member of 1987 NFL All-Rookie Team
- 1987 NFL Defensive Rookie of the Year
- Three-time Pro Bowl selection (1988, 1989, and 1990)
- Three-time Second-Team All-Pro selection (1987, 1988, and 1990)
- 1988 First-Team All-AFC selection
- 1990 Second-Team All-AFC selection

# 30
# JIM DUNAWAY

An important member of Bills teams that won three consecutive division titles and two AFL championships, Jim Dunaway spent nine seasons in Buffalo starting at left-defensive tackle. Combining with Tom Sestak to give the Bills a virtually impenetrable interior to their defensive line, Dunaway did an exceptional job of clogging up the middle against the run, helping his team consistently place near the top of the league rankings in fewest yards allowed per rush. A solid pass-rusher as well, Dunaway recorded as many as 6 sacks in a season, with his strong all-around play earning him four trips to the AFL All-Star game and one All-AFL nomination. Yet Dunaway is largely remembered today for his suspected involvement in the mysterious death of his ex-wife.

Born in Columbia, Mississippi, on September 3, 1941, James Kenneth Dunaway first exhibited his exceptional athletic ability at Columbia High School, where he earned three letters in football and four in track. A two-time All-Big Eight Conference selection, Dunaway also gained unanimous prep All-America recognition his senior year for his outstanding play on the gridiron.

After accepting an athletic scholarship to the University of Mississippi, Dunaway continued to excel in track and football, setting a new school record in the shotput with a throw of 55 feet, 4.5 inches, while also earning All-America honors twice as a two-way lineman. Establishing himself as a top pro prospect at Ole Miss, Dunaway, who stood close to 6'5" and weighed 260 pounds during his collegiate days, helped lead the Rebels to an overall record of 29-2-1, two Southeastern Conference (SEC) titles, and a share of two national championships.

Selected by the Bills in the second round of the 1963 AFL Draft, with the ninth overall pick, and by Minnesota with the third overall pick of that year's NFL Draft, Dunaway seriously considered signing with the Vikings, who, according to *Pioneer Press* accounts of the story, had him rated as the top lineman in college football. In fact, after Vikings chief scout

Jim Dunaway combined with Tom Sestak to give the Bills the AFL's best pair of defensive tackles for much of the 1960s.

Joe Thomas said of Dunaway, "He should develop into an All-Pro tackle someday," the Ole Miss grad expressed interest in joining the organization, stating, "It's a great honor being chosen on the first round. In fact, I'm so shook I don't know what to say. I'm sure my wife and I would enjoy Minnesota hunting." However, after the Vikings reportedly offered Dunaway a two-year deal worth $54,000, he chose to sign with the Bills, who offered more than $60,000 over the same period.

Making a major impact as a rookie, Dunaway joined the starting unit during the early stages of the 1963 campaign, after which he helped lead the Bills to a record of 7-6-1 that nearly earned them their first division title with his stellar play up front. Playing alongside perennial All-Pro Tom Sestak, Dunaway, who spent most of his pro career playing at somewhere between 275 and 290 pounds, proved to be virtually impossible to move out of the middle, as former Bills linebacker Harry Jacobs noted when he said, "Jimmy was a really strong guy. He was a big guy, bigger than Tom. He was a solid mass in the middle."

Dunaway's size, strength, and girth helped make him an integral member of an outstanding defense that ranked first in the AFL against the run three straight times, with the Bills holding opposing rushers without a touchdown for a record seventeen consecutive games from 1964 to 1965. More than just a space eater, though, Dunaway also possessed surprising speed and agility for a man of his proportions, making him an effective pass-rusher as well, with his career-high 6 sacks in 1967 tying him with line-mate Ron McDole for the second-highest total on the team. Recognized by the mid-1960s as one of the finest all-around interior defensive linemen in the league, Dunaway earned four straight AFL All-Star nominations and one First-Team All-AFL selection from 1965 to 1968, despite having to compete against teammate Sestak and other outstanding tackles such as Buck Buchanan, Ernie Ladd, Tom Keating, and Houston Antwine for postseason honors.

Although Dunaway failed to gain All-Star recognition again in 1969, both the Newspaper Enterprise Association (NEA) and the *New York Daily News* accorded him unofficial Second-Team All-AFL honors. Meanwhile, Dunaway continued his string of consecutive seasons in which he appeared in every game that the Bills played, a streak that lasted through 1971—two years after the AFL merged with the more established NFL.

Released by the Bills following the conclusion of the 1971 campaign, Dunaway left Buffalo with career totals of 22.5 sacks, 1 interception, 7 fumble recoveries, and an unrecorded number of tackles and forced fumbles. Never missing a game in his nine seasons with the Bills, Dunaway appeared in 126 consecutive contests as a member of the team, starting 114 of those at his familiar position of left-defensive tackle. After being released by the Bills, Dunaway spent the 1972 season with the Miami Dolphins, starting six games at right-defensive tackle and registering 1 sack for the only undefeated team in NFL history, before announcing his retirement at the end of the year.

Following his playing days, Dunaway remained largely out of the limelight for more than two decades, although his name surfaced briefly in 1995, when his longtime wife, Nonniel, received 800 acres of land, $1,800 a month in alimony, and half of his NFL pension as part of a divorce settlement. Three years later, Dunaway figured far more prominently in the news when she was found dead in a half-empty swimming pool. After the autopsy revealed that she had a fractured skull and had been unconscious when her killer placed her in the water, police arrested Dunaway on suspicion of murder. Although a grand jury subsequently chose not to indict Dunaway, his own children filed a wrongful death civil lawsuit against him in 2002, alleging that he had been responsible for their mother's death. Voicing his objections over their claims, Dunaway's attorney, Gary Honea, stated, "This is just a vendetta. They [Dunaway's children] want to punish him because they're angry about the divorce. Do you think a grand jury and the DA's office would let someone who's guilty go free? This is the most horrible thing I've ever seen . . . suing your daddy for more money."

Nevertheless, after being found liable, Dunaway had to pay over half a million dollars in damages to his children, prompting him to say, "I'm extremely disappointed. I had absolutely nothing to do with Nonniel's death. I looked both my children in the eye and told them that."

Dunaway lived another sixteen years, before passing away at the age of seventy-six on May 12, 2018.

## BILLS CAREER HIGHLIGHTS

### Best Season

Although Dunaway recorded a career-high 6 sacks the following year, he played his best ball for the Bills in 1966, when he earned one of his four consecutive trips to the AFL All-Star Game and his lone First-Team All-AFL selection.

### Memorable Moments/Greatest Performances

- Helped anchor a Bills defense that surrendered just 44 yards rushing and 137 yards of total offense during a 48-17 manhandling of the Houston Oilers on October 11, 1964.
- Performed extremely well in the 1965 AFL Championship Game, recording a sack, blocking a field-goal attempt, and helping to limit the Chargers to just 223 yards of total offense during a 23-0 Bills win.
- Led the defensive charge when the Bills recorded 5 sacks and allowed just 48 yards rushing and 171 yards of total offense during a 29-0 shutout of Miami on November 6, 1966.

- Earned AFL Defensive Player of the Week honors by scoring the only touchdown of his career on a 72-yard return of a blocked field goal attempt during a 14-3 win over the Jets on November 13, 1966.

## Notable Achievements

- Never missed a game in nine seasons, appearing in 126 consecutive contests
- Scored 1 touchdown on special teams
- Four-time division champion (1963, 1964, 1965, and 1966)
- Two-time AFL champion (1964 and 1965)
- 1966 Week 10 AFL Defensive Player of the Week
- Four-time AFL All-Star selection (1965, 1966, 1967, and 1968)
- 1966 First-Team All-AFL selection

# 31
## TONY GREENE

**A**n outstanding defensive back who spent his entire nine-year professional career in Buffalo, Tony Greene established himself as one of
the NFL's finest safeties after initially playing cornerback when he
first entered the league. Excelling as the Bills' last line of defense, Greene
recorded the second most interceptions and amassed the second most
interception-return yards in franchise history, earning in the process one
trip to the Pro Bowl, one All-Pro selection, and two All-AFC nominations.
Displaying a nose for the football throughout his career, Greene also ranks
extremely high in team annals in fumble recoveries, accomplishing all he
did for the Bills at safety after originally signing with them as an undersized,
undrafted free agent corner.

Born in Gaithersburg, Maryland, on August 29, 1949, Anthony
Jerome Greene got his start in organized football at Gaithersburg High
School, performing so well for the Trojans on the gridiron that he received
several scholarship offers as graduation neared. Ultimately choosing to
remain in-state, Greene enrolled at the University of Maryland, where he
spent three seasons competing in track as a sprinter and starting for the
Terrapins at cornerback, serving as one of the team captains his senior year.

Ignored by all twenty-six teams in the 1971 NFL Draft due to his
size, or lack thereof, Greene recalled, "I was a little disappointed I didn't
get drafted. I knew I wasn't going in the first or second round, or even on
the first day. But back then they had, like, 16 or 17 rounds, so I thought
someone would take me eventually. But, hey, 5-10 and 165, realistically,
maybe not."

Subsequently contacted by several NFL teams, Greene carefully
weighed his options, eventually deciding to sign with the Bills since he
believed they offered him the best chance of competing for a roster spot. In
discussing his thought process at the time, Greene remembered, "There was
a coach in Buffalo at the time, Ralph Hawkins, and I knew him from when
he was coaching at Maryland. He was one of the main reasons I signed

Tony Greene ranks second in franchise history in interceptions and interception-return yards.

with Buffalo. I could have signed with several teams, including the Dallas Cowboys or Washington Redskins, two teams who had also contacted me, but I just felt as though I had a better chance of making it with the Bills. It just happened that I was in the right place at the right time."

But shortly after he arrived in Buffalo in 1971, the smallish Greene had a difficult time gaining admittance to War Memorial Stadium prior to a preseason game against the New Orleans Saints, recalling, "The guard at the door didn't think I looked like a football player. One of the Bills trainers came out and told the guy who I was. He said he was sorry, and I got in."

Elaborating further on his initial experience at the Bills' home venue, Greene said, "I was just a scared rookie walking up to that gate. He [the guard] said, 'Where do you think you're going?' And I said, 'I'm going to get dressed.' He just shook his head and said, 'Guys try this all the time. Go buy a ticket.'"

Greene continued, "I was there for, like, five minutes, pleading with him. And I told him, 'Go get Tony Marchetti.' He was the Bills equipment guy at the time. And Marchetti came walking out with his big voice and he said, 'Oh, yeah, he's on the team, let him in. He ain't going to be here long anyway.'"

Despite concerns about his size, Greene ended up earning a spot on the Bills roster, after which he spent his first pro season backing up starting cornerbacks Robert James and Alvin Wyatt. Replacing Wyatt as the starter on the right side of Buffalo's defense the following year, Greene performed fairly well, recording 3 interceptions, one of which he returned 39 yards for a touchdown. Nevertheless, the 5'10", 170-pound Greene sometimes felt physically overmatched at corner, stating, "Cornerbacks, in that era, we played a lot of bump-and-run, hitting receivers all the way down the field. I got overpowered by some receivers who were bigger than I was. I mean, I did a decent job, but it was tough."

Moved to free safety prior to the start of the 1973 campaign, Greene thrived at his new post, picking off one pass and recovering 2 fumbles his first season there, before earning First-Team All-Pro and All-AFC honors the following year by finishing second in the league with 9 interceptions. Continuing to perform at an elite level the next three seasons while serving as a team captain, Greene recorded a total of 20 interceptions, amassed 360 interception-return yards, and scored another touchdown, earning in the process his second All-AFC nomination and his lone Pro Bowl selection.

Able to make better use of his outstanding speed and ball-hawking ability at the safety position, Greene consistently ranked among the league leaders in interceptions, saying, "It's a combination of a whole lot of things. You'd like to say you're good and can read offenses, but a lot of interceptions come off bad throws. You've got to get into the area to make the reception and be quick and fast. I had some good coaching and could read offenses and where plays were going. You just have to give yourself an opportunity to get there."

Greene continued to patrol the back end of the Bills secondary for two more years, picking off another 4 passes, before announcing his retirement following the conclusion of the 1979 campaign with career totals of 37 interceptions, 628 interception-return yards, 13 fumble recoveries, 1 sack, 1 safety, and 2 touchdowns. Extremely durable, Greene missed just two games his nine years in the league.

Following his playing days, Greene, who currently resides in Atlanta, Georgia, received several honors, including being named the winner of the Ralph C. Wilson, Jr. Distinguished Service Award in 1995, an honor presented to former Bills for their long and meritorious contributions to the organization. Greene also gained induction into the Maryland Athletics Hall of Fame in 2007.

One of the most popular Bills of his era, Greene looks back favorably on the time he spent in Buffalo, saying, "I had a really good time in Buffalo. Just a country boy from Maryland going out there playing the game that I love."

Expressing his fondness for Bills fans as well, Greene says, "They're crazy. They loved us. Too bad we couldn't give them more wins. You know what that stadium is like—20 degrees out there and they're wearing no shirts, which I don't really understand, but they do what they do. They were always very generous to us."

Now seventy-three years of age, Greene remains in relatively good health, although he says, "I know I can't run a 40 anymore." Nevertheless, Greene admitted that the passing of former teammates Jim Braxton and Bob Chandler affected him deeply, saying, "The three of us were very close and were like the three musketeers. I roomed with both of those guys. We learned a lot about each other. We talked a lot with each other. We were close. We had a very special relationship. They were a big part of my life and now they're gone and I'm the only one left of the three. I miss them."

## CAREER HIGHLIGHTS

### Best Season

Greene earned Pro Bowl and Second-Team All-AFC honors in 1977 by finishing second in the NFL with 9 interceptions, which he returned for a total of 144 yards. But Greene had his finest all-around season in 1974, when, despite missing the final two games with a knee injury, he gained consensus First-Team All-Pro recognition by picking off 9 passes and amassing 157 interception-return yards. Performing especially well during the early stages of the campaign, Greene recorded an interception in six of the Bills' first seven games.

### Memorable Moments/Greatest Performances

- Recorded his first career interception during a 27-20 win over the San Francisco 49ers on September 24, 1972.
- Although the Bills ended up losing to the Miami Dolphins by a score of 30-16 on November 5, 1972, Greene brought them to within 3 points of their Eastern Division rivals just before halftime by returning his interception of an Earl Morrall pass 39 yards for a touchdown.

- Began a string of four straight games during which he recorded an interception by picking off a Ken Stabler pass during a 21-20 win over the Oakland Raiders in the opening game of the 1974 regular season.
- Continued his streak in Week 3 by intercepting Joe Namath during a 16-12 win over the Jets on September 29, 1974.
- Picked off another pass during a 27-7 victory over the Packers on October 6, 1974, extending his streak to four games.
- Contributed to a 15-10 win over the Cleveland Browns on November 24, 1974, by picking off a pair of Mike Phipps passes.
- Punctuated a 50-17 rout of the Kansas City Chiefs on October 3, 1976, by returning his interception of a Tony Adams pass 101 yards for a touchdown in the final period, recording in the process the longest pick-six in franchise history. Looking back on his memorable TD return, Greene said, "All I remember is that I caught the ball and just took off with it. A few key blocks were thrown, and I was on my way."

**Notable Achievements**

- Missed just two games in nine seasons, appearing in 128 out of 130 contests
- Scored 2 defensive touchdowns
- Recorded at least 5 interceptions four times
- Amassed more than 100 interception-return yards three times
- Finished second in NFL in interceptions twice
- Led Bills in interceptions three times
- Ranks among Bills career leaders with 37 interceptions (2nd), 628 interception-return yards (2nd), and 13 fumble recoveries (3rd)
- 1977 Pro Bowl selection
- 1974 First-Team All-Pro selection
- 1974 First-Team All-AFC selection
- 1977 Second-Team All-AFC selection

# 32

## JOE FERGUSON

Underappreciated by the hometown fans much of his time in Buffalo, Joe Ferguson spent twelve seasons starting behind center for the Bills, giving everything that he had to the team. Playing through injuries that would have felled a lesser man, Ferguson started every game the Bills played in all but two of his twelve years in Western New York, earning him the respect of his teammates. Blessed with a strong throwing arm, Ferguson proved to be one of the league's better signal callers, passing for more than 3,000 yards and 25 touchdowns twice each. Second only to Jim Kelly in franchise history in pass attempts, pass completions, passing yards, and touchdown passes, Ferguson led the Bills to one division title and three playoff appearances, with his many contributions to the team eventually gaining him induction into the Bills Wall of Fame.

Born in Alvin, Texas, on April 23, 1950, Joseph Carlton Ferguson Jr. moved with his family at a young age to Shreveport, Louisiana, where he got his start in football when the coach of his school's eighth-grade team conducted a search in all the gym classes for the biggest boys. Recalling his introduction to the sport years later, Ferguson said, "He picked out three of us and gave us a football and looked at us throwing it. I never played any football before."

Eventually emerging as a star quarterback at Shreveport's Woodlawn High School, Ferguson led the team to the state championship in 1968, with his three-year total of 6,710 passing yards and 86 TD passes earning him a scholarship to the University of Arkansas. Continuing his outstanding play with the Razorbacks, Ferguson set numerous school records, including most career pass attempts (611) and most consecutive pass completions in a game (31). Performing especially well his junior year, Ferguson gained recognition as the Southwest Conference (SWC) Offensive Player of the Year by leading the SWC with 2,203 passing yards and 11 touchdown passes, while also running for 6 TDs.

Joe Ferguson ranks second only to Jim Kelly in franchise history in most passing categories.

Selected by the Bills in the 3rd round of the 1973 NFL Draft, with the 57th overall pick, Ferguson found himself faced with the unenviable task of going to a city he knew nothing about, remembering, "The farthest north I had ever been before was where I went to college. I didn't know where Buffalo was, I had to go find it on a map, but I knew it was cold up there."

Arriving at Bills training camp later that year, Ferguson seemed very much out of place at first, with Reggie McKenzie later describing him as "basically a square," and stating, "I don't think he drank Kool-Aid. I know he didn't drink beer." But McKenzie added that, by 1976, his teammate had begun to occasionally consume alcohol and "even started looking at women, too."

McKenzie also spoke of the favorable impression that Ferguson made on him and the rest of the team at his first pro training camp, saying, "As soon as he got here after the college all-star game, he was our best passer."

With the Bills having compiled an overall record of just 5-22-1 the previous two years and Dennis Shaw struggling behind center, Buffalo head coach Lou Saban anointed Ferguson the team's new starting quarterback prior to the start of the 1973 regular season. Although Ferguson subsequently spent most of his rookie year handing the ball off to O. J. Simpson, passing for just 939 yards and 4 touchdowns, he guided the Bills to a record of 9-5 that represented their best mark in seven seasons. Continuing to function primarily as a game-manager the following year, Ferguson threw for just 1,588 yards and 12 TDs. Nevertheless, those figures proved to be enough to lead the Bills to another 9-5 record that earned them a spot in the playoffs as a wild card. However, they ended up losing to the eventual Super Bowl champion Pittsburgh Steelers in the opening round of the postseason tournament by a score of 32-14. Acquitting himself fairly well in his first playoff start, Ferguson completed nearly 50 percent of his passes for 164 yards and 2 touchdowns against Pittsburgh's "Steel Curtain" defense.

Allowed to throw the ball more often in 1975, Ferguson had one of his finest statistical seasons, passing for 2,426 yards, completing 52.6 percent of his passes, posting a QBR of 81.3, and leading the league with 25 touchdown passes, although the Bills' record of 8-6 left them on the outside looking in when the playoffs began. Ferguson subsequently performed well during the first half of the 1976 campaign, ranking among the league leaders with 1,086 yards passing, 9 TD passes, and a QBR of 90.0 through the season's first seven weeks. But, with the Bills having won just two games, many of the hometown fans began clamoring for him to be replaced behind center by third-year signal caller Gary Marangi, who finally got his chance to start when Ferguson suffered a season-ending back injury during a Week 7 loss to the New England Patriots. However, Marangi proceeded to cement Ferguson's position as the no. 1 quarterback by failing to lead the Bills to a single victory the rest of the year.

Fully recovered by the start of the 1977 campaign, Ferguson started every game the Bills played for the first of seven consecutive seasons, leading the NFL with 2,803 passing yards, but also compiling a poor QBR of 54.8 and throwing only 12 TD passes and a league-high 24 interceptions for a team that finished just 3-11 under new head coach Jim Ringo. Posting slightly better overall numbers the following year after ownership replaced Ringo with Chuck Knox, Ferguson passed for 2,136 yards and 16 touchdowns, threw 15 interceptions, and compiled a QBR of 70.5 for a Bills team that finished the season with a record of 5-11. Although Ferguson helped the Bills improve their record to 7-9 in 1979 by finishing in the league's top 10 with 3,572 passing yards, the team's lack of overall talent prevented the coaching staff from better utilizing his passing skills, with the quarterback lamenting years later, "We weren't doing what other teams were doing, but we weren't a very good football team a few of those years. We had some protection problems, and we didn't have the talent that some of the other teams had that were turning their quarterbacks loose. So, you understand a little of why we didn't do it, but, yet, in your mind, you were wishing you were able to see if it could have helped the football team."

A true pocket-passer, Ferguson, who stood 6'1" and weighed just under 200 pounds, possessed one of the NFL's stronger throwing arms and quickest releases, making him a threat to deliver the ball deep downfield any time he received adequate protection from his offensive line. However, Ferguson's lack of mobility often made him a prime target for opposing defenses, which typically applied a significant amount of pressure to him in the pocket. Ferguson also found himself being hampered by the freezing temperatures and swirling winds at Rich Stadium, once saying, "You have to be in the top three or four quarterbacks the first half of the season, then grit your teeth. The cold isn't so bad, except when the wind is blowing. Your hands are the worst part. A lot of times, I can't grip the ball, and I just sort of palm it."

Sympathizing with his Bills counterpart, Jets quarterback Richard Todd, who had to contend with the notoriously strong winds at New York's Shea Stadium, commented, "The wind, the cold. That's the only reason why Joe Ferguson never winds up with the great stats."

Despite posting relatively modest numbers throughout his career, Ferguson earned the respect of his teammates with his grit, determination, and exceptional leadership ability, with Joe DeLamielleure stating, "Besides being extremely talented, Joe was an unbelievable leader. He was the best leader of all the team sports I've ever played. He led by example."

Meanwhile, Reggie McKenzie spoke of Ferguson's ability to perform well under pressure, saying, "In my mind, Joe Ferguson is the best two-minute quarterback in the NFL. There is no one, absolutely no one, better than him with two minutes to go in the game or in the half. We're playing Oakland a couple of years ago, and we're down by five or six points with 50 seconds to go against a very formidable Oakland Raiders team. Ferg hit Ahmad Rashad with six seconds to go, and Buffalo wins."

Also known for his mental and physical toughness, Ferguson performed heroically during the latter stages of the 1980 campaign, starting Buffalo's final two games on a severely injured ankle. Punctuating a season in which he led the Bills to an 11-5 record and their first AFC East title by completing 57.2 percent of his passes, while also throwing for 2,805 yards and 20 touchdowns, Ferguson directed his team to a division-clinching 18-13 victory over the San Francisco 49ers at soggy Candlestick Park in the regular-season finale, after injuring his ankle the previous week against the Patriots. Two weeks later, Ferguson left a lasting impression on his teammates and the fans of Buffalo with the courage and determination he displayed by nearly leading the Bills to a victory over the San Diego Chargers in their first playoff game since 1974.

Revealing the severity of his injury years later, Ferguson recalled, "We taped that ankle up as much as we could. But it really hurt. I just couldn't get going with it. When I got back home and had it examined a final time, it was discovered that the ankle had been sprained, torn, pulled, and stretched. And there was a cracked bone in the back of my ankle to top it off."

Although Ferguson earned a newfound respect from Bills fans with his gritty performance, he never felt truly comfortable in Buffalo, once saying, "I like Buffalo and the people here. But I don't own a house here, and I don't really care to. I know I wouldn't enjoy the winters."

Ferguson had one more successful season with the Bills, leading them to a record of 10-6 and their second straight playoff appearance in 1981 by passing for 3,652 yards and 24 touchdowns. After tossing a league-high 16 interceptions and throwing for 1,597 yards and 7 touchdowns during the strike-shortened 1982 campaign, Ferguson passed for 2,995 yards, threw 26 TD passes, and tossed 25 interceptions for a Bills team that finished 8-8 in 1983. Relieved of his starting duties during the second half of the ensuing campaign after leading the Bills to just one win in their first eleven games, Ferguson spent the season's final few weeks sitting behind Joe Dufek, before being traded to the Detroit Lions during the off-season.

Recalling his final days in Buffalo, Ferguson said, "Near the end of my career with Buffalo, the press seemed to get on my physical ability. When we were winning, I was fine. But, when we lost, I was considered 'over the hill.' That's why, when I was traded, I was ready for a change. I felt it was time to move on and let somebody else take over. I had no regrets about leaving."

Ferguson, who left Buffalo with career totals of 4,166 pass attempts, 2,188 pass completions, 27,590 passing yards, 181 touchdown passes, and 190 interceptions, a 52.5 percent pass-completion percentage, and a QBR of 68.9, ended up spending the next two years in Detroit, starting only five games for the Lions, before splitting his final three seasons between the Tampa Bay Buccaneers and Indianapolis Colts, serving both teams almost exclusively as a backup. Announcing his retirement following the 1990 season, Ferguson ended his playing career with 29,817 passing yards, 196 touchdown passes, and 209 interceptions.

After retiring as an active player, Ferguson returned to the University of Arkansas, where he spent four seasons serving as quarterbacks coach. He also pursued a career in real estate, spending many years working primarily with people who frequently relocated. Diagnosed with Burkitt's lymphoma in 2005 and acute myeloid leukemia in 2008, Ferguson overcame both forms of cancer, later saying, "I didn't feel great, but I never thought I was close to not being around."

Looking back on the time he spent in Buffalo, the seventy-three-year-old Ferguson, who has been living with his wife, Sandy, at his lakefront property near Dallas, Texas, since he retired to private life early in 2021, says, "I would have liked to have left on a winning note. That's my biggest regret. The fans will always wonder if I was the right quarterback for this team. I want to be remembered as a guy who tried."

## BILLS CAREER HIGHLIGHTS

### Best Season

Although Ferguson led the NFL with 25 touchdown passes in 1975 and 2,803 passing yards in 1977, he had his finest all-around season in 1981, when he led the Bills into the playoffs by throwing for a career-high 3,652 yards and tossing 24 TD passes.

### Memorable Moments/Greatest Performances

- Led the Bills to a 21-20 come-from-behind victory over the Raiders in the 1974 regular-season opener by throwing a pair of TD passes to Ahmad Rashad in the final two minutes of regulation, hitting Rashad with the game-winner with just six seconds left on the clock. ·
- Threw three touchdown passes in one game for the first time as a pro during a 30-28 win over the Patriots on October 20, 1974, hooking up with O. J. Simpson from 29 yards out, and collaborating with Paul Seymour on scoring plays of 10 and 40 yards.
- Passed for 296 yards and 3 touchdowns during a 24-23 victory over the Jets on November 2, 1975, collaborating with O. J. Simpson on a 64-yard scoring play in the final period.

- Led the Bills to a 45-31 win over the Patriots on November 23, 1975, by throwing for 276 yards and 4 touchdowns, the longest of which went 77 yards to J. D. Hill.
- Although the Bills lost to the Dolphins by a score of 31-24 on September 17, 1978, Ferguson collaborated with Frank Lewis on a career-long 92-yard TD connection during the contest.
- The combination of Ferguson and Jerry Butler proved to be too much for the Jets to handle on September 23, 1979, with Ferguson throwing for 367 yards and 5 touchdowns during a 46-31 Bills win, and Butler making 4 TD receptions, two of which exceeded 70 yards.
- Followed that up with another strong outing, passing for 317 yards and 3 touchdowns during a 31-13 victory over the Colts on September 30, 1979.
- Continued to perform well in the month of October, throwing for 339 yards and 1 touchdown during a 20-17 win over the Lions on October 28, 1979, with his 7-yard TD pass to tight end Reuben Gant late in the fourth quarter providing the margin of victory.
- Gave the Bills a 31-24 win over the Jets on November 9, 1980, by connecting with Frank Lewis from 31 yards out late in the final period for the last of his 3 TD passes.
- Led the Bills to a convincing 35-3 victory over the Colts on September 13, 1981, by passing for 261 yards and 4 touchdowns, the longest of which went 54 yards to Jerry Butler.
- Turned in a solid effort against the Dolphins at home on October 12, 1981, completing 20 of 29 pass attempts for 338 yards and 3 touchdowns during a 31-21 Bills win, with two of his TD tosses going to Jerry Butler and the other to Joe Cribbs.
- Directed the Bills to a 22-13 win over the Browns on November 1, 1981, by throwing for 297 yards and 3 touchdowns, all of which went to Cribbs.
- Came up big for the Bills on September 16, 1982, leading them back from a 19-0 first-half deficit against the Vikings by passing for 330 yards and 3 touchdowns, with his 11-yard TD pass to Jerry Butler in the final period giving the Bills a 23-22 win.
- Experienced his finest moment on October 9, 1983, when he led the Bills to a 38-35 overtime victory over the Dolphins in Miami by throwing for a career-high 419 yards and 5 touchdowns, the longest of which went 30 yards to Byron Franklin. Physically and emotionally drained after the game, which ended the Bills' Orange Bowl drought, Ferguson said, "I feel as good as I ever felt. It's taken me 11 years to win down

here in Miami, and it's a great win for us. This is something I really wanted to do before I got out of football. It really hasn't sunk in yet what we did against the Dolphins because you just don't do that. It was the most emotional game I've ever played in. I'm happy for everybody, especially Joe Ferguson."

## Notable Achievements

- Passed for more than 3,000 yards twice
- Threw at least 25 touchdown passes twice
- Posted passer rating of at least 90.0 once
- Led NFL in passing yards once and touchdown passes once
- Finished third in NFL in passer rating once
- Ranks second in Bills history in pass attempts (4,166), pass completions (2,188), passing yards (27,590), and touchdown passes (181)
- 1980 division champion
- Inducted into Bills Wall of Fame in 1995

# 33
## NATE CLEMENTS

A versatile cornerback who did an excellent job in both pass coverage and run support, Nate Clements spent the first six years of his NFL career in Buffalo, appearing in every game the Bills played during that time. The first player in franchise history to lead the team in interceptions in four consecutive seasons, Clements picked off a total of 23 passes while wearing the Red, White, and Blue, placing him among the franchise's all-time leaders. Clements, who also ranks extremely high in team annals in interception-return yards, forced fumbles, and touchdowns scored on defense, proved to be a standout performer on special teams as well, returning 2 punts for touchdowns. Also known for his ability to deliver hard hits to the opposition, Clements established himself as one of the NFL's most complete corners from 2001 to 2006, before leaving Buffalo when the San Francisco 49ers offered him a massive free agent contract following the conclusion of the 2006 campaign.

Born in Shaker Heights, Ohio, on December 12, 1979, Nathan D. Clements grew up in modest means knowing that he wanted to go to Ohio State and play in the NFL. Informed at an early age by his father, Nate Sr., who worked as an electrician and firefighter, that he needed to obtain a scholarship to achieve his goals, Clements recalled being told, "Then you'd better concentrate on football. What I do is nothing to be ashamed of, but it's important that each generation do a little better for themselves."

Clements's father also instilled in his son a sense of humility, remembering the time he visited Nate Jr.'s school and heard his friends expressing their admiration for his athletic ability by shouting, "You're the man, Nate!" Trying to dispel such notions, Nate Sr. told his son after he arrived home later that day, "Nathan, let me tell you. You're NOT the man. Your dad is the man. You're not the man until you put a roof over your family's head and put food on their table. All you've done is run back some touchdowns in high school. Don't get caught up in the hype."

Nate Clements led the Bills in interceptions four straight times.

A star defensive back at Shaker Heights High School, Clements earned First-Team All-Ohio honors and gained All-America recognition from *USA Today*, *Blue Chip Illustrated*, and *Super Prep* his senior year by intercepting 6 passes and scoring 3 touchdowns, 2 of which came on kickoff returns. Working extremely hard to attain the individual accolades he received, Clements woke up early every morning so he could work out before going to school. Self-motivated and disciplined, Clements also applied himself in the classroom, often staying up until midnight in his junior and senior years to finish his homework and study for the SATs.

Having set the Shaker career record for most interceptions (14), Clements received a football scholarship to The Ohio State University, where, after spending his freshman year playing behind starting cornerbacks

Ahmed Plummer and Antoine Winfield, he eventually emerged as arguably the best of the three. Starting twenty-four of the thirty-six games in which he appeared as a member of the Buckeyes, Clements recorded 7 interceptions and 177 tackles, performing especially well his junior year, when he earned First-Team All-Big Ten honors by picking off 4 passes, recording 60 solo tackles, and amassing 470 punt-return yards.

Electing to forego his final season of college eligibility, Clements entered the 2001 NFL Draft, where the Bills selected him in the 1st round, with the 21st overall pick. Claiming afterward that the Bills made a wise choice, Clements's agent, Neil Cornrich, said of his client, "He clearly established he was the top corner [in the draft]. He possesses superior size and speed."

After spending the first few weeks of his rookie campaign assuming a backup role on defense, Clements replaced Ken Irvin as the starter at right cornerback. Performing well the rest of the year, Clements earned a third-place finish in the NFL Defensive Rookie of the Year voting by recording 3 interceptions, 3 forced fumbles, 67 tackles, and 1 sack, while also accumulating 709 kickoff- and punt-return yards and scoring 2 touchdowns. Establishing himself as one of the league's top players at his position over the course of the next two seasons, Clements picked off 9 passes, amassed 136 interception-return yards, registered 127 tackles, forced 4 fumbles, and scored 2 touchdowns, although the Bills' poor play as a team likely prevented him from garnering postseason honors either year. Finally named to the Pro Bowl in 2004, Clements earned that distinction by finishing third in the league with 6 interceptions and 5 forced fumbles, recording 79 tackles, amassing 327 punt-return yards, and scoring a pair of touchdowns.

A well-rounded cornerback with no glaring weaknesses in his game, the 6', 205-pound Clements possessed good size, speed, and strength, making him equally effective against the run and the pass. Capable of covering virtually any receiver in the league one-on-one, Clements played the cornerback position with an unmatched level of tenacity and a knack for finding the football, recording 23 interceptions, 87 passes defensed, and 12 forced fumbles during his time in Buffalo. Displaying the same type of intensity in run support, Clements registered 446 tackles as a member of the Bills, with his aggressiveness and willingness to engage the opposition anywhere on the playing field making him an intimidating presence in their defensive secondary.

In describing his style of play, Clements said, "I like to think that I am known as somebody that can tackle forcefully. I've done that all through my career. I play full speed, aggressive."

With opposing quarterbacks typically choosing not to throw to his side of the field in 2005 and 2006, Clements recorded just 5 interceptions, although he still managed to force 3 fumbles and make a career-high 102 tackles in the first of those campaigns. Offered an eight-year, $80 million contract by the 49ers on March 2, 2007, Clements had no choice but to accept, becoming in the process the highest paid defensive player in the league. In addition to leaving Buffalo with career totals of 23 interceptions, 446 tackles, and 12 forced fumbles, Clements amassed 341 interception-return yards, recovered 6 fumbles, recorded 1.5 sacks, accumulated 1,259 punt- and kickoff-return yards, and scored 7 touchdowns as a member of the Bills, scoring five times on defense and twice on special teams.

Failing to experience the same level of success in San Francisco, Clements spent four seasons with the 49ers, picking off a total of 10 passes, before being released by them on July 28, 2011. Signed by the Bengals a few days later, Clements received rave reviews from Cincinnati head coach Marvin Lewis and Bengals defensive coordinator Mike Zimmer, with the former saying, "He's the epitome of a defensive back."

Meanwhile, Zimmer gushed, "He's extremely versatile and valuable to us. He's a great veteran leader and a terrific player. He's a pro's pro."

Once again failing to regain his earlier form, Clements picked off just 3 passes over the course of the next two seasons, before announcing his retirement at the end of 2012 with career totals 36 interceptions, 508 interception-return yards, 826 tackles, 22 forced fumbles, 8 fumble recoveries, and 4.5 sacks.

Since retiring from football, Clements has spent most of his time serving as a member of an investment group that deals in commercial real estate, saying, "What's kind of unique about it is that my investment group are guys that I played with in Buffalo."

Looking back favorably on the time he spent in Buffalo, Clements says, "It was an excellent organization with good coaches. It wasn't a city like Miami or Atlanta. It was a hidden blessing. I wasn't able to always go out. I didn't have distractions off the field."

## BILLS CAREER HIGHLIGHTS

### Best Season

Clements had an outstanding year for the Bills in 2002, ranking among the league leaders with 6 interceptions and 19 passes defended, recording 65 tackles, and scoring 1 touchdown on defense. But he performed even better in 2004, earning his only trip to the Pro Bowl by finishing third in the NFL with 6 interceptions and 5 forced fumbles, registering 79 tackles, and scoring 2 touchdowns, with one coming on defense and the other on special teams.

### Memorable Moments/Greatest Performances

- Although the Bills suffered a 42-26 defeat at the hands of the Indianapolis Colts on September 23, 2001, Clements scored the game's first points when he returned the first interception of his career 48 yards for a touchdown.
- Once again starred in defeat in the second meeting between the two teams on November 4, 2001, returning a punt 66 yards for a touchdown during a 30-14 loss to the Colts.
- Known as one of the NFL's hardest-hitting cornerbacks, Clements first began to make a name for himself in that area during a 12-9 overtime loss to the Patriots on December 16, 2001, when he delivered a vicious blow to Tom Brady at the line of scrimmage that the GOAT identified some 20 years later as the hardest hit he ever took.
- Earned AFC Defensive Player of the Week honors by recording 3 interceptions during a 23-10 win over the Dolphins on October 20, 2002, returning one of his picks 29 yards for a touchdown.
- Contributed to a 27-9 victory over the Cincinnati Bengals in the final game of the 2002 regular season by recording 9 tackles and an interception, which he returned 42 yards.
- Gave the Bills the only points they scored during a 17-7 loss to the Dolphins on September 21, 2003, when he returned 1 of his 2 interceptions 54 yards for a touchdown.
- Crossed the opponent's goal line again on November 21, 2004, when he returned a punt 86 yards for a touchdown during a 37-17 win over the St. Louis Rams.

- Lit the scoreboard again when he returned his interception of a Tommy Maddox pass 30 yards for a touchdown during a 29-24 loss to the Steelers in the 2004 regular-season finale.
- Recorded the last of his five career-pick-sixes when he returned his interception of a Chad Pennington pass 58 yards for a TD during a 31-13 win over the Jets on December 10, 2006.

### Notable Achievements

- Never missed a game in six seasons, appearing in ninety-six consecutive contests
- Scored 5 defensive touchdowns
- Returned 2 punts for touchdowns
- Recorded 6 interceptions twice
- Recorded more than 100 tackles once
- Finished third in NFL in interceptions once and forced fumbles once
- Led Bills in interceptions four times
- Holds share of franchise record for most touchdowns scored on defense (5)
- Ranks among Bills career leaders with 23 interceptions (tied for 7th), 341 interception-return yards (9th), 12 forced fumbles (6th), and 617 punt-return yards (6th)
- 2002 Week 7 AFC Defensive Player of the Week
- 2004 Pro Bowl selection

# 34

## JOE CRIBBS

A n outstanding all-around back who excelled for the Bills as both a runner and a receiver out of the backfield, Joe Cribbs spent five seasons in Buffalo, leading the team in rushing in four of those. A huge contributor to Bills teams that won one division title and made two playoff appearances, Cribbs gained more than 1,000 yards on the ground and amassed more than 1,500 yards from scrimmage three times each, en route to establishing himself as one of the franchise's all-time leaders in both categories. The 1980 AFC Rookie of the Year, Cribbs also earned three Pro Bowl selections and two First-Team All-AFC nominations, before being dealt to the San Francisco 49ers at the end of 1985 due to differences with team management.

Born in Sulligent, Alabama, on January 5, 1958, Joe Stanier Cribbs began playing organized football in the seventh grade, when he joined his grade school's varsity team as a defensive back. Eventually emerging as a standout athlete at Sulligent High School, Cribbs starred in football, basketball, and track, performing especially well on the gridiron, where he earned *Parade* All-American honors twice.

Offered an athletic scholarship to Auburn University, Cribbs spent four seasons playing for head coach Doug Barfield, distinguishing himself at running back despite sharing playing time with future NFL stars James Brooks and William Andrews. Particularly outstanding in his final two seasons, Cribbs rushed for 1,205 yards and 16 touchdowns his junior year, before gaining 1,120 yards on the ground and scoring 15 TDs as a senior.

Impressed with Cribbs's exceptional play for the Tigers, the Bills selected him at the beginning of the 2nd round of the 1980 NFL Draft, with the 29th overall pick. Recalling how he learned of his selection, Cribbs said, "Actually, I was supposed to have been a higher pick than I was, and I remember being at Auburn . . . in my apartment. I had I think three networks, three local networks, that were there waiting for the phone call. That's how we were notified. We had to wait a long time because I was

214

Joe Cribbs earned AFC Rookie of the Year honors in 1980.

the 29th pick and everybody thought I'd probably be the second running back taken, and it ended up not going that way. . . . Now I look back and realize that the 29th pick is not low. It's still really good, but, at that time, I expected to be higher. So, anyway, I just kind of made up my mind that I was going to make a lot of people regret the fact that they passed on me. So, I did."

Replacing Terry Miller as the starter at halfback shortly after he arrived in Buffalo, Cribbs became the Bills' primary offensive weapon before long, earning Pro Bowl, First-Team All-AFC, and AFC Rookie of the Year honors by rushing for 1,185 yards and 11 touchdowns, making 52 receptions for 415 yards and 1 TD, accumulating another 186 yards on punt and kickoff returns, and ranking among the league leaders with 1,600 yards from scrimmage and 1,786 all-purpose yards. Cribbs followed that up with another outstanding season, gaining Pro Bowl recognition again in 1981 by rushing for 1,097 yards, making 40 receptions for 603 yards, and scoring 10 touchdowns, with his strong all-around play prompting the Newspaper Enterprise Association to accord him unofficial Second-Team All-Pro honors.

A swift and elusive runner, the 5'11", 190-pound Cribbs hit the hole quickly and had the ability to run away from defenders once he broke into the open field. Despite his somewhat smallish frame, Cribbs also possessed good strength, enabling him to run the ball well between the tackles. Perhaps Cribbs's greatest asset, though, lay in his ability to excel as a receiver coming out of the backfield, making him one of the NFL's finest all-purpose backs.

Commenting on the importance of Cribbs to Buffalo's offense when the running back requested a five-year contract extension worth $3.47 million prior to the start of the 1982 campaign, his agent, Dr. Jerry Argovitz, argued, "Without Joe Cribbs, the Buffalo Bills are like an airplane without wheels—they can't take off, and they can't land."

But, with notoriously frugal Bills owner Ralph Wilson running the team's finances, Buffalo offered Cribbs just $1.2 million over four years, prompting the latter to call out the organization when he said, "It's the little things that show the Bills are a no-class operation. I always have to give in."

After holding out through the first two weeks of the 1982 regular season, Cribbs decided to report to the team, play under the terms of his existing contract, and hope for the best the following offseason. But, with a players' strike shortening the campaign to just nine games, Cribbs ended up appearing in only seven contests, finishing the year with 633 yards rushing, 732 yards from scrimmage, and 3 touchdowns.

Still unhappy over what he considered to be his shabby treatment by the Bills, Cribbs signed with the Birmingham Stallions of the United States Football League (USFL) when they came calling in the spring of 1983. Claiming they had a right of first refusal, the Bills took Cribbs to court, after which U.S. District Court judge John T. Elfvin ruled in the running back's favor, but also decreed that he had to return to the Bills for one more season.

Putting aside all the outside distractions, Cribbs performed exceptionally well for the Bills in 1983, earning his third Pro Bowl selection and second First-Team All-AFC nomination by rushing for 1,131 yards and 3 touchdowns, making 57 receptions for 524 yards and 7 TDs, and ranking among the league leaders with 1,655 yards from scrimmage. Commenting on the effort he put forth that year, Cribbs said, "I'm a guy who, whenever I walk between those white lines, I am always going to give my best. And I did everything I could do that year."

Looking back years later on his decision to leave Buffalo when he did, Cribbs stated, "If you truly understand the game and statistics, I was playing on a team where, basically, I was probably 60 to 70 percent of our offense at that time. I had guys who were backing me up that were making more than I was making. That was just total injustice. But the thing that I feel that I would have done differently is, I would have at least kept my doors open as opposed to just saying, 'Hey, okay, they don't want me. I'm leaving.' Then, when they came back, I said, 'Nah, it's too late.' I would have done that differently."

Cribbs subsequently led the USFL in rushing in each of the next two seasons, before returning to the Bills, who retained his NFL rights, when the upstart league disbanded following the conclusion of the 1985 campaign. Failing to regain his earlier form, Cribbs found himself being used sparingly, later saying, "I don't think I was going to be allowed to shine too much," and adding that, had he known the USFL would fold, he never would have left in the first place.

After Cribbs rushed for just 399 yards, amassed only 541 yards from scrimmage, and scored just 1 touchdown in 1985, the Bills traded him to San Francisco for a pair of draft picks at the end of the year, with 49ers head coach Bill Walsh saying at the time, "We've been following Cribbs's career for several years, and his statistics speak for themselves. Any time you can add a player of that caliber to your roster, naturally you'd like to do it."

Cribbs, who left Buffalo with career totals of 4,445 rushing yards, 21 rushing touchdowns, 180 pass receptions, 1,783 receiving yards, 15 TD catches, 6,228 yards from scrimmage, 6,405 all-purpose yards, and 36 touchdowns, ended up spending two years in San Francisco, starting alongside Roger Craig in one of those, before announcing his retirement after splitting the 1988 campaign between the Indianapolis Colts and Miam Dolphins. Over eight NFL seasons, Cribbs rushed for 5,356 yards, gained another 2,199 yards on 224 pass receptions, amassed 7,555 yards from scrimmage and 8,922 all-purpose yards, and scored 43 touchdowns.

Following his playing days, Cribbs, who is sixty-five years old as of this writing, returned with his wife, Daphne, to his home state of Alabama, where he became an insurance broker, saying in 2019, "For the last, maybe, 20-something years, I've been in the financial services industry. Primarily, on the insurance side of setting up supplemental retirement plans for guys, for individuals. I do all types of insurance—business, personal, everything on the insurance side. That's pretty much what I've done since I retired."

Despite the problems that Cribbs experienced with Bills management, he continues to hold the city of Buffalo and its fans close to his heart, saying, "I love Buffalo. I have always loved the fans of Buffalo. They are the most supportive fans in the NFL. Just the way they show up in some of the conditions they show up in, that's a commitment, that's a real commitment. Players appreciate that. I know I did."

## BILLS CAREER HIGHLIGHTS

### Best Season

Cribbs performed brilliantly for the Bills in 1980, 1981, and 1983, gaining Pro Bowl recognition in each of those three seasons by rushing for more than 1,000 yards, amassing more than 1,500 yards from scrimmage, and scoring at least 10 touchdowns. But Cribbs also gained 173 yards on the ground, amassed 237 yards from scrimmage, and scored 3 TDs during the 1981 playoffs, making that the most impactful season of his career.

### Memorable Moments/Greatest Performances

- Excelled in his first game as a pro, amassing a total of 166 all-purpose yards during a 17-7 win over the Miami Dolphins in the opening game of the 1980 regular season. In addition to rushing for 60 yards, Cribbs made 9 receptions for 71 yards, accumulated another 35 yards returning kickoffs and punts, and sealed the victory late in the fourth quarter by scoring his first career touchdown on a two-yard run.
- Turned in another outstanding all-around effort during a 31-13 win over the Patriots on October 26, 1980, rushing for 118 yards, making 3 receptions for 41 yards, and scoring 2 touchdowns.
- Contributed to an 18-13 victory over the San Francisco 49ers in the 1980 regular-season finale by gaining a season-high 128 yards on the ground.
- Had another strong game against the Colts on October 4, 1981, carrying the ball seventeen times for 159 yards during a 23-17 Bills win.
- Proved to be a one-man wrecking crew against Cleveland on November 1, 1981, leading the Bills to a 22-13 victory by gaining 85 yards on the ground and making 5 receptions for 163 yards and 3 TDs, which came on passes from Joe Ferguson that covered 58, 15, and 60 yards.
- Performed brilliantly once again during a 19-10 win over the Patriots on December 13, 1981, rushing for 153 yards and making 3 receptions

for 48 yards and 1 touchdown, which he scored on a 39-yard pass from Joe Ferguson.

• Helped lead the Bills to a hard-fought 31-27 victory over the Jets in the 1981 AFC wild card game by rushing for 83 yards, making 4 receptions for 64 yards, and scoring the game-winning touchdown on a 45-yard fourth-quarter run.

• Contributed to a 13-0 win over the Pittsburgh Steelers on December 12, 1982, by rushing for a season-high 143 yards on 30 carries.

• Led the Bills to a 28-23 win over the Colts on September 18, 1983, by rushing for 82 yards and scoring 3 touchdowns, the last of which came on a 2-yard pass from Joe Ferguson late in the final period that provided the margin of victory.

• Helped the Bills end a ten-game losing streak to the Houston Oilers on September 25, 1983, by carrying the ball 22 times for 166 yards and 1 touchdown during a 30-13 win.

• Gained a career-high 185 yards on the ground during a 14-9 win over the Kansas City Chiefs on December 4, 1983.

## Notable Achievements

• Rushed for more than 1,000 yards three times
• Surpassed 50 receptions and 500 receiving yards twice each
• Surpassed 1,500 yards from scrimmage three times
• Scored at least 10 touchdowns three times
• Finished third in NFL with 11 rushing touchdowns in 1980
• Led Bills in rushing four times, receptions once, and receiving yards once
• Ranks among Bills career leaders with 4,445 yards rushing (4th), 6,228 yards from scrimmage (6th), 6,405 all-purpose yards (7th), and 36 touchdowns (9th)
• 1980 division champion
• Member of 1980 NFL All-Rookie Team
• 1980 United Press International AFC Rookie of the Year
• Three-time Pro Bowl selection (1980, 1981, and 1983)
• Two-time First-Team All-AFC selection (1980 and 1983)

# 35

## AARON SCHOBEL

One of the more underappreciated defensive players in Bills history, Aaron Schobel spent his entire nine-year NFL career in Buffalo, performing valiantly for teams that posted just one winning record. A good pass-rusher who led the Bills in sacks eight times, Schobel brought down opposing quarterbacks behind the line of scrimmage at least ten times in four different seasons, en route to recording the second-most sacks in franchise history. Strong against the run as well, Schobel also registered the fourth most tackles of any Bills defensive lineman and ranks third in team annals in forced fumbles, with his solid all-around play earning him two Pro Bowl selections and one All-Pro nomination.

Born in Columbus, Texas, on September 1, 1977, Aaron Ross Schobel grew up some seventy miles west of Houston, where he earned All-District honors at both outside linebacker and tight end while attending Columbus High School. Offered a football scholarship to Texas Christian University, Schobel spent four years starting on defense for the Horned Frogs, gaining First-Team All-WAC recognition in each of his final three seasons. Particularly outstanding his senior year, Schobel earned WAC Defensive Player of the Year and Second-Team All-America honors, prompting the Bills to select him in the 2nd round of the 2001 NFL Draft, with the 46th overall pick.

After spending the first few weeks of his rookie season serving the Bills as a situational player, Schobel established himself as the starter at right-defensive end—a role he maintained for the rest of his career. Gradually developing into one of the AFC's better pass-rushers, Schobel, who recorded a total of 15 sacks his first two years in the league, ranked among the conference leaders with 11.5 sacks in 2003, while also placing near the top of the league rankings with 15 tackles for loss. Continuing to perform well for the Bills over the course of the next two seasons, Schobel registered 20 sacks and 144 tackles, before earning Pro Bowl, Second-Team All-Pro,

Aaron Schobel recorded the second most sacks of any player in franchise history.
Courtesy of Mark Cromwell.

and First-Team All-AFC honors in 2006 by recording 14 sacks and 4 forced fumbles.

Although Schobel, who stood 6'4" and weighed close to 250 pounds, possessed neither great size nor outstanding athleticism, he became, arguably, the most productive Bills defender of his era because of his hard work, hustle, and unwillingness to give up on a play. Relying primarily on his wits, superb technique, and tremendous determination, Schobel developed the ability to overpower blockers much larger than himself, consistently applying pressure to opposing quarterbacks on the pass rush, while also preventing big runs to the outside by controlling his side of the line of scrimmage. Also extremely effective at batting down passes, Schobel recorded 31 passes defended over the course of his career, which represents the highest total by a Bills defensive lineman.

Praising Schobel for his excellent work in the trenches, Bills coach Dick Jauron said, "Tremendous player. He's a guy that wins a lot of matchups. One of the premier players in the league at his position, and, when he's not on the field, we definitely miss him."

Longtime friend and teammate Chris Kelsay added, "His play speaks for itself. You turn the game film on Monday mornings, and that's a guy that plays his heart out on the field."

In trying to describe himself as a player, Schobel said, "I just feel I'm not flashy. As long as the guys around the league respect me, the coaches respect me. As far as the fans, I hope they at least see a good player."

Schobel appeared in every game the Bills played for the seventh straight time in 2007, earning his second consecutive Pro Bowl nomination by recording 6.5 sacks, 57 tackles, and 5 forced fumbles, before missing eleven games with a foot injury the following year. Healthy again by the start of the 2009 campaign, Schobel had a solid season, registering 10 sacks, 56 tackles, 3 forced fumbles, and a career-high 17 tackles for loss. But, with new Bills coach Chan Gailey announcing that he planned to switch from a 4-3 to a 3-4 defense in 2010, Schobel informed the team that he had begun to seriously consider retirement.

Ultimately released by the Bills on August 4, 2010, Schobel left Buffalo harboring no ill feelings toward the team, saying at the time, "I have no regrets, and I appreciate the organization, Buffalo, their fans, and (Bills owner) Ralph (Wilson) for putting me in this position where I was able to play for nine years. I'm not going to say anything bad about them, and I wish them the best."

Officially announcing his retirement less than two weeks later, Schobel said during a phone interview with the Associated Press, "I really didn't have a lot of fun playing last year. The passion wasn't there, so it was time. I took as much time as I felt like I needed to make a decision, and I think I made the right one. . . . The decision came down to whether I wanted to play. I didn't really feel like I wanted to do it. A lot of people probably think I'm crazy, but, whenever you feel like it's time, it's time."

Schobel, who had four years left on a $50.5 million contract extension he signed with the Bills in 2007, added, "It's always hard to pass up money, but there's more to life than that. If I wanted to play, I felt like I still could've. But it was time. . . . My kids are getting older, and I didn't feel like it [the annual move from his home in Texas to New York] was fair.

It was getting to the point where it was starting to affect them, so that was the reason not to go back to Buffalo."

During his nine seasons with the Bills, Schobel recorded 78 sacks, 483 tackles, 334 solo stops, 98 tackles for loss, 21 forced fumbles, 8 fumble recoveries, and 3 interceptions, one of which he returned for a touchdown. Most noted for the success he experienced against Tom Brady and the Patriots, Schobel sacked the New England quarterback more times (14) than any other NFL player.

Following his playing days, Schobel retired to his ranch in Texas, where he continues to maintain a low profile, rarely attending team celebrations, reunions, or autograph signings.

## CAREER HIGHLIGHTS

### Best Season

Schobel turned in his most dominant all-around performance in 2006, when he earned his lone All-Pro and All-AFC nominations by finishing third in the league with a career-high 14 sacks and registering 22 hits on opposing quarterbacks, while also making 53 tackles and forcing 4 fumbles.

### Memorable Moments/Greatest Performances

- Recorded the first sack of his career when he brought down Mark Brunell behind the line of scrimmage during a 13-10 win over the Jacksonville Jaguars on October 18, 2001.
- Contributed to a 45-39 overtime victory over the Minnesota Vikings on September 15, 2002, by registering 2.5 sacks and 5 tackles, two of which resulted in a loss.
- Recorded the first of his three career interceptions during a 22-16 win over the Cincinnati Bengals on October 5, 2003.
- Earned AFC Defensive Player of the Week honors by recording 3 sacks, recovering a fumble, and registering 4 tackles for loss during a 24-7 win over the Giants on November 30, 2003.
- Excelled during a 20-13 win over the Dolphins on October 17, 2004, recording 2.5 sacks and 8 tackles, two of which resulted in a loss.
- Earned AFC Defensive Player of the Week honors by recording 3 sacks, 9 tackles, and 1 forced fumble during a 31-13 win over the Jets on December 10, 2006.

- Scored the only points of his career when he returned his interception of a Tom Brady pass 26 yards for a touchdown during a 25-24 loss to the Patriots in the opening game of the 2009 regular season.

**Notable Achievements**

- Appeared in 112 consecutive games from 2001 to 2007
- Scored 1 defensive touchdown
- Finished in double digits in sacks four times
- Finished third in NFL in sacks once and forced fumbles once
- Led Bills in sacks eight times
- Led Bills defensive linemen in tackles four times
- Ranks among Bills career leaders with 78 sacks (2nd) and 21 forced fumbles (3rd)
- Two-time AFC Defensive Player of the Week
- Two-time Pro Bowl selection (2006 and 2007)
- 2006 Second-Team All-Pro selection
- 2006 First-Team All-AFC selection

# 36
## JOE DEVLIN

**P**erhaps the most overlooked and underrated player in franchise history, Joe Devlin spent thirteen seasons in Buffalo, proving to be a pillar of strength on the right side of the Bills' offensive line during that time. Starting all but two of the 177 contests in which he appeared his last twelve years in the league, Devlin, who missed the entire 1983 campaign due to injury, provided the Bills with consistently excellent play from his right tackle position. Yet even though Devlin served as an integral member of teams that won three division titles and made four playoff appearances, the overall lack of success the Bills experienced during his time in Buffalo prevented him from ever gaining Pro Bowl or All-Pro recognition.

Born in Phoenixville, Pennsylvania, on February 23, 1954, Joseph Gregory Devlin grew up in nearby Malvern, where he starred on the gridiron as a two-way lineman while attending Great Valley High School. Offered a football scholarship to the University of Iowa, Devlin started at left guard for the Hawkeyes for three seasons, earning All-Big Ten and First-Team All-America honors his senior year.

Subsequently selected by the Bills in the 2nd round of the 1976 NFL Draft, with the 52nd overall pick, Devlin transitioned to tackle following his arrival in Buffalo, after which he spent his first pro season assuming a backup role. However, after starting just two games as a rookie, Devlin replaced Donnie Green as the full-time starter at right tackle the following year. Although the Bills managed to compile an overall record of just 15-31 over the course of the next three seasons, Devlin established himself as one of the league's better players at his position, helping to pave the way for Terry Miller to rush for more than 1,000 yards in 1978, while also providing solid pass protection for quarterback Joe Ferguson.

Dramatically improving their performance in 1980 following the emergence of Fred Smerlas as a dominant force on defense and the arrival of AFC Rookie of the Year Joe Cribbs, the Bills posted a regular season record of 11-5 that earned them their first AFC East division title. Contributing

Joe Devlin helped the Bills win three division titles and advance to the playoffs four times.

to the success of the team with his outstanding blocking up front, Devlin helped Cribbs gain 1,185 yards on the ground and amass 1,600 yards from scrimmage. The Bills advanced to the playoffs once again the following year, this time as a wild card, after compiling a record of 10-6 during the regular season. However, they failed to post a winning mark in any of the next six seasons, twice finishing just 2-14, with their poor play preventing Devlin from receiving significant support for postseason honors.

Nevertheless, the 6'5", 280-pound Devlin earned the respect and admiration of his teammates with his blue-collar attitude and strong work ethic, with Kent Hull, who joined him on the Bills offensive line in 1986, saying during the latter stages of his own career, "The big thing is the older players here now had some great teachers like Joe Devlin and Fred Smerlas. I can remember in 1988, going into the championship game in Cincinnati. Joe Devlin stood up and said, 'Guys, I got to tell you, play as hard as you can because you never know when you're going to be in this situation again.' I was 26 then, and that didn't mean anything to me, because I'm thinking I'm going to get back there next year. It doesn't work like that."

Hall of Fame guard, Joe DeLamielleure, who spent three seasons starting alongside Devlin on Buffalo's offensive line, said of his former teammate, "One of the best tackles I've ever played with. Never went to a Pro Bowl, which was a joke. Literally one of the best players I've ever played with."

New York Jets pass-rusher extraordinaire Mark Gastineau expressed similar sentiments in 1984 when he stated, "Joe Devlin is the toughest offensive tackle I've played against. That he's never been picked as an All-Pro is an indictment of the selection process."

In discussing his former teammate in his book *Tales from the Buffalo Bills*, Steve Tasker said, "Joe Devlin was one of the best offensive tackles in football and probably the most intimidating guy I ever played with. He was big—280 pounds of lean muscle on a 6-foot-5 frame—and he was mean."

Tasker continued, "Joe was tight with guys like Freddy Smerlas and some of the older offensive linemen, but he had no use for wide receivers, defensive backs, or kickers. So, when you saw him in the locker room, you'd take a real wide route to avoid him, like you would if you were in the presence of a bear."

Tasker then added, "I always felt it was a shame he never made it to a Pro Bowl. This was a guy who used to own great pass-rushers such as Mark Gastineau, but for some reason opponents never gave him the accolades he deserved. Perhaps it was because he spent so much of his career playing on losing teams."

With the Bills establishing themselves as the class of the AFC East in 1988, Devlin spent his final two seasons in Buffalo playing for winning teams, manning his familiar position of right tackle in 1988, before moving inside to guard the following year to make room on the outside for future Pro Bowler Howard Ballard. Released by the Bills following the conclusion of the 1989 campaign, Devlin announced his retirement, ending his career with 191 games played, 179 of which he started. Aside from missing two contests in 1978 and the entire 1983 season, Devlin appeared in every nonstrike game the Bills played his thirteen years in the league, with his longevity, durability, and outstanding play earning him a spot on the Bills 25th Anniversary Team.

Choosing to remain in western New York following his retirement, Devlin currently lives a quiet life, spending most of his time away from the spotlight, just as he did during his playing days. Still in good health at sixty-nine years of age, Devlin exercises often, leaving him fit, trim, and in excellent shape.

## CAREER HIGHLIGHTS

**Best Season**

Devlin received his highest grade from Pro Football Reference in four different seasons, with that source assigning him an "Approximate Value" of "9" in 1981, 1986, 1988, and 1989. But, while the Buffalo offensive line surrendered more than 30 sacks in each of the other three seasons, opposing defenders got to quarterbacks Joe Ferguson and Matt Robinson just sixteen times in 1981. Furthermore, the Bills posted a regular season record of 10-6 that earned them a playoff berth, with Buffalo running backs averaging a solid 4.1 yards per carry. All things considered, the 1981 campaign ranks as the finest of Devlin's career.

**Memorable Moments/Greatest Performances**

- Helped the Bills rush for 209 yards and amass 455 yards of total offense during a 51-24 mauling of the Bengals on September 9, 1979.
- Along with his line-mates, turned in another dominant performance two weeks later, with the Bills amassing 497 yards of total offense during a 46-31 win over the Jets on September 23, 1979, gaining 348 of those yards through the air and the other 149 on the ground.
- His strong blocking at the point of attack helped the Bills amass 469 yards of total offense during a 22-13 win over the Cleveland Browns on November 1, 1981.
- His powerful lead-blocking helped the Bills gain a season-high total of 280 yards on the ground during a 31-17 victory over the Miami Dolphins on October 29, 1988.

**Notable Achievements**

- Appeared in every nonstrike game the Bills played twelve times from 1976 to 1989
- Started ninety-two consecutive nonstrike games from 1984 to 1989
- Ranks fourth in franchise history with 191 games played
- Three-time division champion (1980, 1988, and 1989)

# 37

## STEFON DIGGS

A big-play receiver with good speed, soft hands, and exceptional route-running ability, Stefon Diggs has proven to be one of the AFC's most productive wideouts since he first joined the Bills in 2020. The favorite target of quarterback Josh Allen the past three seasons, Diggs, who spent his first five years in the league combining with Adam Thielen in Minnesota to give the Vikings an extremely formidable pass-receiving duo, has surpassed 100 receptions and 1,200 receiving yards three straight times, earning in the process three Pro Bowl selections and two All-Pro nominations. Arriving in Buffalo with a reputation as something of a malcontent, Diggs has displayed no such tendencies during his time in western New York, serving as one of the leaders of Bills teams that have won three straight division titles.

Born in Gaithersburg, Maryland, on November 29, 1993, Stefon Diggs had responsibility thrust upon him at the early age of fourteen when he lost his father to congestive heart failure. Looking back on how his father's untimely passing affected him, Diggs said, "Not having a father is big. You need guidance. I know, personally, when my father died, I needed guidance; I needed somebody to show me how to be a man, how to grow up, basically how to do the right thing."

Serving as a father figure to his younger brothers throughout the remainder of his teenage years, Diggs had to assume numerous roles while attending Our Lady of Good Counsel High School, where he played football and ran track. Excelling on the gridiron on both sides of the ball, Diggs earned a runner-up finish in the Gatorade Maryland Player of the Year voting as a junior by amassing 810 receiving yards and scoring 23 touchdowns. Performing equally well his senior year, Diggs accumulated 1,047 yards from scrimmage, scored 11 touchdowns, and recorded 31.5 tackles on defense, with his exceptional all-around play gaining him recognition from *The Washington Post* as a First-Team All-Metro selection. Starring in track as well, Diggs competed in both the 100-meter and 200-meter dashes, posting

Stefon Diggs holds single-season franchise records for most pass receptions and most receiving yards.
Courtesy of Keith Allison and All-Pro Reels Photography.

a personal best time of 22.30 seconds in the latter event at the Darius Ray Invitational as a senior in 2012.

Subsequently offered athletic scholarships to several major colleges, including Florida, USC, Cal, Ohio State, and Auburn, Diggs elected to remain close to home and enroll at the University of Maryland, where he spent three seasons playing for head football coach Randy Edsall. Performing brilliantly for the Terrapins in his freshman year, Diggs earned a second-place finish to Duke's Jamison Crowder in the ACC Rookie of the

Year balloting by making 54 receptions for 848 yards and amassing 1,896 all-purpose yards. After being limited to 34 receptions and 587 receiving yards the following year by a broken right fibula that forced him to miss the season's final six games, Diggs earned Second-Team All-Big Ten honors as a junior by making 62 receptions for 792 yards and 5 TDs, despite missing another three games due to injury.

Choosing to forgo his final year of college, Diggs declared himself eligible for the 2015 NFL Draft, where Minnesota selected him in the 5th round, with the 146th overall pick. After earning a starting job during the early stages of the 2015 campaign, Diggs acquitted himself extremely well his first year in the league, earning a spot on the NFL All-Rookie Team by leading the Vikings with 52 receptions and 720 receiving yards, while also finishing second on the team with 4 TD catches. Continuing to perform well the next two seasons, Diggs totaled 148 receptions, 1,752 receiving yards, and 11 touchdowns, before establishing new career highs in 2018, when he caught 102 passes, amassed 1,021 receiving yards, and scored 9 TDs.

Although Diggs compiled excellent numbers again in 2019, concluding the campaign with 63 receptions for 1,130 yards and 6 touchdowns, he became increasingly unhappy over the Vikings' reliance on their running game and his role in the offense as the season progressed, causing tensions to mount between him and the team at various times. After the Vikings fined Diggs $200,000 for missing a practice following a Week 4 loss to the Chicago Bears, Ben Goessling of the *Star Tribune* wrote: "His absence stemmed from frustrations that had been building since the spring over the direction of the offense and his role in it. When asked whether he wished to be traded upon his return to the team, Diggs responded, 'I feel like there's truth to all rumors, no matter how you dress it up. I won't be saying nothing on it. I won't be speaking on it at all. But there is truth to all rumors, I guess.'"

Despite performing well the rest of the year, Diggs continued to express his dissatisfaction with the organization during the subsequent off-season, tweeting on separate occasions, "I don't forget or forgive," "I hate people that do you wrong then try to play the victim," "People don't appreciate things until they're gone," and "It's time for a new beginning."

Left with little choice, the Vikings worked out a trade with the Bills on March 16, 2020, that sent the disgruntled receiver and a 7th round pick in the 2020 NFL Draft to Buffalo for three picks in that year's draft (a first, fifth, and sixth rounder) and a 4th round selection in the 2021 draft.

Given a new lease on life following his arrival in Buffalo, Diggs emerged as one of the premier receivers in the game in 2020, earning Pro Bowl, First-Team All-Pro, and First-Team All-AFC honors by catching 8 touchdown passes and leading the league with 127 receptions and 1,535 receiving yards, setting in the process new single-season franchise records in the last two categories. Diggs followed that up with another outstanding season, gaining Pro Bowl recognition again in 2021 by making 103 receptions for 1,225 yards and 10 touchdowns.

Although the 6', 191-pound Diggs lacks elite speed, he possesses several other qualities that have enabled him to establish himself as one of the league's top big-play threats. An outstanding route runner who is extremely adept at running all kinds of pass patterns, Diggs also does an excellent job of using his quickness to separate himself from his defender and evade would-be tacklers in the open field.

In discussing his greatest strengths, Diggs said, "I can separate very well. I can do everything I need to do as a player. I'm not the fastest guy always, or the strongest guy, or the biggest guy, but I always get the job done. I'm a workaholic. . . . I don't just study my opponent; I study myself. It's something you have to do to get better. . . . You've got to bring something to the table that someone else is not. I love football too much."

Although portrayed in Minnesota as a somewhat selfish player, Diggs soon emerged as one of the Bills team leaders, developing an especially strong bond with quarterback Josh Allen, who he has helped fulfill his enormous potential. Voted a team captain prior to the start of the 2021 season, Diggs received high praise for his leadership ability from teammate Dion Dawkins, who stated, "He's one of the best teammates I've ever had. Dude is obsessed with making the people around him better. . . . Whether it's staying after practice with Gabe [Davis] and working him through a ball cart of reps. Or it's speaking up in a meeting and making sure him and Cole [Beasley] have their timing on a crossing pattern down to the split second. Or it's just doing whatever is needed to lead his group like a true unit. Or it's making the type of play where the entire sideline is left speechless. Whether it's any of those things, man. Stefon has been there for it."

Dawkins added, "It's funny, but like—I don't think I'd ever really understood what a 'superstar' is before. . . . The definition of a superstar is: You know it when you see it. . . . You know it when you see Stefon Diggs. I think what I've realized with Stefon is that being a superstar . . . it's not about having a higher ceiling. It's about having no ceiling. . . . In other words, Stefon has redefined what good football means for our squad."

Following his outstanding 2021 campaign, Diggs signed a four-year, $96 million contract extension with the Bills that promises to keep him in Buffalo through the 2026 season. Expressing his joy upon inking his deal, Diggs said, "It's crazy because when I first got traded to Buffalo, besides the Mafia and the people who are fans of Buffalo, not too many people thought it would work out. A lot of people were like this, 'The Bills are dah dah dah dah.' Two years later, I can smile and say, you know, 'God works in mysterious ways, and I am with my family, I am with the right people. I got the right support system.'"

Continuing to perform at an elite level in 2022, Diggs helped the Bills capture their third straight division title by ranking among the league leaders with 108 receptions, 1,429 receiving yards, and 11 touchdown catches, earning in the process Pro Bowl and Second-Team All-Pro honors. Already among the franchise's all-time leaders in all three categories, Diggs has caught 338 passes, amassed 4,189 receiving yards, and made 29 TD catches in his three years with the Bills. Meanwhile, Diggs boasts career totals of 703 receptions, 8,812 receiving yards, and 59 touchdowns heading into the 2023 campaign.

## BILLS CAREER HIGHLIGHTS

### Best Season

Diggs had his finest season to date in 2020, when he gained consensus First-Team All-Pro recognition by leading the NFL with 127 receptions and 1,535 receiving yards, finishing fourth in the league in yards from scrimmage and all-purpose yards, and scoring 8 touchdowns, with his 127 catches and 1,535 receiving yards breaking single-season franchise marks previously held by Eric Moulds.

### Memorable Moments/Greatest Performances

- Had a huge game against the Miami Dolphins on September 20, 2020, making 8 receptions for 153 yards and 1 touchdown during a 31-28 Bills win.
- Contributed to a 26-15 win over the Pittsburgh Steelers on December 13, 2020, by making 10 receptions for 130 yards and 1 touchdown, which came on a 19-yard pass from Josh Allen.

- Followed that up with another strong outing, making 11 receptions for 147 yards during a lopsided 48-19 victory over the Denver Broncos on December 19, 2020.
- Continued his exceptional play one week later, earning AFC Offensive Player of the Week honors by making 9 receptions for 145 yards and 3 touchdowns during a convincing 38-9 win over the New England Patriots on December 28, 2020, with the longest of his TDs coming on a 50-yard connection with Josh Allen.
- Played an important role in the Bills' 27-24 win over the Indianapolis Colts in the 2020 AFC Wild Card game, making 6 receptions for 128 yards and 1 touchdown, which came on a 35-yard pass from Josh Allen early in the final period that increased Buffalo's lead to 14 points.
- Contributed to a 45-17 rout of the Jets on November 14, 2021, by making 8 receptions for 162 yards and 1 touchdown, which came on a 12-yard pass from Josh Allen.
- Helped lead the Bills to a 31-10 victory over the defending Super Bowl champion Los Angeles Rams in the 2022 regular season opener by catching 8 passes for 122 yards and 1 TD, which came on a 53-yard fourth-quarter connection with Allen that closed out the scoring.
- Had another huge game the following week, making 12 receptions for 148 yards and 3 touchdowns during a 41-7 thrashing of the Tennessee Titans on September 19, 2022, with the longest of his TD catches covering 46 yards.
- Helped the Bills avenge their playoff loss to Kansas City the previous year by making 10 receptions for 148 yards and 1 TD during a 24-20 win over the Chiefs on October 16, 2022.

### Notable Achievements

- Has surpassed 100 receptions and 1,000 receiving yards three times each
- Has scored at least 10 touchdowns twice
- Led NFL with 127 receptions and 1,535 receiving yards in 2020
- Has led Bills in receptions and receiving yards three times each
- Holds Bills single season records for most receptions (127) and most receiving yards (1,535)
- Ranks among Bills career leaders with 338 receptions (5th), 4,189 receiving yards (8th), and 29 touchdown receptions (tied for 6th)
- Three-time division champion (2020, 2021, and 2022)
- 2020 Week 16 AFC Offensive Player of the Week
- Three-time Pro Bowl selection (2020, 2021, and 2022)

- 2020 First-Team All-Pro selection
- 2022 Second-Team All-Pro selection
- 2020 First-Team All-AFC selection

# 38

# MARK KELSO

An unsung member of Bills teams that won five division titles and four AFC championships, Mark Kelso spent eight years in Buffalo, starting at free safety in seven of those. A classic overachiever who served as the quarterback of the Bills' defensive secondary from 1987 to 1993, Kelso led the team in interceptions three times, en route to recording the third-most picks in franchise history. Yet despite the many contributions Kelso made to the Bills on the playing field, he is largely remembered today for his invention of the "Pro Cap," a large helmet with an extra layer of padding that helped prolong his career.

Born in Pittsburgh, Pennsylvania, on July 23, 1963, Mark Alan Kelso attended North Hills High School, where his exceptional play on the gridiron earned him a scholarship to the College of William & Mary in Virginia. A star defensive back at the Division I-AA level, Kelso recorded a total of 20 interceptions during his college career and registered 141 tackles one year, with the last figure representing the third-highest single season mark in school history.

Despite his outstanding play at William & Mary, Kelso ended up slipping to the 10th round of the 1985 NFL Draft due to concerns over his somewhat limited natural athletic ability. Ultimately selected by the Philadelphia Eagles with the 261st overall pick, Kelso failed to earn a roster spot, allowing the Bills to sign him as a free agent the following year.

Arriving in Buffalo in 1986, Kelso appeared in only three games, failing to make a significant contribution to a Bills team that finished just 4-12. However, after joining the starting unit the following year, Kelso helped the Bills improve their record to 7-8 by making a team-high 6 interceptions and recovering 2 fumbles, one of which he returned 56 yards for a touchdown. Continuing to perform well the next two seasons for Bills teams that captured back-to-back division titles, Kelso recorded a total of 13 interceptions, amassed 281 interception-return yards, and scored a pair of touchdowns, with one of those coming on defense and the other on special teams.

Mark Kelso recorded the third-most interceptions in franchise history.

An extremely opportunistic player who always seemed to be in the right place at the right time, the 5'11", 181-pound Kelso used his instincts, intelligence, and knowledge of opposing offenses to compensate for his lack of elite speed. Recording at least 6 interceptions on four separate occasions, Kelso proved to be one of the NFL's better ball hawks, consistently ranking among the league leaders in picks. A sure tackler as well despite his some-what smallish frame, Kelso did an excellent job of serving as the Bills' last line of defense, often bringing down opposing ball carriers in the open field.

Eventually emerging as one of the Bills' team leaders, Kelso experienced tremendous popularity with his teammates, with Steve Tasker saying in his book, *Tales from the Buffalo Bills*, "He was as well-grounded and as big-hearted as anybody I've ever met. I never heard anybody say a bad word about him. We tried to bust his chops for being such a straight arrow, but we could never get a rise out of him."

Beloved by the hometown fans as well for his kindness and generosity, Kelso, who won the Byron "Whizzer" White NFL Man of the Year Award in 1993 for his contributions to the community, spent much of his free time at Buffalo's Roswell Park Cancer Institute, where he helped brighten the lives of children stricken with the disease. Typically remaining at the institute for hours, Kelso drew praise for his dedication to youngsters in distress from the head of the pediatric ward, Dr. Marty Brecher, who said, "His involvement is on a different level. He spends hours at a bedside. He helps walk the children to the bathroom, he talks to them, he plays with them. He cares about them."

When asked about his commitment to helping others, Kelso stated, "There is a great verse in the Bible that says, 'To whom much is given, much is expected.' I disagree with the people who say that athletes don't have the obligation to be role models, to be part of their communities. I think they do. . . . This is not a one-sided thing. It's a two-way street. Sometimes, I think I get more out of this than the children do. I get to see the fight in these kids."

During his time in Buffalo, Kelso also became known for wearing an oversized helmet with an extra layer of padding that earned him the nickname "The Great Gazoo" (after the alien from *The Flintstones* animated TV series, who wore a similarly-shaped head covering).

Kelso, who began donning the so-called Pro Cap in 1989 after he sustained two serious concussions early in his career, later explained, "I had a concussion here or there, and then I had a problem with migraines. After I'd make a hit, it would cause vision problems. It's difficult to play when you're unable to see. You lose your peripheral vision. . . . It helped me, and I certainly don't think I would have played much longer without it. It was a great protector for me. It prolonged my career. There's no question about it."

Kelso added, "I wanted to be a viable part of this community when I was done playing football. I wasn't going to continue to risk my head if I couldn't protect myself in a more effective manner. I felt like I could play with the aggression I was accustomed to without risking additional injury."

Often referred to as "the guy with the giant helmet," Kelso garnered a considerable amount of attention from television commentators, who frequently paused game action to point out and circle the helmet, further endearing him to Bills fans.

Kelso continued to start at free safety for the Bills for four more years, helping them advance to the Super Bowl each season by recording another 11 interceptions. Choosing to announce his retirement following the conclusion of the 1993 campaign, Kelso ended his career with 30 interceptions, 327 interception-return yards, 8 fumble recoveries, 3 touchdowns, and an unrecorded number of tackles.

Following his playing days, Kelso coached briefly at Buffalo State University, before receiving his teaching certification from Canisius College in Buffalo and becoming an elementary school teacher in the East Aurora, New York, school system and, later, the director of development at a Buffalo-area Catholic school. Returning to football in 2006, Kelso spent the next thirteen years serving as the color commentator for Bills radio broadcasts on both WGRF 96.9 FM and WGR 550, before leaving the broadcast booth at the end of 2018 to focus more on his role with NASCAR's JTG Daugherty Racing.

## CAREER HIGHLIGHTS

### Best Season

Kelso played his best ball for the Bills from 1987 to 1989, recording a total of 19 interceptions during that three-year stretch. The 1988 campaign stood out as perhaps Kelso's finest, since in addition to registering a career-high 7 interceptions, he led the NFL with 180 interception-return yards, returning one of his picks 78 yards for a touchdown.

### Memorable Moments/Greatest Performances

- Recorded the first interception of his career during a 31-28 loss to the Jets in the opening game of the 1987 regular season.
- Scored his first touchdown as a pro when he ran 56 yards to paydirt after recovering a fumble during a 27-21 loss to the Cleveland Browns on November 15, 1987.
- Contributed to a 27-3 victory over the Indianapolis Colts on December 13, 1987, by picking off 2 passes in one game for the first time in his career.
- Earned AFC Defensive Player of the Week honors by recording 2 interceptions, which he returned a total of 70 yards, during a 36-28 win over the Steelers on September 25, 1988.
- Lit the scoreboard for the second time in his career when he returned his interception of a Don Majkowski pass 78 yards for a TD during a 28-0 win over the Packers on October 30, 1988.

- Made a key interception during the Bills 17-10 win over the Houston Oilers in the divisional round of the 1988 playoffs.
- Turned in a tremendous all-around effort on September 24, 1989, helping the Bills record a 47-41 overtime victory over the Houston Oilers by picking off a pass, which he subsequently returned 43 yards, and returning a blocked field goal attempt by Tony Zendejas 76 yards for a touchdown.
- Recorded a career-high 3 interceptions during a 27-17 win over the Denver Broncos on December 12, 1992.

**Notable Achievements**

- Scored 3 touchdowns
- Recorded at least 6 interceptions four times
- Amassed more than 100 interception-return yards twice
- Led NFL with 180 interception-return yards in 1988
- Finished second in NFL with 6 interceptions in 1987
- Finished third in NFL with 7 interceptions in 1992
- Led Bills in interceptions three times
- Ranks among Bills career leaders with 30 interceptions (3rd) and 327 interception-return yards (11th)
- Five-time division champion (1988, 1989, 1990, 1991, and 1993)
- Four-time AFC champion (1990, 1991, 1992, and 1993)
- 1988 Week 4 AFC Defensive Player of the Week
- 1993 Byron "Whizzer" White NFL Man of the Year

# 39

# AL BEMILLER

A true iron man who never missed a game his entire career, Al Bemiller spent nine seasons in Buffalo anchoring the Bills' offensive line from his center position. One of the better offensive linemen in the ten-year history of the AFL, Bemiller helped lead the Bills to three division titles and two league championships, earning in the process one All-Star selection and a place on Pro Football Reference's All-1960s Second Team.

Born in Hanover, Pennsylvania, on April 18, 1938, Albert Delane Bemiller grew up some nineteen miles southwest of York, where he made a name for himself as a standout football player and wrestler at Hanover High School. After accepting a wrestling scholarship to Syracuse University, Bemiller soon found himself being recruited for the school's football team by legendary head coach Ben Schwartzwalder, under whom he spent three seasons starring at center, while continuing to wrestle.

Recalling how he ended up on the offensive line after never playing there before, Bemiller said, "I didn't want to be a center. When I was in high school, I was an end—a tall, skinny end. Prep school—tall, skinny end. Went to Syracuse—tall, skinny end my freshman year. In my sopho-more year, one day we were playing basketball in the gym—that's how we got in shape. Coach Dailey came in and he said, 'Okay, I've got a football here. Any of you can center this damn ball?' We all said, 'We'll try.' So, he marked it off and said, 'There's a doorknob. Whoever hits that doorknob is gonna be my center.' I hiked the ball and hit the doorknob. From that time on, I was a center."

Eventually establishing himself as one of the finest interior offensive linemen in the nation, Bemiller helped lead Syracuse to the 1959 National Championship, before earning All-East and Third-Team All-America hon-ors as a senior the following year.

Subsequently selected by the Bills in the 7th round of the 1961 AFL Draft, with the 52nd overall pick, and by the St. Louis Cardinals in the same round of that year's NFL Draft, with the 94th overall pick, Bemiller

Al Bemiller never missed a game his entire career.

chose to sign with the Bills, saying years later, "That was a tough decision. I could have made almost twice as much money [if he signed with the Cardinals]. We just thought it over, and we wanted to be closer to home, so that's why we came here."

Bemiller added, "I didn't know how good I was. I figured I had a better shot at making the Bills. Then I had a coach up at Syracuse who used to play here, and he was telling me how great the town is, how great the people were, and so on."

Joining the Bills in just their second year of existence, Bemiller made an immediate impact as a rookie, starting every game at center after beating out Dan McGrew for the starting job. Remaining a pillar of strength on the interior of the Bills' offensive line for the next eight years, Bemiller started every contest, although he spent the 1964 and 1965 campaigns playing right guard, before returning to his more natural position of center for his final four seasons.

An excellent straight-ahead blocker who did an outstanding job of creating holes up the middle for running backs Cookie Gilchrist and Wray Carlton, the 6'3", 243-pound Bemiller served as a key contributor to

Buffalo's vaunted running attack that ranked either first or second in the league three straight times from 1962 to 1964. Solid in pass-protection as well, Bemiller moved well between the tackles, where he used his strength, athleticism, and wrestling background to hold his own against opponents who sometimes outweighed him by thirty or forty pounds.

One of the Bills' leaders on offense, Bemiller assumed the critical role of giving the other linemen their blocking assignments, recalling, "The center, myself, I was always the one who called the blocking techniques we were supposed to use on the line. Thank God I had a guy like Billy Shaw. When I had a tough guy in front of me, I'd always call him over to help. It worked out very well."

More than anything, though, Bemiller became known for his tremendous durability that enabled him to start 126 straight contests from 1961 to 1969. Looking back on his amazing streak, Bemiller said, "I always ran scared. Somebody's looking for your job—I was very conscious of that all the time. When you're a marginal player like I was, you just want to keep playing. You don't want to get out of the game. You never take time off. As soon as somebody else steps in there, and especially in those days, if they did better than you, you were gone."

Bemiller's string of consecutive starts ended when he suffered a serious knee injury in the final game of the 1969 season. Although he planned to return to the Bills in 1970, head coach John Rauch decided to go in a different direction, with Bemiller recalling, "The next year, I went back, and I was fully recovered. I was in great shape, and Rauch let me go."

Bemiller continued, "I could have gone on, but I chose not to because I had my restaurant in Hamburg—Al Bemiller's Turfside. And it was going great guns. I had the restaurant for 15 years. . . . We always had live bands. Then disco came in and all these other places started to pop up, and it went down the tubes."

Aside from managing his restaurant, Bemiller operated several other businesses in the Buffalo area for over twenty-five years following his retirement. He also became a decorated wrestling coach at St. Francis High School in Athol Springs and a certified official for both high school wrestling and football.

Explaining why he chose to remain in the Buffalo area after his playing career ended, Bemiller said, "The one main thing was the great people here. I met up with some great people. Another thing, we didn't make enough money to move."

Eighty-five years old at the time of this writing, Bemiller stills lives in northwest New York.

## CAREER HIGHLIGHTS

### Best Season

Bemiller earned his lone trip to the AFL All-Star Game in 1965. But Buffalo running backs averaged just 3.3 yards per carry that year. Meanwhile, they averaged 4.1 yards per carry during the championship campaign of 1964, with the Bills also boasting the league's top offense. All things considered, Bemiller made his greatest overall impact in 1964.

### Memorable Moments/Greatest Performances

- Helped the Bills rush for a season-high 206 yards during a 22-12 victory over the Houston Oilers on October 8, 1961.
- Anchored an offensive line that enabled the Bills to rush for 303 yards and amass 439 yards of total offense during a 35-10 win over the San Diego Chargers on October 13, 1962.
- Along with his line-mates, dominated the Oakland Raiders at the point of attack on November 24, 1966, with the Bills rushing for 226 yards and amassing 465 yards of total offense during a convincing 31-10 victory.

### Notable Achievements

- Never missed a game entire career, appearing in 126 consecutive contests
- Three-time division champion (1964, 1965, and 1966)
- Two-time AFL champion (1964 and 1965)
- 1965 AFL All-Star selection
- Pro Football Reference All-1960s Second Team

# 40

## ELBERT DUBENION

The Bills' first true deep threat at wide receiver, Elbert Dubenion proved to be one of the most exciting players in the brief ten-year history of the AFL. Nicknamed "Golden Wheels" for his tremendous running speed, Dubenion helped generate fan interest in the fledgling league with his ability to score from anywhere on the field. The first player in franchise history to amass more than 1,000 receiving yards in a season, Dubenion accomplished the feat in 1964, when he helped lead the Bills to the first of their back-to-back AFL championships. A one-time AFL All-Star and two-time Second-Team All-AFL selection, Dubenion continues to rank among the Bills' all-time leaders in several offensive categories more than fifty years after he donned the team's colors for the last time.

Born in Griffin, Georgia, on February 16, 1933, Elbert D. Dubenion moved with his family at an early age to Columbus, Ohio, where he starred in football, basketball, and track at South High School. Choosing to enlist in the military following his graduation, Dubenion spent three years in the service, before enrolling at tiny Bluffton College, a university located in northwest Ohio that is affiliated with the Mennonite Church.

Continuing to excel in multiple sports at Bluffton, Dubenion once registered 23 rebounds in a basketball game and never lost a 100-yard dash to another small-college athlete in his four years on the track team. But Dubenion became better known for his exploits on the football field, where he earned All-Mid-Ohio League honors four straight times by gaining a total of 4,734 yards on the ground, averaging 9.4 yards per carry, and scoring 57 touchdowns. Yet even though Dubenion also gained First-Team Little All-America recognition his senior year by ranking third in the nation with 1,288 yards rushing, his small-college background and relatively old age (he was twenty-six years old at the time) scared off most pro teams, causing him to fall to the 14th round of the 1959 NFL Draft, where the Cleveland Browns finally selected him with the 167th overall pick.

The Bills' first true deep threat, Elbert Dubenion became the first player in franchise history to surpass 1,000 receiving yards in a season in 1964.

Failing to earn a roster spot with the Browns after spraining his knee while practicing for the college all-star game, Dubenion signed as a free agent with the Bills the following year, joining them in time for the start of the AFL's inaugural season of 1960. Beginning his pro career in ignominious fashion, Dubenion struggled terribly in his first game, recalling, "I dropped about four or five balls and fumbled a handoff from Tommy O'Connell on a reverse. [Bills head coach] Buster [Ramsey] didn't take too kindly to that. I didn't think I'd make it past that first game."

Given a second chance by Ramsey, Dubenion went on to establish himself as one of the new league's most explosive players, earning team MVP honors and gaining unofficial Second-Team All-AFL recognition from UPI as a rookie by making 42 receptions for 752 yards and 7 touchdowns, while also carrying the ball sixteen times for 94 yards and another TD. Later crediting Bills assistant coach Johnny Mazur for his early success, Dubenion stated, "Johnny Mazur was the receivers coach, and he used to keep me after practice, and it paid off. He'd throw me 200 or 300 balls after practice. I'd have my back to him, then I'd turn around and he'd throw at me. He told me, 'Either catch or work for a living.'"

Posting solid numbers in each of the next two seasons as well, Dubenion concluded the 1961 campaign with 31 receptions, 461 receiving yards, 634 yards from scrimmage, 966 all-purpose yards, and 8 touchdowns, before gathering in 33 passes, accumulating 571 receiving yards, 611 yards from scrimmage, and 842 all-purpose yards, and scoring 6 touchdowns the following year. Still, the best had yet to come.

After further developing his game by improving his route-running and learning not to depend solely on his great speed, Dubenion reached the apex of his career in 1963 and 1964, earning consecutive Second-Team All-AFL nominations by making 53 receptions for 959 yards and 4 touchdowns, accumulating 333 yards on special teams, and amassing 1,292 all-purpose yards in the first of those campaigns, before catching 42 passes for 1,139 yards and 10 touchdowns the following year.

Recalling how his former teammate gradually matured into a more complete receiver, cornerback Booker Edgerson, who joined the Bills in 1962, said, "When I first got here, he was just running basic routes. No patterns at all. But he got better with that."

Edgerson then added, "Duby was our touchdown man. They loved to throw him the bomb."

Perhaps the AFL's fastest player, the 5'11", 187-pound Dubenion created excitement in the stands any time he touched the football. Capable of beating his man deep downfield or turning short passes into long gains, Dubenion possessed tremendous open field running ability, with fellow Bills wideout Charley Ferguson stating, "I don't think Duby ever knew how fast he could really run. He was that kind of person. He ran accordingly, in order to beat somebody. Whatever it took, he could do it. . . . He had the speed. He was a sure catcher out there. He caught the big ones. He was so reliable, and no one could cover him."

Unfortunately, Dubenion sustained an injury during the early stages of the 1965 campaign that ended up robbing him of much of his blinding speed. With the Bills hosting the New York Jets in the third game of the regular season, Dubenion gathered in an 11-yard touchdown pass from Jack Kemp. However, in so doing, he seriously injured his knee, recalling, "Willie West landed on top of me. We just landed the wrong way. My body was bent back over him, and my leg was underneath."

248 THE 50 GREATEST PLAYERS IN BUFFALO BILLS HISTORY

Forced to undergo season-ending surgery, Dubenion subsequently spent the entire offseason trying to regain his earlier form by lifting weights and doing various exercises to strengthen his knee. Nevertheless, when Dubenion returned to action in 1966, it soon became apparent that he had lost a step. Although Dubenion ended up posting respectable numbers, concluding the campaign with 50 receptions for 747 yards and 2 touchdowns, he no longer possessed the ability to separate himself from his defender, making him more of a possession receiver. After catching just 25 passes and amassing only 384 receiving yards the following year, Dubenion announced his retirement four games into the 1968 season, ending his career with 294 receptions, 5,294 receiving yards, 326 rushing yards, 5,620 yards from scrimmage, 970 kickoff- and punt-return yards, 6,590 all-purpose yards, 35 touchdown receptions, 3 rushing TDs, and 39 total touchdowns.

Following his playing days, Dubenion became a scout for the Bills and, later, the Miami Dolphins and Atlanta Falcons. While in Miami, he also served as the team's assistant director of player personnel. After leaving Atlanta, Dubenion retired to Westerville, Ohio, where he remained until December 26, 2019, when he died at the age of eighty-six following a lengthy battle with Parkinson's and Alzheimer's disease.

Remembered by those who knew him for his humility and great sense of humor, Elbert Dubenion should also be remembered for the excitement he created in Buffalo and the impact he made on the AFL, which he helped become a viable entity.

## CAREER HIGHLIGHTS

### Best Season

Dubenion performed exceptionally well for the Bills in 1963, earning Second-Team All-AFL honors for the first of two straight times by ranking among the league leaders with 959 receiving yards, scoring 4 touchdowns, and establishing career-high marks with 53 receptions and 1,292 all-purpose yards. But he had his finest all-around season in 1964, earning his lone trip to the AFL All-Star Game by making 42 receptions, placing near the top of the league rankings with 1,139 receiving yards and 10 touchdown receptions, and averaging a league-best 27.1 yards per catch, which represents the highest single-season mark in pro football history for players with at least 40 receptions.

## Memorable Moments/Greatest Performances

- Scored the first two touchdowns of his career during a 27-21 loss to the Denver Broncos on September 18, 1960, collaborating with quarterback Tommy O'Connell on scoring plays that covered 53 and 40 yards.
- Helped the Bills forge a 38-38 tie with the Broncos on November 27, 1960, by catching 6 passes for 134 yards and 1 touchdown, which covered 76 yards.
- Although Dubenion made just 2 receptions for 18 yards during a 38-14 win over the Patriots on December 4, 1960, he contributed significantly to the victory by recording a 66-yard TD run.
- Displayed his explosiveness during a 41-31 win over the New York Titans on September 17, 1961, scoring a pair of touchdowns on a career-long 72-yard run and a 33-yard pass from Richie Lucas.
- Began a memorable fourth-quarter comeback against the Broncos on October 28, 1962, by gathering in a 75-yard touchdown pass from Warren Rabb that reduced Denver's lead to 8 points midway through the period. The Bills went on to score another two touchdowns, with Rabb's 3-yard TD run in the closing moments giving them a 45-38 win.
- Scored his lone touchdown on special teams when he returned a kickoff 93 yards for a TD during a 28-28 tie with the Patriots on November 3, 1962.
- Collaborated with Jack Kemp on an 89-yard touchdown reception during a 35-26 win over the Kansas City Chiefs on October 13, 1963.
- Scored the only points the Bills tallied during their 26-8 loss to the Patriots in the divisional round of the 1963 AFL playoffs when he hooked up with Daryle Lamonica on a 93-yard touchdown reception.
- Contributed to a 48-17 rout of the Houston Oilers on October 11, 1964, by making 5 receptions for 183 yards and 1 touchdown, which came on a 19-yard pass from Jack Kemp.
- Followed that up with another strong outing, catching 5 passes for 122 yards and 2 touchdowns during a 35-22 win over the Chiefs on October 18, 1964, with his TDs coming on passes of 55 and 22 yards from Kemp.
- Made five receptions for a career-high 218 yards and 2 touchdowns during a 34-24 victory over the Jets on October 24, 1964, scoring his TDs on a pair of 44-yard receptions.

**Notable Achievements**

- Surpassed 50 receptions twice
- Surpassed 1,000 receiving yards once
- Amassed more than 1,000 all-purpose yards twice
- Scored 10 touchdowns in 1964
- Returned 1 kickoff for a touchdown
- Led AFL with an average of 27.1 yards per reception in 1964
- Finished third in AFL in touchdown receptions once, touchdowns once, and yards per reception once
- Led Bills in receptions once and receiving yards five times
- Ranks among Bills career leaders with 294 receptions (11th), 5,294 receiving yards (4th), 5,620 yards from scrimmage (8th), 6,590 all-purpose yards (6th), 35 touchdown receptions (4th), and 39 touchdowns (tied for 6th)
- Three-time division champion (1964, 1965, and 1966)
- Two-time AFL champion (1964 and 1965)
- 1964 AFL All-Star selection
- Two-time Second-Team All-AFL selection (1963 and 1964)
- Inducted into Bills Wall of Fame in 1993

# 41

# STEVE CHRISTIE

icknamed "Mr. Clutch" for his ability to perform well under pressure, Steve Christie established himself as the finest kicker in Bills history during his nine seasons in Buffalo, setting franchise records for most points scored, field goals made, and extra points made. A huge contributor to Bills teams that made eight playoff appearances and won two division titles and two AFC championships, Christie scored more than 100 points eight times and successfully converted more than 80 percent of his field goal attempts five times, despite having to contend with the strong winds and frigid temperatures at Rich Stadium. Nevertheless, it took some time for Bills fans to warm up to Christie, who received a cool reception in Buffalo after he replaced the popular Scott Norwood as the team's regular placekicker.

Born in Hamilton, Ontario, on November 13, 1967, Geoffrey Stephen Christie grew up in the nearby town of Oakville, where he spent much of his youth playing soccer some eighty miles northwest of Buffalo. A standout player at Trafalgar High School, Christie earned a spot on the Canadian Junior World Cup soccer team, before turning his attention to football after accepting an athletic scholarship to The College of William & Mary in Virginia. Serving as the Tribe's placekicker and punter for the next four years, Christie set school records for most career points (279) and longest punt (69 yards), performing especially well as a senior in 1989, when he gained Division 1-AA All-America recognition as both a punter and kicker.

After being selected by the Edmonton Eskimos in the first round of the 1990 CFL Draft and being bypassed by all twenty-eight teams in that year's NFL Draft, Christie chose to sign with the Tampa Bay Buccaneers as an undrafted free agent. He then spent the next two seasons in Tampa Bay, earning First-Team All-NFC honors and a spot on the NFL All-Rookie Team in 1990, before signing with the Bills as a Plan B free agent when the Buccaneers left him unprotected following the conclusion of the ensuing campaign.

Steve Christie kicked more field goals and scored more points than anyone else in team annals.

Recalling the circumstances surrounding his decision to join the Bills, Christie said, "I called my dad, and he was in Oakville at the time. I said, 'Yeah, dad, it looks like I'm going to Buffalo. I got a call from Bill Polian [Bills GM and former Montreal Alouettes scout].' My dad said, 'You know Marv [Levy] coached in the CFL?' That's the first thing he said. 'And he went to William & Mary.' I said, 'I know. That's part of why I'm flying up right now. I'll see you tomorrow. I'm signing.' That was part of it, the fact that he did have a connection up there, and that he had success, and that he coached at William & Mary."

Expressing his glee over becoming part of a first-rate organization located so close to the Canadian border after inking his deal with the Bills, Christie stated, "I'm really flattered and really happy to be able to come home. I had my seed well-planted in Tampa, but an opportunity like this only comes up once. Money was a factor, but not the only factor; playing with some very established players was as well."

However, Bills fans failed to welcome their team's new kicker with open arms, with Christie remembering, "I was on the plane the next day. Got to Buffalo with my agent and my parents in a limo, and there were about 1,500 Scott Norwood fans protesting my arrival. I said, 'Well, I respect that.' And I realized quickly how loyal the fans were in Buffalo."

After beating out Norwood for the starting job during training camp, Christie performed well his first year in Buffalo, helping the Bills advance to the playoffs for the fifth straight time by successfully converting 24 of his 30 field goal attempts and all but one of his 44 extra point attempts, en route to scoring a total of 115 points that placed him fifth in the league rankings.

Remaining one of the NFL's most reliable kickers the next several years, Christie connected on more than 80 percent of his field goal attempts in four of the next six seasons, with his 140 points scored in 1998 representing the second-highest total in the league.

Having spent his youth playing north of the border, the 6', 195-pound Christie quickly proved himself capable of handling the freezing temperatures and unpredictable winds ever-present at Rich Stadium. Blessed with a strong leg, Christie had the ability to drive the ball through the uprights from well over 50 yards out, with his 59-yard field goal in 1993 establishing a franchise record that still stands. More importantly, Christie demonstrated during his time in Buffalo that he had the ability to come through in the clutch, kicking 13 game-winning field goals in the final minute of regulation or in overtime.

In discussing the faith that the team placed in Christie in pressure situations, longtime Bills special teams coach Bruce DeHaven stated, "In terms of a pressure kicker, he's got to be as good as there ever has been. The more the kick means, the better he is. He makes us all look good."

Meanwhile, Kent Hull marveled at his teammate's dependability, saying, "The guy is so reliable it's scary. I've never been around a field-goal kicker in my career where, once you get him to a certain point, it's automatic. That's the feeling we all have on this team."

While Christie's clutch kicking helped make him one of the Bills' more popular players, he further endeared himself to the hometown fans by contributing to the community as a member of the board of directors of the Buffalo and Erie County Historical Society and helping to raise thousands of dollars for Camp Good Days and Special Times.

Somewhat less proficient in 1999 and 2000, Christie converted just under 75 percent of his field goal attempts both years, although he still managed to score more than 100 points each season. Placed on the "reserved-injured" list after pulling his groin just prior to the 2001 regular season opener, Christie rejected an injury settlement with the Bills, leading to his eventual release. Christie subsequently signed with the San Diego Chargers, with whom he spent the next three seasons, before ending his NFL career with the New York Giants in 2004. Over fifteen seasons, Christie kicked 336 field goals, scored 1,476 points, and converted 78 percent of his field goal attempts, successfully converting 234 field goals and scoring 1,011 points during his time in Buffalo.

After spending the 2007 campaign kicking for Toronto in the CFL, Christie officially retired from football, doing so as a member of the Bills, with whom he signed a one-day contract in March 2008. Upon inking his deal with the Bills, Christie stated, "Regardless of where I ended up playing following my career in Buffalo, I knew that I wanted to retire a Bill. My best years and really the bulk of my career was in Buffalo. So, to retire here was not only closure, for me it was a necessity."

Following his playing days, Christie settled with his family in Bradenton, Florida, where he and his wife became real estate agents, with the Bills' all-time leading scorer saying during a 2019 interview: "My wife Kelly and I do real estate down here, and most of our clients are from Western New York—the Buffalo area, some from Chicago, but a lot of Northeasterners come down and we handle a lot of their real estate stuff."

Christie has also served as an analyst for The Score Television Network, done radio color commentary for University of Buffalo football, and served as president of Relative Goal Sports and Entertainment Management LLC, with whom he has represented numerous musical acts in both the United States and Scotland. In his spare time, Christie enjoys painting, saying, "I majored in fine arts at William & Mary—mostly oil painting. Now I do acrylic—I do a lot of painting still. It's very therapeutic."

When asked what he misses most about playing in the NFL, Christie, who has had two surgeries at the Cleveland Clinic in Cleveland, Ohio, after being diagnosed with colorectal cancer in 2014, said, "I think I miss Sunday afternoon at 1 o'clock. I miss coming out of the locker room and regardless of the weather, knowing that the Bills fans would be there. The stadium would be packed, and you know, I think that goes back to another question, 'What do you remember most about playing for the Bills,' and that's the fans. No matter what our record was, no matter how cold it was . . . they still packed the house. And to come out of the tunnel in Buffalo was incredible. That was something you never forget. That's a feeling that you don't get everywhere."

# BILLS CAREER HIGHLIGHTS

## Best Season

Christie scored a career-high 140 points in 1998, finishing second in the NFL in that category in the process. But he missed 8 of his 41 field-goal attempts, giving him a rather mediocre field-goal percentage of 80.5 that did not even rank among the ten best in the league. Meanwhile, even though Christie finished just eighth in the NFL with 110 points scored in 1994, he proved to be far more consistent, compiling a career-high 85.7 field goal percentage by successfully converting 24 of his 28 attempts, including 17 straight at one point.

## Memorable Moments/Greatest Performances

- Proved to be the difference in a 26-20 win over the Miami Dolphins on November 16, 1992, kicking 4 field goals, the longest of which came from 54 yards out.
- Put the finishing touches on the Bills' miraculous comeback against Houston in the 1992 AFC Wild Card Game that saw them overcome a 35-3 third-quarter deficit by kicking a 32-yard field goal in overtime that gave them a 41-38 victory.
- Subsequently had a huge hand in the Bills' 29-10 win over Miami in the 1992 AFC Championship Game, successfully converting 5 of his 6 field goal attempts, the longest of which traveled 38 yards.
- Although the Bills lost to the Dolphins by a score of 22-13 on September 26, 1993, Christie kicked a career-long and franchise-record 59-yard field goal during the contest.
- Helped the Bills record a 19-10 win over the Jets on October 24, 1993, by successfully converting all 4 of his field-goal attempts, the longest of which split the uprights from 37 yards out.
- After sending the game into overtime by kicking a 27-yard field goal late in the final period, Christie gave the Bills a 13-10 win over the Patriots on November 7, 1993, by driving the ball through the uprights from 30 yards out during the OT session.
- Earned AFC Special Teams Player of the Week honors by successfully converting all 3 of his field-goal attempts during a 16-14 win over the Jets on December 26, 1993, with his 40-yard kick in the closing moments clinching the division title for the Bills.

- Although the Bills ended up losing Super Bowl XXVIII to Dallas by a score of 30-13, Christie briefly tied the game at 3-3 by kicking a 54-yard field goal in the first quarter that remains the longest in Super Bowl history.
- Earned AFC Special Teams Player of the Week honors by accounting for all 15 points the Bills scored during a 15-7 win over the Houston Oilers on September 18, 1994, with 2 of his 5 field goals coming from 48 yards out.
- Again kicked 5 field goals during a 29-10 win over the Jets on October 8, 1995, splitting the uprights once from 51 yards out.
- Came up big for the Bills twice during the latter stages of a 23-20 overtime win over the Giants in the 1996 regular season opener, sending the game into OT by kicking a 39-yard field goal with just thirty-four seconds left in regulation, and then driving the ball through the uprights from 34 yards out as time expired in overtime.
- Provided further heroics on October 6, 1996, giving the Bills a 16-13 overtime victory over the Colts by kicking a 39-yard field goal, after earlier sending the game into OT by splitting the uprights from 37 yards out with just fifteen seconds left in regulation.
- Proved to be the difference in a 25-22 win over the Jets on October 20, 1996, earning AFC Special Teams Player of the Week honors by kicking 6 field goals, 3 of which traveled more than 45 yards, with his 47-yarder with just ten seconds left in the final period providing the margin of victory.
- Although a 33-yard field goal by Jason Elam gave Denver a 23-20 overtime win over the Bills on October 26, 1997, Christie earlier came up big in the clutch for Buffalo, sending the game into OT by driving the ball through the uprights from 55 yards out with just under a minute remaining in regulation.
- Earned AFC Special Teams Player of the Week honors by successfully converting all 4 of his field-goal attempts during a 33-20 win over Cincinnati on December 6, 1998, with the longest of his kicks coming from 52 yards out.
- Displayed his ability to excel under pressure on four separate occasions in 2000. After giving the Bills a 16-13 win over the Tennessee Titans in the regular season opener by kicking a 33-yard field goal with just thirty-one seconds left in the final period, Christie enabled them to come away with a 27-24 victory over the San Diego Chargers on October 15 by driving the ball through the uprights from 46 yards out midway through the overtime session.

Two weeks later, Christie gave the Bills a 23-20 win over the Jets by kicking a 34-yard field goal as time expired in regulation. Christie then experienced perhaps his finest moment against the Patriots on November 5, 2000, when, after sending the game into overtime by kicking a 48-yard field goal with just four seconds remaining in the final period, he gave the Bills a 16-13 victory over their Eastern Division rivals by splitting the uprights from 32 yards out 4:32 into the OT session.

## Notable Achievements

- Never missed a game in nine seasons, appearing in 144 consecutive contests
- Scored more than 100 points eight times, topping 120 points twice
- Converted more than 80 percent of field goal attempts five times
- Finished second in NFL in points scored once and field goals made once
- Finished third in NFL in field goals made once
- Holds Bills career records for most points scored (1,011), field goals made (234), and extra points made (309)
- Two-time division champion (1993 and 1995)
- Two-time AFC champion (1992 and 1993)
- Seven-time AFC Special Teams Player of the Week
- Two-time AFC Special Teams Player of the Month

# 42

## WRAY CARLTON

An outstanding all-around running back who excelled as a runner, blocker, and receiver out of the backfield, Wray Carlton spent his entire eight-year career in Buffalo, seeing a significant amount of action at both fullback and halfback. Twice the Bills' leading rusher, Carlton gained more than 500 yards on the ground four times and amassed more than 1,000 yards from scrimmage once, earning in the process AFL All-Star and All-AFL honors twice each. A member of teams that won three division titles and two league championships, Carlton later received the additional honor of being inducted into the Bills Wall of Fame.

Born in Wallace, North Carolina, on June 18, 1937, Linwood Wray Carlton developed a love for sports at an early age, spending his formative years playing ball in his yard with older brothers Harry and Ralph, while also deriving great pleasure from chatting with Thell Overman, the local high school football coach who lived just a few houses away. Recalling his conversations with Overman, Carlton said, "Coach Overman was a wonderful man, a very moral man. He believed in sports as a way of developing character. I could not have had a better mentor than him."

Eventually emerging as a standout athlete at Wallace-Rose Hill High School, Carlton starred in multiple sports, once scoring 48 points in a prep basketball game, and attracting the attention of pro baseball scouts with his exceptional play on the diamond. However, Carlton experienced his greatest success on the gridiron, where, under the tutelage of Overman, he earned All-State honors at halfback, later saying, "I learned early that football was my best shot to move on."

After also fielding offers from Wake Forest and North Carolina, Carlton accepted a scholarship to Duke University, where he earned First-Team All-Atlantic Conference and honorable mention All-America honors his final two seasons. Carlton, who ended his three-year college career with 1,774 yards rushing, 2,798 all-purpose yards, 17 touchdowns, 148 points, and 5 interceptions, later received praise for his exceptional all-around play

Wray Carlton excelled at both fullback and halfback during his time in Buffalo.

from longtime college coach Jerry McGee, who said of his former Blue Devils teammate, "Unbelievable athletic ability. He was a great one, and such a good guy, easy to get along with."

Carlton was selected by the Philadelphia Eagles in the 3rd round of the 1959 NFL Draft, with the 26th overall pick. Instead, he chose to head north and play for the Toronto Argonauts of the Canadian Football League after failing to come to terms on a contract with the Eagles. However, after rejecting a trade to Vancouver just four games into the 1959 campaign, Carlton decided to return home and work at a bank until Lou Saban, then head coach of the Boston Patriots, convinced him to play for him in the newly formed American Football League. Signed by the Patriots early in 1960, Carlton appeared with them briefly during the preseason, before being dealt to the Bills for defensive tackle Al Crow prior to the start of the regular season.

Making an extremely favorable impression on the Bills coaching staff upon his arrival in Buffalo, Carlton drew special praise from head coach Buster Ramsey, who told the *Buffalo Courier Express*, "He has speed, power, is a great blocker, and can catch the ball."

Living up to the hype, Carlton proved to be the Bills' top offensive performer in their inaugural season, gaining Second-Team All-AFL recognition by rushing for 533 yards, gaining another 477 yards on 29 pass receptions, and scoring 11 touchdowns as the team's starting fullback. Splitting time with Art Baker in 1961, Carlton posted somewhat less impressive numbers, concluding the campaign with 311 yards rushing, 17 receptions for 193 yards, and just 4 touchdowns. Joined in the Buffalo backfield by Cookie Gilchrist the following year, Carlton moved to halfback, where, despite carrying the ball only 94 times, he rushed for 530 yards, giving him a league-leading average of 5.6 yards per carry. Plagued by injuries in each of the next two seasons, Carlton assumed a far less prominent role, appearing in a total of just eight games while serving as Gilchrist's backup.

Growing increasingly unhappy over his lack of playing time and inability to remain healthy, Carlton seriously considered retiring at the end of 1963, recalling, "I was really discouraged, and I considered retirement. I wrote a letter to the Bills, and to [general manager] Dick Gallagher in particular, and I said, 'I'm not really healing up that well. I don't think I can play anymore. I really don't want to play.' So, he announced my retirement, and I was all done. But then I got a call from Jack Kemp, and he said, 'What are you doing? You can't quit now. You're only 25 years old!' I said, 'Well, I'm not sure that I want to play anymore.' He said, 'You've got to come back. We're on the verge here of something really good. With you back, I think we can do something, and maybe even win the championship.' So, I was thinking about it, and Ralph [Wilson] called, and so I decided to come back."

Carlton's 1964 campaign got off to an inauspicious start when he sat out the first several games after breaking three ribs during the preseason. However, he ended up making significant contributions down the stretch, helping the Bills win their first AFL championship after being approached by head coach Lou Saban during the latter stages of the campaign, with Carlton remembering, "We started to stall out a little bit toward the end there, and Saban called me into his office and said, 'Are you ready? I think we need you in there. We need your blocking and your power running because of the weather. It's getting cold. I'm going to activate you.' So, he activated me for the last three games, and we went on to beat San Diego [in the AFL Championship Game]."

With the Bills trading Cookie Gilchrist during the subsequent offseason after he experienced differences with Saban, Carlton stepped to the forefront once again, gaining AFL-All-Star recognition by rushing for 592 yards, amassing 788 yards from scrimmage, and scoring 7 touchdowns for the eventual AFL champions. Carlton followed that up with another outstanding season, earning AFL All-Star and Second-Team All-AFL honors in 1966 by gaining 696 yards on the ground, accumulating 976 yards from scrimmage, and scoring 6 touchdowns.

Although Carlton lacked Gilchrist's explosiveness, he ran the ball extremely well between the tackles and proved to be nearly the equal of his running mate in terms of his blocking ability and pass-receiving skills. Standing 6'2" and weighing 225 pounds, Carlton possessed good size and strength and excelled in short-yardage situations, as former teammate Charley Ferguson noted, "Wray didn't have the best speed, but he was a very reliable halfback. He was a very good short yardage back. He could get those short yards for you and was very dependable."

Billy Shaw expressed similar sentiments when he stated, "He was dependable, durable, a great teammate, a very special guy. He's in my Hall of Fame."

Carlton remained with the Bills for one more year, rushing for 467 yards, amassing 564 yards from scrimmage, and scoring 3 touchdowns in 1967, before announcing his retirement when the team cut him during the following preseason. Leaving Buffalo with career totals of 3,368 rushing yards, 110 receptions, 1,329 receiving yards, 4,697 yards from scrimmage, 29 rushing touchdowns, and 5 TD catches, Carlton retired as the franchise's all-time leading rusher.

Following his playing days, Carlton remained in the Buffalo area, where he entered the trucking business and helped raise three children with his wife, Susan. Eighty-six years old at the time of this writing, Carlton still lives in Orchard Park, New York.

## CAREER HIGHLIGHTS

### Best Season

Although Carlton rushed for a career-high 696 yards, amassed 976 yards from scrimmage, and scored 6 touchdowns in 1966, he had his finest all-around season as a rookie in 1960, earning the first of his two Second-Team All-AFL nominations by gaining 533 yards on the ground and ranking among the league leaders with 1,010 yards from scrimmage and 11 TDs.

### Memorable Moments/Greatest Performances

- Made history on September 18, 1960, when, during the second quarter of a 27-21 loss to Denver in the Bills' home opener, he scored the first touchdown in franchise history on a 1-yard run. Commenting on his TD years later, Carlton said, "I was listening to the radio a couple years ago, to a Buffalo station, and a trivia question popped up. The guy said, 'Who scored the Bills' first touchdown?' Everybody was saying, 'I don't know. I don't know.' And I'm thinking, 'I don't know who it was.' Then some guy called in and said, 'Wray Carlton.' I said, 'Whoa! That's amazing! I didn't even know that.' I never really thought about it. It never occurred to me that I was the one that scored the first touchdown."
- Starred in defeat on October 16, 1960, gaining 98 yards on just 9 carries and scoring a touchdown during a 17-13 loss to the New York Titans, with his TD coming on a 54-yard run.
- Followed that up with another strong outing, making 5 receptions for 110 yards and 3 TDs during a 38-9 win over the Raiders on October 23, 1960, with Bills QB Johnny Green stating in the book, *Legends of the Buffalo Bills*, "Running back Wray Carlton is the guy who made me look good that day. He scored three touchdown passes from me on a day that was very rainy and muddy. And, on most of my passes to him, Wray was the secondary target. He would just catch the ball and run with it after he caught it. Wray did most of the work."
- Again displayed his pass-receiving skills one week later, leading the Bills to a 25-24 victory over the Houston Oilers on October 30, 1960, by making 6 receptions for 177 yards and 1 touchdown, which came on a career-long 70-yard catch-and-run on a pass thrown by Green.
- Continued to be a thorn in the side of the Oilers on October 8, 1961, carrying the ball 10 times for 87 yards and 1 touchdown during a 22-12 Bills win, with his 27-yard TD run in the fourth quarter sealing the victory.
- Contributed to the Bills 20-7 win over San Diego in the 1964 AFL Championship Game by rushing for 70 yards and the go-ahead touchdown.
- Topped 100 yards rushing for the only time in his career when he carried the ball 11 times for 148 yards and 1 touchdown during a 29-28

victory over the Oilers on December 5, 1965, scoring his TD on a career-long 80-yard run.

- Had a big game against the Raiders on November 24, 1966, rushing for 97 yards and 2 touchdowns during a 31-10 victory.
- Contributed to a 35-13 win over the Dolphins on November 5, 1967, by carrying the ball 15 times for 97 yards and 2 touchdowns.

### Notable Achievements

- Amassed more than 1,000 yards from scrimmage once
- Scored 11 touchdowns in 1960
- Averaged more than 5 yards per carry once
- Led AFL in rushing touchdowns and rushing average once each
- Led Bills in rushing yards twice
- Ranks among Bills career leaders with 3,368 rushing yards (7th), 29 rushing touchdowns (6th), and 34 touchdowns (tied for 11th)
- Three-time division champion (1964, 1965, and 1966)
- Two-time AFL champion (1964 and 1965)
- Two-time AFL All-Star selection (1965 and 1966)
- Two-time Second-Team All-AFL selection (1960 and 1966)
- Inducted into Bills Wall of Fame in 1993

# 43

## TREMAINE EDMUNDS

A somewhat polarizing figure among Bills fans due to his inability to fully reach his enormous potential during his time in Buffalo, Tremaine Edmunds nonetheless established himself as one of the NFL's better inside linebackers and a true team leader his five seasons in Western New York. The centerpiece of an outstanding Bills defense that consistently ranked among the league's best, Edmunds recorded more than 100 tackles five straight times, leading the team in stops on four separate occasions. A two-time Pro Bowler who ranks among the franchise's all-time leaders in tackles, Edmunds made huge contributions to Bills teams that won three division titles.

Born in Danville, Virginia, on May 2, 1998, Tremaine Edmunds grew up in a football family, with his father, Ferrell Edmunds, earning back-to-back Pro Bowl selections with the Miami Dolphins in 1989 and 1990, and his older brothers, Trey and Terrell, playing in the NFL at the same time. Emerging as a standout himself on the gridiron at Dan River High School in nearby Ringgold, Edmunds spent three years playing tight end on offense and linebacker and end on defense, performing especially well as a junior, when he earned consideration for Virginia's Defensive Player of the Year by recording 123 tackles, 4 sacks, 2 interceptions, and 2 forced fumbles. Although Edmunds subsequently missed most of his senior year due to injury, he gained All-State recognition at both tight end and linebacker, setting off a recruiting frenzy that included offers from Virginia Tech, Cincinnati, East Carolina, Kentucky, Maryland, and North Carolina, among others.

Ultimately choosing to follow in his brothers' footsteps and enroll at Virginia Tech, Edmunds spent two seasons starting at outside linebacker for head coaches Frank Beamer and Justin Fuente, being named a finalist for the Butkus Award as the nation's best linebacker his junior year after registering 108 tackles and 5.5 sacks. Feeling that he had nothing left to prove, Edmunds elected to forgo his final year of college eligibility and enter the

Tremaine Edmunds led the Bills in tackles in four of his five seasons in Buffalo. Courtesy of Keith Allison and All-Pro Reels Photography.

2018 NFL Draft, where, after trading up six spots, the Bills selected him in the 1st round, with the 16th overall pick.

Chosen by the Bills just days before he celebrated his twentieth birthday, Edmunds arrived in Buffalo as the second youngest player ever drafted into the NFL. Still extremely rough around the edges, Edmunds faced the difficult task of transitioning from outside linebacker to inside backer, stating at one point during his rookie year, "It's a big change. Anybody who has made that change can tell you that. I've just been all ears trying to get advice from everybody and hearing what the coaches have to say. I'm still trying to take steps forward now. I feel the sky is the limit to where I can get to. Personally, I feel I'm nowhere close to being as good as I can be. I just have to keep working and keep learning the game more and keep developing."

Despite his youth and relative lack of experience, Edmunds ended up recording a team-high 121 tackles, while also registering 2 sacks, 2 forced fumbles, and a pair of interceptions. Performing better and better as the season progressed, Edmunds earned NFL Defensive Rookie of the Month honors for December. Nevertheless, Edmunds realized that he still had a lot to learn, admitting, "I've definitely had challenges along the way. I'm a rookie in this league, I'm a young guy. It's definitely going to bring different things each week. I've been trying to just get better each week, just focus on things that I can. I know it hasn't been perfect. My whole goal for myself is just improve each week."

After hearing his young teammate's comments, veteran linebacker Lorenzo Alexander stated, "That's what you want. That's the sign of a leader. He wants to play so well that he puts guys on his back and leads us to victory. Being a young guy and a high draft pick and the mike linebacker, there's a lot that's associated with that position and that role."

Alexander continued, "The good thing is he's so long and tall that he can hold additional weight and not lose any speed. He's going to be a freak. He'll probably become that new standard that everyone is trying to look for, that big, fast, athletic guy who can run and cover and hit in the middle of the field. He gets to so many balls, disrupts so many things that he doesn't always get credit for, but quarterbacks have a hard time hitting targets in the middle of the field because he's there. I don't know what he's going to look like in two or three years, but he's going to be in that All-Pro caliber conversation."

Extremely impressed with Edmunds's play his first year in the league, Bills GM Brandon Beane said, "He's come a long way, and I think everybody forgets, especially if you're around him all the time, that he's 20. He's still growing into his body. Mentally, this was a big step. A lot was asked of him that was not asked at Virginia Tech. For all that was thrown at him, I thought he really progressed."

Bills defensive tackle Star Lotulelei agreed with Beane's assessment, saying of the 6'5", 250-pound rookie linebacker, "He was a lot more confident with his calls in the second half of the season. The defense was slowing down for him. . . . There's no real limit on what he can do. He's a big, athletic guy who, once things really start slowing down for him and he gets a little more experience, I know he's going to be real scary."

Fully embracing the responsibility of aligning his teammates and calling the team's defensive signals even at such a young age, Edmunds stated, "A lot of people look at it as me being young, but I've been comfortable since day one being the voice of the defense. I know the type of person I am. There are different ways that people can lead. I think I'm a natural-born leader. Sometimes it's going to be vocal and sometimes it's by example, but in the end, I'm trying to lead and bring guys along with me."

Praising Edmunds for his leadership ability and strong work ethic, Bills defensive coordinator Leslie Frazier said, "His preparation is off the charts when he's away from the building, because he'll come back with great questions about things he's seen, and then you go like man this guy's been studying. That's a sign of a future leader on your team."

Kyle Williams, then in his final season with the Bills, added, "He's a guy who displays the right habits. He works hard. He plays hard. He does the right things. He wants to be better at everything."

Named a team captain prior to the start of the 2019 campaign, Edmunds had another strong season, earning Pro Bowl honors by recording 115 tackles, 1.5 sacks, and 1 interception. Despite spending most of the following year playing with a shoulder injury he sustained during a victory over the Jets in the regular-season opener, Edmunds gained Pro Bowl recognition again by registering 119 tackles and 2 sacks for a Bills team that won their first division title in twenty-five years.

Yet even though Edmunds made significant contributions to the success the Bills experienced, his failure to reach truly elite status drew criticism from some of the team's fanbase, which expected his rare combination of size and speed to make him a perennial All-Pro. Criticized in particular for his occasional struggles in pass coverage, Edmunds perhaps failed to live up to the huge expectations fans of the team set for him his first few years in the league. Nevertheless, he established himself as arguably the best player on one of the NFL's best defenses.

Continuing to perform well in 2021, Edmunds helped the Bills capture their second straight AFC East title by making a team-high 108 tackles. He followed that up with another strong season, making 102 stops for a Bills team that won their third consecutive division title, before signing a four-year, $72 million contract with the Chicago Bears when he became a free agent at season's end. Edmunds leaves Buffalo with career totals of 565 tackles, 6.5 sacks, 5 interceptions, and 2 forced fumbles.

## BILLS CAREER HIGHLIGHTS

### Best Season

Although Edmunds recorded more tackles in both 2018 and 2020, he had his finest all-around season in 2019, when he earned his first Pro Bowl nomination by registering 115 tackles, including a career-high 10 tackles for loss, 1.5 sacks, 1 interception, and his lone safety, while also successfully defending nine passes.

### Memorable Moments/Greatest Performances

• Turned in an outstanding all-around performance in the 2018 regular-season finale, recording an interception, a sack, and 11 solo tackles during a 42-17 rout of the Miami Dolphins.
• Scored the only points of his career when he sacked Baker Mayfield in the end zone for a safety during a 19-16 loss to the Cleveland Browns on November 10, 2019.
• Although the Bills lost to the Houston Texans in overtime by a score of 22-19 in the wild card round of the 2019 AFC playoffs, Edmunds performed extremely well in his first postseason appearance, recording a sack and a game-high 12 tackles.
• Recorded a season-high 13 tackles during a 30-23 win over the Las Vegas Raiders on October 4, 2020.
• Earned AFC Defensive Player of the Week honors by intercepting a pass and recording 6 tackles during a 40-0 manhandling of the Houston Texans on October 3, 2021.
• Helped lead the Bills to a 27-17 win over the Packers on October 30, 2022, by making a career-high 16 tackles, including 13 of the solo variety.

### Notable Achievements

• Recorded more than 100 tackles five times
• Led Bills in tackles four times
• Ranks ninth in Bills history with 565 tackles
• Three-time division champion (2020, 2021, and 2022)
• 2021 Week 4 AFC Defensive Player of the Week
• Two-time Pro Bowl selection (2019 and 2020)

# 44

## LEE EVANS

ampered by the lack of a quality quarterback and a true No. 2 receiver most of his time in Buffalo, Lee Evans never quite attained the level of excellence the Bills expected from him when they made him their first selection in the 2004 NFL Draft. Nevertheless, the speedy Evans established himself as one of the finest wideouts in team annals during his seven-year stint in Orchard Park, recording the fourth-most receptions, amassing the third-most receiving yards, and making the third-most TD catches in franchise history, despite playing for teams that posted just one winning record.

Born in Sandusky, Ohio, on March 11, 1981, Lee Evans III grew up some seventy miles east, in the Cleveland suburb of Bedford, where he spent his youth rooting for the Browns. A star in multiple sports at Bedford High School, Evans excelled as a receiver in football and a hurdler in track, posting personal best times of 13.59 seconds in the 110-meter hurdles and 37.32 seconds in the 300-meter hurdles.

Offered an athletic scholarship to the University of Wisconsin, Evans spent three seasons starting at wide receiver for the Badgers, making 175 receptions, amassing 3,468 receiving yards, and scoring 27 touchdowns, despite missing a fourth year after tearing his left ACL during a spring intrasquad game. A two-time First-Team All-Big Ten selection, Evans earned the honor for the first time as a sophomore in 2001, when he made 75 receptions for 1,545 yards and 9 touchdowns. After sitting out the ensuing campaign following his injury, Evans gained All-Big Ten recognition again in 2003 by making 64 receptions, amassing 1,213 receiving yards, and scoring 13 touchdowns.

Later crediting Badgers head football coach Barry Alvarez for instilling in him a strong competitive fire, Evans said, "He taught me about competing, being aggressive going for the ball, and not being afraid to make mistakes; things that I still remember to this day. I don't know where I would be without him."

Lee Evans ranks among the Bills' all-time leaders in receptions, receiving yards, and touchdown catches.
Courtesy of Guy Harbert.

Choosing to forgo his final year of college eligibility, Evans entered the 2004 NFL Draft, where the Bills selected him with the 13th overall pick. Commenting on his team's new wideout shortly thereafter, Bills head coach Mike Mularkey told *The Buffalo News*, "Rarely do you find guys with this kind of speed who have hands as good as his are."

After spending the first few weeks of his rookie campaign assuming a part-time role, Evans started opposite veteran receiver Eric Moulds the rest of the year, finishing his first NFL season with 48 receptions, 843 receiving yards, 928 yards from scrimmage, and 9 TD catches. Particularly effective down the stretch, Evans caught 27 passes for 406 yards and 7 touchdowns in the season's final five games, leading the Bills to believe they had found the deep threat they had been seeking. However, with Buffalo releasing starting quarterback Drew Bledsoe at the end of the year, Evans failed to take a step forward in 2005, once again making 48 receptions, while amassing fewer receiving yards (743) and scoring fewer touchdowns (7).

Stepping into the role of No. 1 wide receiver after the Bills traded Moulds to the Houston Texans the following off-season, Evans posted the best numbers of his career, concluding the 2006 campaign with 82 receptions, 1,292 receiving yards, and 8 TD catches. But, with Evans consistently drawing double coverage in subsequent seasons, he never again reached such heights, although he still managed to surpass 50 receptions two more times and amass 1,017 receiving yards in 2008.

Certainly, the lack of another downfield threat in Buffalo's offense contributed greatly to Evans's inability to reach his full potential. From the time Eric Moulds left at the end of 2005 until Terrell Owens joined him on the starting unit in 2009, Evans served as the only legitimate threat in the Bills' passing game, allowing opposing teams to focus almost exclusively on stopping him. Evans also suffered from a lack of consistent quarterback play, with Kelly Holcomb, J. P. Losman, Trent Edwards, and Ryan Fitzpatrick all taking turns directing the Bills offense following the departure of Drew Bledsoe.

Nevertheless, Evans posted solid numbers year after year, earning the respect of his teammates with his talent and strong work ethic. Blessed with excellent speed, soft hands, and superb route-running ability, the 5'10", 210-pound Evans, who seemed to glide downfield, drew praise from teammate Nate Clements, who said, "He is definitely a complete receiver. He's capable of going deep, stretching the defense. He has good hands."

One of the team's most popular players, Evans also became a favorite of the local media, which found his modesty and unassuming nature refreshing. Quiet and reserved, Evans preferred not to draw attention to himself, merely nodding his head and flipping the ball to an official after scoring a touchdown.

In discussing his rather subdued celebration, Evans said, "I was told when I was young to act like you've been there before. I take a lot of pride in getting there. . . . It's not that I don't celebrate. Sometimes I get excited. But I'm not about to do a dance or anything like that."

Meanwhile, Evans addressed his calm demeanor thusly: "I'm just not as wild and outspoken as some other guys. It's about the way you play, the way you interact with your team, and the way you perform on Sunday."

Expressing the belief that Evans's failure to display his inner emotions prevented him from garnering as much attention as he deserved, Bills teammate Donte Whitner stated, "He doesn't have to change his personality or anything, but just show that he's here. If he does a little bit of that, it'll bring a little more attention to him, and maybe he'll get one of those Pro Bowl nods that he deserves."

After making 63 receptions for 1,017 yards and 3 touchdowns in 2008, Evans underwent minor shoulder surgery the following off-season. Although fully recovered by the start of the ensuing campaign, Evans found himself taking a backseat to Terrell Owens in the Buffalo offense, limiting him to just 44 catches and 612 receiving yards. Even less productive in 2010, Evans made only 37 receptions for 578 yards and 4 touchdowns, prompting the Bills to trade him to the Baltimore Ravens for a 4th round pick in the 2012 NFL Draft just prior to the start of the 2011 regular season.

Praising his latest acquisition upon completion of the deal, Ravens GM Ozzie Newsome said, "He's a quality veteran receiver who stretches the field and gives us a significant downfield presence. He's the type of person you want on your team. He brings leadership and maturity to the locker room."

Evans ended up spending just one injury-marred season in Baltimore, making only 4 receptions for 74 yards and no touchdowns in nine games with the Ravens, before signing a one-year deal with the Jacksonville Jaguars in the spring of 2012. Released by the Jaguars prior to the start of the regular season, Evans announced his retirement, ending his career with 381 receptions, 6,008 receiving yards, 6,153 yards from scrimmage, and 43 touchdowns.

Settling with his wife and two sons in Northern Virginia following his retirement from football, Evans became a real estate investor and junior high school football, basketball, and baseball coach. He also organizes youth football camps and is involved in the wine business.

# BILLS CAREER HIGHLIGHTS

## Best Season

Evans has his finest season for the Bills in 2006, when, in addition to scoring 8 touchdowns, he established career-high marks with 82 receptions and 1,292 receiving yards, with the last figure placing him sixth in the league rankings.

## Memorable Moments/Greatest Performances

- Scored the first touchdown of his career when he gathered in a 46-yard pass from Drew Bledsoe during a 16-14 loss to the Jets on October 10, 2004.
- Topped 100 receiving yards for the first time as a pro on December 5, 2004, when he made 4 receptions for 110 yards and 2 TDs during a 42-32 win over Miami, with his longest scoring play covering 69 yards.
- Provided much of the offensive firepower when the Bills recorded a 14-3 victory over Kansas City on November 13, 2005, scoring both their touchdowns on hookups of 33 and 29 yards with J. P. Losman.
- Starred in defeat on December 4, 2005, making 5 receptions for 117 yards and 3 touchdowns during a 24-23 loss to the Dolphins, with his TDs coming on passes from Losman that covered 4, 46, and 56 yards.
- Turned in the finest performance of his career on November 19, 2006, leading the Bills to a 24-21 win over the Houston Texans by making 11 receptions for a franchise-record 265 yards and 2 touchdowns, both of which covered 83 yards.
- Displayed his big-play ability again on October 28, 2007, when he punctuated a five-catch, 138-yard performance with an 85-yard fourth-quarter touchdown reception that sealed a 13-3 victory over the Jets.
- Followed that up by making 9 receptions for 165 yards and 1 touchdown during a 33-21 win over the Cincinnati Bengals on November 4, 2007.
- Although the Bills lost to the Baltimore Ravens in overtime by a score of 37-34 on October 24, 2010, Evans had a big game, making 6 receptions for 105 yards and 3 touchdowns, which came on passes from Ryan Fitzpatrick that covered 33, 20, and 17 yards.

**Notable Achievements**

- Surpassed 80 receptions once (82 in 2006)
- Surpassed 1,000 receiving yards twice
- Finished sixth in the NFL with 1,292 receiving yards in 2006
- Led Bills in receptions and receiving yards three times each
- Holds Bills single-game record for most receiving yards (265 vs. Houston on November 19, 2006)
- Ranks among Bills career leaders with 377 receptions (4th), 5,934 receiving yards (3rd), 6,079 yards from scrimmage (7th), 6,079 all-purpose yards (9th), 43 touchdown receptions (3rd), and 43 touchdowns (5th)

# 45

# BRIAN MOORMAN

One of the NFL's premier punters for more than a decade, Brian Moorman spent parts of thirteen seasons in Buffalo, amassing more yards with his kicks than any other player in franchise history. Known for his ability to pin the opposition deep inside their own territory, Moorman proved to be one of the few bright spots on Bills teams that typically finished well under .500, gaining Pro Bowl and First-Team All-Pro recognition twice each. Later accorded the additional honor of being named to the NFL 2000s All-Decade Second Team, Moorman accomplished all he did after being bypassed by all thirty teams in the 1999 NFL Draft.

Born in Wichita, Kansas, on February 5, 1976, Brian Donald Moorman grew up in nearby Sedgwick, where he starred in multiple sports while attending Sedgwick High School. An outstanding all-around athlete, Moorman excelled in football, basketball, and track, earning All-State honors on the gridiron as a defensive back and punter, while also winning three state championships as a hurdler.

Continuing to display his athletic prowess at Division II Pittsburg State University in Kansas, Moorman, in addition to becoming the first player in school history to earn All-America honors in football four times, gained First-Team All-America recognition three straight times in track by winning consecutive national championships in the 400-meter intermediate hurdles.

Despite Moorman's many achievements at the collegiate level, no NFL team selected him on draft day, prompting him to sign with the Seattle Seahawks as an undrafted free agent on April 24, 1999. Recalling his feelings at the time, Moorman said, "When I signed with Seattle, I was just thrilled to be in the league. I was just thrilled to have a jersey with my name on it. I started to improve, though, and I realized this was not some pipe dream."

With Moorman subsequently failing to earn a roster spot in Seattle in either of the next two seasons, the Seahawks allocated him to the Berlin Thunder of NFL Europe, with whom he spent 2000 and 2001, leading the league in punting both years.

Brian Moorman amassed more yards with his kicks than any other punter in franchise history.
Courtesy of Mark Cromwell.

Looking back on his two-year stint in Berlin, Moorman said, "It was a great experience. Nothing is different for kickers and punters. The ball is the same, the uprights are the same. The competition might be different for some of the guys, but for kickers it shows people how capable we really are."

Signed by the Bills as a free agent following his return to the United States in 2001, Moorman beat out veteran punter Chris Mohr for the starting job during training camp, after which he had a solid first season, averaging just under 41 yards per punt, while also handling kickoff duties. Establishing himself as one of the NFL's top punters the following year, Moorman began a string of five straight seasons during which he averaged better than 43 yards per kick, performing especially well in 2005, when he earned Pro Bowl, First-Team All-Pro, and First-Team All-AFC honors for the first of two straight times by leading the league with an average of 45.7 yards per punt.

Although Moorman never again led the NFL in punting average, he typically placed near the top of the league rankings in net yards per punt, demonstrating his ability to place the ball all over the field and drive it high enough in the air to allow his coverage team the opportunity to get down-field. Blessed with a strong leg, Moorman twice delivered the NFL's longest punt of the season, with his 84-yard kick in 2002 representing the longest of his career. Also extremely adept at getting the ball off under pressure, Moorman had only 2 of his 979 career punts blocked.

Perhaps as much as anything, though, Moorman became known for his exceptional athletic ability, which separated him from virtually every other player who ever manned his position. Occasionally reverting to his college days as a track star, the 6', 175-pound Moorman took off with the football from time to time, scoring 5 touchdowns over the course of his career, and twice throwing TD passes off fake field goal attempts.

In discussing Moorman's outstanding athleticism, Bills' special teams coach Bobby April said, "He is a tremendous athlete. He's really fast, and he's got tremendous leg speed, like a runner. His ability to strike the sweet spot on a ball is better than most other punters."

Remaining a weapon for the Bills on special teams for five more years, Moorman averaged more than 44 yards per punt three times between 2007 and 2011, posting a career-high mark of 48.2 yards per kick in the last of those campaigns. However, after Moorman fell out of favor with special teams coach Bruce DeHaven, the Bills cut him three games into the 2012 regular season, replacing him with Shawn Powell. Moorman subsequently signed with the Dallas Cowboys, for whom he averaged 44.6 yards per punt the rest of the year, before resigning with the Bills when they relieved DeHaven of his duties at the end of 2012.

Expressing his happiness to be returning to Buffalo after inking his deal with the Bills, Moorman said, "I've been kind of at a loss for words since I got back. It means the world to me. I'd obviously love to finish my career as a Buffalo Bill. And to have that opportunity now is great."

Moorman spent one final season in Buffalo, averaging 41.2 yards per punt in 2013, before announcing his retirement shortly after the Bills released him just prior to the start of the ensuing campaign. Posting a "Thank You" letter on the Bills website after the team announced its cuts, Moorman wrote, "Today is certainly bittersweet. But I can truly tell you that wherever the road takes us, we will always consider ourselves members of the Buffalo Bills family. It may be the end of a career, but it's certainly not the end of a friendship."

Following his retirement from football, Moorman, who as a member of the Bills amassed 40,370 punting yards and averaged 43.7 yards per punt, moved with his wife, Amber, and their young son, Cooper, to Ponte Vedra Beach, Florida, where he became a real estate agent. Now part-owner of a Sotheby's brokerage firm, Moorman also remains active in the PUNT Foundation he and his wife created in 2004 to help make a difference in the lives of western New York children facing life-threatening illnesses.

Still holding the city of Buffalo and its fans close to his heart, Moorman says, "Buffalo is like a college town. When I was playing, we always said, 'Once we make the playoffs, this place is gonna go nuts.' We were close a few times, and you could see it boiling up and start to bubble over for the town ready to explode. So, I can only imagine what it's like in that area right now."

## BILLS CAREER HIGHLIGHTS

### Best Season

Although Moorman averaged a career-best 48.2 yards per punt in 2011, that represented just the fifth-highest mark in the league. Meanwhile, Moorman's 45.7-yard average in 2005 topped the circuit, earning him First-Team All-Pro honors. Factoring everything into the equation, the 2005 campaign would have to be considered the finest of Moorman's career.

### Memorable Moments/Greatest Performances

- Recorded the longest punt in the NFL for the entire 2002 season when he drove the ball 84 yards all the way down to the Green Bay 2-yard line during a 10-0 loss to the Packers on December 22.
- Earned AFC Special Teams Player of the Week honors for the first of five times by averaging 53 yards per punt during a 20-13 win over the Dolphins on October 17, 2004, with two of his three kicks resulting in touchbacks.
- Earned that distinction again by punting the ball eight times for 379 yards (47.4-yard average) during a 24-10 win over Green Bay on November 5, 2006, with three of his kicks pinning the Packers inside their own 10-yard line.

- Contributed to a 34-10 victory over the Seahawks in the opening game of the 2008 regular season by completing a 19-yard TD pass to Ryan Denney off a fake field goal attempt.
- Combined with Denney again to give the Bills the only points they scored during a 27-7 loss to the Saints on September 27, 2009, with Moorman hitting Denney with a 25-yard TD pass off a fake field goal attempt early in the second quarter.
- Earned AFC Special Teams Player of the Week honors for the final time by averaging 45 yards per punt during a 20-9 win over Carolina on October 25, 2009, with 6 of 8 eight kicks pinning the Panthers inside their own 20-yard line.

## Notable Achievements

- Averaged more than 45 yards per punt three times
- Recorded 2 punts of at least 80 yards
- Recorded longest punt in NFL twice
- Threw 2 touchdown passes
- Led NFL in punting average once
- Finished second in NFL in punting average once
- Finished third in NFL in total punting yards twice
- Holds Bills record for longest punt (84 yards)
- Holds Bills single season record for highest punting average (48.2 in 2011)
- Holds Bills career record for most total punting yards (40,370)
- Ranks among Bills career leaders with 43.7-yard punting average (3rd) and 190 games played (5th)
- Five-time AFC Special Teams Player of the Week
- Three-time AFC Special Teams Player of the Month
- Two-time Pro Bowl selection (2005 and 2006)
- Two-time First-Team All-Pro selection (2005 and 2006)
- Two-time First-Team All-AFC selection (2005 and 2006)
- NFL 2000s All-Decade Second Team

# 46
## LESEAN MCCOY

Although Lesean Mccoy is most closely associated with the Phila-delphia Eagles, the star running back spent four seasons in Buffalo, serving as the centerpiece of the Bills offense in three of those. After setting the Eagles career record for most yards rushing, McCoy gained more than 1,000 yards on the ground twice and amassed more than 1,000 yards from scrimmage three times for the Bills from 2015 to 2018, earning in the process three Pro Bowl selections. More importantly, McCoy's exceptional all-around play helped the Bills end a seventeen-year playoff drought in 2017, when they advanced to the postseason for the first time this century.

Born in Harrisburg, Pennsylvania, on July 12, 1988, Lesean Kamel McCoy acquired the nickname "Shady" as a child due to his pronounced mood swings that saw him go from laughing one minute to crying the next. Eventually emerging as a standout on the gridiron at Bishop McDevitt High School, McCoy rushed for 406 yards in one game as a sophomore, before earning Associated Press (AP) First-Team All-State, AP Class AAAA Player of the Year, and Mid-Penn Commonwealth Conference Offensive MVP honors his junior year by running for 2,828 yards and scoring 35 touchdowns. Performing brilliantly once again in his final season, McCoy gained AP First-Team All-State recognition for the second straight time, with a 2006 ESPN evaluation describing him as "lightning in a bottle every time he touches the ball."

Rated by recruiting analyst Tom Lemming the nation's eleventh-ranked high school prospect, McCoy initially committed to the University of Miami before difficulties in the classroom and a serious ankle injury sus-tained his last year at Bishop McDevitt forced him to spend one year at Milford Academy, a prep school located in New Berlin, New York. Follow-ing a coaching change at Miami, McCoy enrolled at the University of Pitts-burgh, where he made an extremely favorable impression during summer practice, with Dave Grdnic writing in an August 2007 edition of the school newspaper, *Panthers Digest*, "After just one week, Lesean McCoy has been

LeSean McCoy gained more than 1,000 yards on the ground for the Bills twice.
Courtesy of Keith Allison.

as amazing as advertised. He's been dynamic on the field and off, banging
up the middle on runs as hard as he bolts around end, and talking just as
good a game to the media."

Excelling in his first year of college ball, McCoy rushed for 1,328
yards and scored 15 touchdowns, prompting Rivals.com to name him to
its Freshman All-American team. Meanwhile, an article in the *Sporting
News* credited McCoy with having "one of the best starts by a freshman
running back at Pittsburgh since Tony Dorsett." Even better as a sophomore, McCoy gained 1,488 yards on the ground, amassed 1,793 yards from
scrimmage, and scored 21 TDs, causing him to forgo his final two seasons
of college and enter the 2009 NFL Draft, where Philadelphia selected him
in the 2nd round, with the 53rd overall pick.

After sharing playing time with Brian Westbrook as a rookie, McCoy
established himself as a force on offense his second year in the league,

scoring 9 touchdowns and ranking among the NFL leaders with 1,080 yards rushing and 1,672 yards from scrimmage, despite suffering a rib injury that sidelined him for one game. Continuing to perform at an elite level the next four years, McCoy surpassed 1,000 yards rushing three times and 1,200 yards from scrimmage each season, earning in the process three trips to the Pro Bowl and two First-Team All-Pro selections. Particularly outstanding in 2013, McCoy led the NFL with 1,607 yards rushing and 2,146 yards from scrimmage, while also scoring 11 touchdowns and averaging 5.1 yards per carry.

But, while McCoy rose to stardom in Philadelphia, he also developed a reputation as someone who often conducted himself inappropriately off the playing field. Accused multiple times of being involved in violent behavior, McCoy was sued in May 2013 for his alleged actions toward a woman using the alias "Mary Roe" aboard a party bus on the New Jersey Turnpike, with Roe testifying that McCoy humiliated her and fifteen other women by spraying them with a beverage before ejecting her from the vehicle. McCoy also found himself being accused at different times of beating his child and dog, spreading STDs to teammates' girlfriends, making derogatory comments about women, and publicly insulting the mother of his children.

Perhaps because of these many indiscretions, the Eagles completed a trade with the Bills on March 5, 2015, that sent their best offensive player to Buffalo for third-year linebacker Kiko Alonso. Expressing his surprise over the deal, which left many people in Philadelphia scratching their heads, McCoy described it as a "panic move" by second-year Eagles head coach Chip Kelly, who he went on to say "got rid of all the good black players" and "doesn't like or respect stars."

Elaborating further on his feelings after examining his situation more closely, McCoy said, "My first reaction, I was definitely disappointed just because my team didn't really . . . I didn't know what was going on. I've been in Philadelphia my whole life—for the six years it was great. But once I kind of sat down, relaxed, and had some thoughts to myself, talked to my family, I thought it was the best move."

Establishing himself as the focal point of the Bills offense immediately upon his arrival in Buffalo, McCoy rushed for 895 yards, accumulated 1,187 yards from scrimmage, and scored 5 touchdowns in 2015, despite missing four games due to injury, with his stellar play earning him Pro Bowl honors for the third of five straight times. Performing even better the next two seasons, McCoy gained 1,267 yards on the ground, caught 50 passes for 356 yards, and scored 14 touchdowns in 2016, before helping the Bills earn a spot in the playoffs as a wild card the following year by rushing for 1,138 yards, making 59 receptions for 448 yards, and scoring 8 TDs.

An explosive runner with outstanding speed and tremendous moves in the open field, the 5'11", 210-pound McCoy possessed the ability to score from anywhere on the field, recording four TD runs of at least 50 yards over the course of his career. Extremely elusive, McCoy tended to carry the ball loosely, allowing him to better evade would-be tacklers. Although known more for his speed and quickness, McCoy also ran the ball well between the tackles, where he used his surprising strength to gain additional yardage after first contact. An excellent receiver out of the backfield as well, McCoy caught at least 50 passes in five different seasons, doing so twice as a member of the Bills.

Running behind an undermanned offensive line in 2018, McCoy gained just 514 yards on the ground, amassed only 752 yards from scrimmage, and scored just 3 touchdowns, contributing greatly to the Bills' decision to cut him during training camp the following year. Nevertheless, with the thirty-year-old McCoy outperforming the team's younger backs in practice, speculation arose as to whether the Bills based their decision, at least in part, on his ill-advised behavior away from the playing field, which garnered him much negative attention in July 2018, when his former girlfriend, Delicia Cordon, accused him on Instagram of battering a woman, beating his son and pet dog, and using illegal steroids. Although McCoy subsequently denied all allegations made against him, court documents later revealed that he had been trying to evict Cordon from a house he owned in Milton, Georgia, for some time, and that Cordon had been robbed and assaulted at the home by a masked assailant on July 10.

Speaking publicly on the matter for the first time some months later, Cordon stated her belief that McCoy had some involvement in the incident and offered a $40,000 reward for information leading to the arrest of the intruder. She went on to say, "I live my life in fear every day not knowing if I'm walking past the man who savagely attacked me. . . . To be clear, very clear, I believe that LeSean McCoy was involved in the attack. The LeSean McCoy that I know behind closed doors is totally different than the LeSean McCoy in front of cameras. This attack was about the jewelry that LeSean expressed that he wanted back from me weeks before the attack."

Released by the Bills after rushing for 3,814 yards, making 175 receptions for 1,334 yards, amassing 5,148 yards from scrimmage, and scoring 30 touchdowns as a member of the team, McCoy subsequently signed with the eventual Super Bowl champion Kansas City Chiefs, for whom he assumed a part-time role in 2019. From Kansas City, McCoy moved on to

Tampa Bay, where he won a second ring in 2020 while serving as a backup for the Buccaneers.

Officially announcing his retirement several months later after signing a ceremonial one-day contract with the Eagles, McCoy ended his playing career with 11,102 rushing yards, 518 pass receptions, 3,898 receiving yards, 15,000 yards from scrimmage, and 89 touchdowns, with 73 of those coming on the ground and the other 16 through the air.

Upon inking his deal with Philadelphia, McCoy received praise from Eagles owner Jeffrey Lurie, who said in a statement, "LeSean possessed a unique combination of speed, elusiveness and an exceptional playmaking ability that made him one of the most dynamic players in the league and one of the most productive players in the history of our franchise. LeSean carried himself with a rare blend of confidence and youthful enthusiasm, but he also was driven by a desire to be one of the all-time greats at the running back position, and that's what made him such an exciting player to be around and watch every week."

Meanwhile, Eric Wood paid his respects to his former Bills teammate by saying, "Shady had one heck of a career. Smart, competitive, really good runner with the football. From the outside, it would appear that he had the worst ball security the way he would carry the ball like a loaf of bread and holding it out at times and almost making basketball type moves with the football. At one point, though, I remember Rex Ryan brought up the stat that he had the least amount of fumbles per carry over the time of his career in the NFL. So, great ball security even though he wasn't a traditional ball carrier."

Wood added, "I truly loved playing with Shady. He was a guy that helped break the longest playoff drought in professional sports. To break that 17-year streak was the highlight of my career, so nothing but respect for Shady for what he did on the football field. If he attacks the next phase of life the way he attacked football, he'll be successful in whatever endeavor he ventures into next."

## BILLS CAREER HIGHLIGHTS

### Best Season

McCoy had an outstanding season for the Bills in 2017, earning his fifth consecutive trip to the Pro Bowl by gaining 1,138 yards on the ground, amassing 1,586 yards from scrimmage, and scoring 8 touchdowns. But he performed even better the previous year, concluding the 2016 campaign with 1,267 yards rushing, 1,623 yards from scrimmage, 13 rushing touchdowns, 14 TDs, and a career-high rushing average of 5.4 yards per carry, all of which placed him near the top of the league rankings.

### Memorable Moments/Greatest Performances

- Helped lead the Bills to a 33-17 win over the Miami Dolphins on November 8, 2015, by carrying the ball sixteen times for 112 yards and 1 touchdown, which he scored on a season-long 48-yard run.
- Followed that up with another strong performance against the Jets just four days later, rushing for 112 yards and gaining another 47 yards on 5 pass receptions during a 22-17 win.
- Contributed to a 30-19 victory over the Los Angeles Rams on October 9, 2016, by gaining 150 yards on 18 carries, with his longest run of the day covering 53 yards.
- Led the Bills to a 45-16 rout of the San Francisco 49ers on October 16, 2016, by rushing for 140 yards and 3 touchdowns, the longest of which covered 18 yards.
- Rushed for 103 yards and 2 touchdowns during a 28-21 win over the Jacksonville Jaguars on November 27, 2016, scoring one of his TDs on a career-long 75-yard run.
- Helped lead the Bills to a 33-13 victory over the hapless Cleveland Browns on December 18, 2016, by rushing for 153 yards and 2 touchdowns.
- Contributed to a 34-14 win over the Oakland Raiders on October 29, 2017, by rushing for 151 yards and 1 touchdown, which came on a 48-yard run late in the fourth quarter.
- Gave the Bills a 13-7 overtime victory over the Indianapolis Colts on December 10, 2017, when he ran the ball in from 21 yards out with just 1:33 left in the OT session. He finished the day with 32 carries for 156 yards and 1 TD.
- Gained more than 100 yards on the ground for the last time as a member of the Bills when he rushed for 113 yards and 2 touchdowns during a 41-10 blowout of the Jets on November 11, 2018.

### Notable Achievements

- Rushed for more than 1,000 yards twice
- Surpassed 1,000 yards from scrimmage three times, topping 1,500 yards twice

- Scored 14 touchdowns in 2016
- Finished third in NFL with rushing average of 5.4 yards per carry in 2016
- Finished fourth in NFL in rushing yards once, yards from scrimmage once, and touchdowns once
- Led Bills in rushing three times and receptions once
- Ranks among Bills career leaders with 3,814 yards rushing (6th), 5,148 yards from scrimmage (9th), and 25 rushing touchdowns (tied for 9th)
- Three-time Pro Bowl selection (2015, 2016, and 2017)

# 47

## PHIL HANSEN

Often overlooked because he spent most of his career playing in the shadow of Bruce Smith, Phil Hansen rarely receives the credit he deserves for being among the finest defensive linemen in franchise history. Nevertheless, Hansen was regarded as one of the Bills' steadiest and most dependable players throughout the 1990s, excelling at left-defensive end for teams that won three division titles and three AFC championships. A relentless defender who had a knack for breaking up plays and getting to the opposing quarterback, Hansen recorded the third-most sacks and tackles in team annals, with his solid all-around play earning him a place in the Bills Wall of Fame.

Born in Ellendale, North Dakota, on May 20, 1968, Phillip Allen Hansen grew up on his family's farm in the nearby city of Oakes. Eventually establishing himself as a standout on the gridiron at Oakes High School, Hansen earned all-conference honors twice by excelling at linebacker, running back, and as both an offensive and defensive lineman.

Choosing to remain close to home, Hansen accepted an athletic scholarship to North Dakota State University, where he became one of the best defensive players in Division II history. A two-time Division II All-American defensive end, Hansen helped lead the Bison to a pair of national championships and an overall record of 42-7-1 by recording a total of 41 sacks and setting a school record with 32 career pass breakups. Named Small College Defensive Lineman of the Year by the NFL Draft Report after his final season, Hansen drew interest from several pro teams heading into the 1991 NFL Draft, with the Bills ultimately selecting him in the 2nd round, with the 54th overall pick.

After assuming a backup role during the early stages of his rookie campaign, Hansen spent most of the year filling in at right-defensive end for an injured Bruce Smith, doing a good enough job to earn a spot on the NFL All-Rookie Team. Moved to the left side of Buffalo's defense prior to the start of the 1992 season, Hansen began a ten-year stint as the team's starting

Phil Hansen ranks among the Bills' all-time leaders in both sacks and tackles.

left-defensive end—a period during which he consistently ranked among the Bills team leaders in sacks and tackles, registering at least 8 sacks three times and more than 100 combined tackles twice.

Although Hansen performed well for the Bills year after year, he never gained Pro Bowl or All-Pro recognition, likely because of the presence of Bruce Smith, whose more spectacular play relegated him to second-tier status among Buffalo defensive linemen. Yet Hansen proved to be one of the league's better all-around linemen, using his burly 6'5", 278-pound frame to plug holes against the run and his quickness and athleticism to apply pressure to opposing quarterbacks.

In addition to the contributions Hansen made to the Bills on the playing field, he helped create an atmosphere of hard work and dedication that greatly influenced the other players around him. A team captain for five years, Hansen set an example for his teammates, who very much appreciated his intensity, professionalism, modesty, and gritty play. Extremely popular with the hometown fans and media as well, Hansen proved to be a perfect fit for the blue-collar city of Buffalo, which embraced his grassroots mentality.

In discussing Hansen, sportswriter Mark Gaughan, who covered the Bills for the *Buffalo News* throughout the defensive lineman's career, said, "He's a first-class guy. He's somebody you want to take into the jungle with you. He was a true professional from the day he walked in until the day he left."

Humble and extremely down to earth, Hansen treated everyone with respect, be it teammates, reporters, or fans, further endearing himself to his fellow Buffalonians by remaining in the city during the offseason and retaining a strong presence in the community.

Unfortunately, after missing only ten games his first nine years in the league, Hansen suffered a knee injury in 2000 that limited him to just ten contests, 2 sacks, and 27 tackles. Appearing in only twelve games the following season, the thirty-three-year-old Hansen recorded just 3 sacks and 31 tackles, prompting him to announce his retirement at the end of the year.

Choosing to wait until after the Bills played their final game to make his decision known to the public, Hansen, who, over the course of his career recorded 61.5 sacks, 876 tackles (496 solo), 8 forced fumbles, 10 fumble recoveries, and 1 interception, said during his retirement press conference, "My body and my heart tell me it's time to move on. I've known for a long time now that this would be my final season. I tried to keep it a secret because I didn't want it to become a distraction to any of my teammates. I always thought the focus should be on the opponent."

Hansen added, "Any time you play for more than a couple years in the National Football League, you always think about retirement, especially Monday mornings after Sunday games. But for a defensive lineman—playing 11 years—that's almost above and beyond the call of duty. I wanted to leave the game on my own terms. I didn't want to be cut or traded."

Following his playing days, Hansen moved with his wife and three children to the Detroit Lakes, Minnesota, area, where he eventually became a high school basketball and football referee. Hansen also hosts a football coaches show on TV and does live radio commentary for his alma mater, North Dakota State. A man of many interests, Hansen ran unsuccessfully for a seat on the Minnesota Senate in 2012, helps his brother manage a 1,300-acre farm in North Dakota, owns and operates his own landscaping business, and, along with his wife, established the Phil and Dianna Hansen Family Fund and The Charitable Champions Fund at DMF.

In discussing his postfootball life, Hansen said, "When people ask me what I do, I first tell them that I'm retired. I do things that keep me busy, but my time is kind of my own. I can decide what I want to do and what I don't want to do. I guess when you're done with football and when you can retire, you try to find purpose in your life, and, when you play at that level, you want to be productive with the time you have. That was the highest level of production in football, so you just find something else in life to be productive with. For me, all of that is surrounded by my family."

Looking back fondly on his eleven years in Buffalo, Hansen stated, "I think of generations of Bills who never even got a sniff of the playoffs. It makes you appreciate what we did, even if we never won one, to go there all those times puts it in perspective for all my Bills colleagues that came after me that didn't get a chance."

## BILLS CAREER HIGHLIGHTS

### Best Season

Hansen performed well for the Bills in 1995, recording 76 tackles and a career-high 10 sacks. But he had his finest all-around season in 1996, when he registered 8 sacks, a career-best 132 combined tackles, 1 forced fumble, and 2 fumble recoveries.

### Memorable Moments/Greatest Performances

- Recorded the first sack of his career during a 16-13 loss to the Patriots on November 24, 1991.
- Contributed to a 20-16 win over the New Orleans Saints on December 20, 1992, by sacking Bobby Hebert twice.
- Proved to be a huge factor in the 1992 AFC Championship Game, recording a sack and intercepting a Dan Marino pass during a 29-10 victory over the Miami Dolphins.
- Recorded a pair of multiple-sack games in 1995, getting to Jim Harbaugh twice during a 20-14 win over the Colts on September 17, and bringing down Boomer Esiason twice during a 28-26 victory over the Jets on November 19.
- Made a huge play during the Bills' 22-13 win over the Detroit Lions on October 5, 1997, giving them a 2-point lead with just over two

minutes remaining in regulation by combining with Bruce Smith to tackle Barry Sanders in the end zone for a safety.
- Scored his only career touchdown when he ran the ball in from 13 yards out after recovering a fumble during a 44-21 win over the Oakland Raiders on December 13, 1998.

## Notable Achievements

- Scored one defensive touchdown
- Recorded 10 sacks in 1995
- Led Bills defensive linemen in tackles three times
- Ranks among Bills career leaders with 61.5 sacks (3rd), 876 tackles (3rd), and 10 fumble recoveries (tied for 6th)
- Three-time division champion (1991, 1993, and 1995)
- Three-time AFC champion (1991, 1992, and 1993)
- Member of 1991 NFL All-Rookie Team
- Inducted into Bills Wall of Fame in 2011

# 48

## ERNIE WARLICK

Although Ernie Warlick posted relatively modest numbers his four years in Buffalo, the tremendous impact he made on the Bills and the American Football League as a whole earned him a spot on this list. A key member of the Bills AFL championship teams of 1964 and 1965, Warlick proved to be a reliable pass catcher and exceptional blocker from his tight end position, with his outstanding all-around play earning him four consecutive AFL All-Star selections. Equally important, Warlick's strong presence and calm demeanor helped make him a central figure in the fight for equal rights of African American players in the infant league.

Born in Washington, DC, on July 21, 1932, Ernest Warlick grew up in Hickory, North Carolina, where he starred in several sports while attending all-black Ridgeview High School. Particularly outstanding in football and basketball, Warlick established himself as a two-way star on the gridiron for the Ridgeview Panthers, excelling at both tight end and defensive back. Meanwhile, the 6'3" Warlick once scored 50 points in a game during a basketball tournament in New York, prompting columnist Al Mallette to write that he gave "a ball-handling show that would make even the fabulous Globetrotters take a second look. As a matter of fact, the Trotters have made overtures to Warlick."

Choosing to further his education rather than join the Globetrotters, Warlick accepted an athletic scholarship to North Carolina Central University, a historically Black school located in the city of Durham. Continuing to compete in multiple sports while in college, Warlick lettered in football and basketball for three seasons, before enlisting in the military following his graduation. After four years in the service, three of which he spent playing for the Bolling Air Force football team, Warlick joined the Calgary Stampeders of the Canadian Football League, for whom he made 192 receptions, amassed 3,332 receiving yards, and scored 16 touchdowns over the course of the next five seasons. A standout two-way player for Calgary,

Ernie Warlick served as a key figure on the Bills' AFL championship teams of 1964 and 1965.

Warlick excelled at both tight end and defensive back, with his strong play on both sides of the ball earning him three West All-Star nominations.

With Warlick having made a name for himself in the CFL, the Bills extended him a contract offer prior to the start of the 1962 campaign. Welcoming a return to the United States, Warlick signed with the Bills, who he subsequently joined at the rather advanced age of thirty.

Claiming that Warlick immediately gained the attention of new head coach Lou Saban upon his arrival in Buffalo, former Bills defensive back Booker Edgerson stated, "Saban saw his athletic ability for catching the ball.

Plus, he was an outstanding blocker, and that's what they used tight ends for a lot back in those days. So, Saban said, 'OK, let's stretch the offense, and let's make the tight end part of our receiving corps.' And the rest is history."

Performing well his first year with the Bills, Warlick led the team with 35 catches, amassed 482 receiving yards, and scored 2 touchdowns, earning in the process the first of his four consecutive trips to the AFL All-Star game. Warlick followed that up with two more solid seasons, totaling 47 receptions and 957 receiving yards from 1963 to 1964, while also doing an exceptional job of blocking for quarterback Jack Kemp and star running back Cookie Gilchrist at the point of attack.

Even though the Bills perhaps never took full advantage of the 6'3", 235-pound Warlick's outstanding pass-receiving skills, choosing to use him more as an in-line blocker, his teammates knew that he had the ability to be more of a factor in the passing game, with Booker Edgerson recalling, "I remember in practice, he went up and caught balls that normally would not be caught. He had the height and everything, but he had these big hands. That was one of the things that everybody used to talk about. They'd say, 'Oh, man, did you see that guy's hands. His one hand is bigger than both of mine.'"

Used almost exclusively as a blocker in 1965, the thirty-three-year-old Warlick made just 8 receptions for 112 yards and 1 touchdown. Nevertheless, he received his fourth straight nomination to the AFL All-Star Game. However, after arriving in the host city of New Orleans, Warlick and the other Black players became the targets of overt racism. Refused service by white taxicab drivers and local business establishments, Black players such as Warlick, Cookie Gilchrist, Ernie Ladd, Earl Faison, Clem Daniels, and Art Powell also reported hearing muttered insults from restaurant and hotel patrons, and bands abruptly stopping music when they entered the room. Meanwhile, in his book *The Birth of the New NFL*, longtime Buffalo sports columnist Larry Felser tells the story that Warlick packed his bags one morning following an incident, writing, "Warlick was able to order breakfast in the dining room of the hotel, but I lost my appetite when an older woman said loud enough for me to hear that she didn't want to eat in the same room with monkeys."

After the entire contingent of twenty-two Black All-Stars on the East and West squads voted to boycott the game, they chose Warlick to be their spokesman, believing that his veteran status and even temperament would make him more acceptable to a wider audience. Reading the statement announcing the walkout, Warlick delivered a particularly strong message when he said, "Because of adverse conditions and discriminatory practices," the league's Black players have "decided to withdraw from the All-Star Game."

With the white players honoring the boycott, the league arranged to move the game to Houston, thereby punishing New Orleans for its atrocious behavior and making men such as Warlick pioneers of sorts for the fair treatment of Black athletes.

Announcing his retirement just weeks later, Warlick ended his four-year AFL career with only 90 receptions, 1,551 receiving yards, and 4 touchdown catches. Nevertheless, he remains a key figure in the history of the Buffalo Bills and the American Football League.

Remaining in Buffalo following his playing days, Warlick broke the city's TV color barrier when, after joining the staff at WGR-TV in 1966, he became the first Black person to anchor a newscast on Buffalo television, serving as that station's nightly 11:00 p.m. sports anchor. Warlick later opened a hamburger stand and eventually landed a job as a sales manager, before being elected to the Buffalo Broadcast Pioneers Hall of Fame in 1998 and being named the winner of the Ralph C. Wilson Distinguished Service Award in 2000 for his years of service to the Bills. Warlick lived until November 24, 2012, when he died at his home in Williamsville, New York, at the age of eighty from an unknown illness after spending nearly two weeks in a Buffalo hospital complaining about pain in his shoulder.

## CAREER HIGHLIGHTS

### Best Season

Warlick made his greatest overall impact in Buffalo in 1964, when, in addition to serving as one of the leaders of a Bills squad that captured the AFL championship, he did an excellent job of blocking up front for an offense that gained more yards and scored more points than any other team in the league.

### Memorable Moments/Greatest Performances

- Scored the first touchdown of his career when he gathered in a 12-yard pass from Al Dorow during a 23-20 loss to the Denver Broncos on September 15, 1962.
- Topped 100 receiving yards for the only time as a member of the Bills when he made 9 receptions for 117 yards and 1 touchdown during a

23-14 win over the Dallas Texans on December 2, 1962, scoring his TD on a 1-yard toss from Jack Kemp.

- Nearly reached that milestone again during a 28-14 loss to the Houston Oilers on October 20, 1963, making 3 receptions for 98 yards and 1 touchdown, which came on a career-long 55-yard connection · with Kemp.
- Made a huge play in the final game of his career, scoring the first points of the 1965 AFL Championship Game on an 18-yard pass from Jack Kemp. Warlick's 18-yard TD catch proved to be the only touchdown the Bills scored on offense in a game they went on to win by a score of 23-0.

**Notable Achievements**

- Never missed a game in four seasons, appearing in fifty-six consecutive contests
- Averaged at least 20 yards per reception twice
- Led Bills with 35 receptions in 1962
- Two-time division champion (1964 and 1965)
- Two-time AFL champion (1964 and 1965)
- Four-time AFL All-Star selection (1962, 1963, 1964, and 1965)

# 49
# BEN WILLIAMS

A mainstay on Buffalo's defensive line for ten seasons, Ben Williams spent his entire career starting at left defensive end for the Bills, providing them with consistently excellent play against both the run and pass. The first African American player to be drafted out of the University of Mississippi, Williams, who acquired the nickname "Gentle Ben" due to his friendly demeanor, recorded at least 10 sacks three times and registered more than 100 tackles once, with his strong all-around play earning him one Pro Bowl selection and three Second-Team All-AFC nominations. A member of Buffalo's 1980 division championship team, Williams recorded the sixth most sacks in franchise history, although his greatest contribution to the Bills may well have been his mentorship of Bruce Smith.

Born in Yazoo City, Mississippi, on September 1, 1954, Robert Jerry Williams got his start on the gridiron at Yazoo City High School, where he earned two letters and served as team captain his senior year. Subsequently offered an athletic scholarship to the University of Mississippi, Williams joined James Reed in breaking the color barrier for the school's football program when he signed a letter of intent in 1971. Establishing himself as one of the nation's top defensive ends over the course of the next four seasons, Williams earned All-SEC honors three times and gained All-America recognition as a senior, when he recorded a career-high 116 tackles.

In discussing Williams, who ended his collegiate career with 37 sacks (including a school record 18 in 1973) and 377 tackles, Keith Carter, Ole Miss vice chancellor for intercollegiate athletics, said, "Gentle Ben's impact on our university, the SEC, and college football as a whole is immeasurable. Ben not only helped break the race barrier for our football program but was also the first African American student to be elected by the student body for what is now known as Mr. Ole Miss. He was a great person, player, and ambassador for our university and will forever be beloved by Rebel Nation."

Commenting on the dominance Williams displayed on the football field, former Rebels teammate Roger Parkes said, "He was just a physically

Ben Williams finished in double digits in sacks for the Bills three times.

superior dude. One man was not going to block him, and sometimes two people couldn't do it. He threw people around like rag dolls."

Jim Carmody, who coached Williams at Ole Miss and later in Buffalo, spoke of the contradictory nature of his former protégé's nickname when he stated, "When Ben Williams was on the football field and the game was on, there was not one thing gentle about him. He annihilated people. On the field, he had more than a little meanness to him. At Ole Miss, he dominated everybody he faced. And I'll tell you something else about Ben. He was a helluva guy, too, one of my favorite people I ever coached."

Carmody added, "People talk about his physical skills and how he threw people around. But he was a smart player as well. He worked at it. He knew how to use his hands and forearms. He listened. He wanted to learn. He wanted to be as good as he could be. His effort was always outstanding."

Selected by the Bills in the 3rd round of the 1976 NFL Draft, with the 78th overall pick, Williams spent the first half of his rookie season assuming a backup role, before replacing Ken Jones as the starter at left defensive end midway through the campaign. Performing well the rest of the year for a Bills squad that won just two games, Williams did an excellent job of defending against the run, while also finishing second on the team with five sacks. Although the Bills posted a losing record in each of the next three seasons as well, Williams developed a reputation as one of the league's better run-stuffers, making good use of his quickness, athleticism, and long arms to ward off blockers. Emerging as an outstanding pass-rusher as well after Buffalo switched to a 3-4 defense in 1979 following the addition of nose tackle Fred Smerlas, Williams helped the Bills capture the division title in 1980 by recording 63 tackles and a team-high 12 sacks, earning in the process Second-Team All-AFC honors for the first of three straight times. Remaining a force on the left side of Buffalo's defense the next three seasons, Williams totaled 231 tackles and 24 sacks, finally gaining Pro Bowl recognition in 1982, after being snubbed by the voters the previous two years.

A hard worker who studied film constantly, the 6'3", 255-pound Williams used his intelligence as well as his physical gifts to succeed at the NFL level. A humble man who took a low-key approach to the game, Williams served as one of the Bills' team leaders, with Joe DeLamielleure saying, "He was a great leader and a great player. He had extremely long arms. He was like a poor man's Elvin Bethea, and he [Bethea] was a Hall of Famer. Just a step below that."

Beloved by his teammates, Williams was a particular favorite of Bruce Smith, who claimed that the veteran defensive end helped him with his technique during their one year together in Buffalo. Citing Williams as a major influence on his development, Smith remembered, "I would always notice he was always using his hands, swiping his hands, and this and that. And he pulled me aside one day and I said, 'Why do you do all that?' He said, 'Because they can't grab you, they can't hold you.' And then, all of a sudden, this piece of the puzzle started coming together, and I started understanding that to be a great pass rusher and a great defensive player, you had to create separation between you and that offensive lineman. So, we could use the best asset that we had in our given athletic ability, and that's your ability to be able to run."

After recording only 3.5 sacks the previous two seasons, Williams chose to announce his retirement on August 19, 1986, just one day after quarterback Jim Kelly signed his rookie contract with the Bills. Williams, who remains tied with Tom Sestak for sixth in franchise history with 52 sacks, spent the next three decades serving his family, community, and alma mater by giving his loyalty, time, and financial support. In addition to owning the LYNCO Construction Company in Jackson, Mississippi, Williams provided leadership at Ole Miss by serving as a member of the Black Alumni Advisory Council, the University of Mississippi Foundation Board of Directors, and the M-Club Board of Directors. Williams also gave back to his community by remaining active in the Easter Seals Society and the Multiple Sclerosis Association. Adopting a more sedentary lifestyle after he suffered a series of strokes and began experiencing memory loss his last few years, Williams lived until May 18, 2020, when he died of natural causes at a hospital in Jackson, Mississippi, at the age of sixty-five.

## CAREER HIGHLIGHTS

### Best Season

Williams earned his lone trip to the Pro Bowl in 1982, when he recorded 4 sacks, 46 tackles, and an interception during the strike-shortened campaign. However, he posted more impressive numbers in a few other seasons, registering 12 sacks and 63 tackles in 1980, before recording 10 sacks and 82 tackles the following year. But Williams had his finest all-around season in 1983, when he recorded 10 sacks, a career-high 103 tackles, and 2 fumble recoveries.

### Memorable Moments/Greatest Performances

- Recorded the first of his two career interceptions during a lopsided 35-3 victory over the Baltimore Colts on September 13, 1981.
- Led the defensive charge when the Bills recorded 7 sacks and allowed just 161 yards of total offense during a 9-7 win over the Denver Broncos on October 25, 1981.
- Scored the only points of his career when he sacked quarterback Matt Cavanaugh in the end zone for a safety during a 19-10 victory over the Patriots on December 13, 1981.
- Helped lead the Bills to a 13-0 win over the Pittsburgh Steelers on December 12, 1982, by recording a sack and an interception, which he subsequently returned 20 yards.
- Starred in defeat in the opening game of the 1983 regular season, recording 3 sacks during a 12-0 loss to the Miami Dolphins.

- Registered another 2 sacks during a 38-35 overtime win over the Dolphins in the second meeting between the two teams on October 9, 1983.

## Notable Achievements

- Finished in double digits in sacks three times
- Recorded 103 tackles in 1983
- Tied for sixth in franchise history with 52 career sacks
- 1980 division champion
- 1982 Pro Bowl selection
- Three-time Second-Team All-AFC selection (1980, 1981, and 1982)

# 50

## TRE'DAVIOUS WHITE

An excellent cover-corner known for his ability to come up with big plays in crucial situations, Tre'Davious White has proven to be one of the NFL's finest one-on-one defenders since he first arrived in Buffalo in 2017. The Bills' starting left cornerback for most of the past six seasons, White has played a key role on teams that have won three division titles, typically covering the opposing team's top wideout. The NFL co-leader in interceptions in 2019, White has led the Bills in picks twice, with his outstanding ball-hawking skills earning him Pro Bowl, All-Pro, and First-Team All-AFC honors twice each.

Born in Shreveport, Louisiana, on January 16, 1995, Tre'Davious White attended Green Oaks High School, where he excelled both in the classroom and on the football field, serving as valedictorian of his graduating class, while also starring on the gridiron at quarterback on offense and cornerback on defense. Rated by Rivals.com as a five-star recruit and the 18th best overall player in his class, White ultimately accepted a scholarship to Louisiana State University, where he spent his college career playing under head coach Les Miles.

A four-year starter at cornerback for the Tigers, White earned All-SEC honors twice by intercepting 6 passes, recording 167 tackles, and scoring 4 touchdowns, 3 of which came on punt returns. Performing especially well his senior year, White gained consensus First-Team All-America recognition, prompting most draft experts to identify him as a potential 1st or 2nd round pick heading into the 2017 NFL Draft.

One of the first corners to come off the board, White headed to Buffalo when the Bills selected him in the 1st round, with the 27th overall pick. Listed as the No. 1 cornerback on the team's depth chart prior to the start of the regular season, White ended up starting every game his first year in the league, earning a spot on the NFL All-Rookie Team and unofficial Second-Team All-Pro honors from *Pro Football Focus* by picking off 4 passes, recording 18 pass deflections, registering 69 tackles, forcing a fumble, and

Tre'Davious White has proven to be one of the league's top cover-corners since he joined the Bills in 2017.
Courtesy of Keith Allison and All-Pro Reels Photography.

recovering two others, one of which he returned 52 yards for a touchdown. White also finished second to New Orleans cornerback Marshon Lattimore in the NFL Defensive Rookie of the Year voting, with his outstanding play helping the Bills advance to the playoffs as a wild card for the first time in eighteen years.

White followed up his excellent rookie year with a solid 2018 campaign, recording 2 interceptions and 54 tackles, although he remained somewhat dissatisfied with the number of penalties he took and his failure to consistently wrap up opposing ball carriers, telling *Good Morning Football* prior to the start of the 2019 season, "I put together two great seasons to start it off, but I've still got a ways to go."

Meanwhile, Bills' defensive coordinator Leslie Frazier spoke highly of his young cornerback, stating that he has the "physical attributes, athletic ability, and mental toughness to match up against the best receivers week in and week out."

Taking his game up a notch in 2019, White gained Pro Bowl, All-Pro, and All-AFC recognition by tying for the league lead with 6 interceptions, registering 58 tackles, forcing 2 fumbles, and recording the first sack of his career. Signed by the Bills to a four-year contract extension worth $70 million at season's end that made him the highest-paid defensive back in the league at the time, White proved his worth by once again earning Pro Bowl, All-Pro, and All-AFC honors in 2020.

The fleet-footed White, who stands 5'11" and weighs 192 pounds, possesses the quickness to employ multiple techniques when guarding opposing wideouts. Very good in press-man coverage, White has the ability to shadow the receiver all over the field, although he rarely uses the bump-and-run. Preferring instead to allow his man to release freely at the line of scrimmage, White mirrors him in and out of his break and then closes quickly, either forcing the quarterback to go elsewhere or engaging the receiver just as the pass arrives.

A playmaker on the defensive side of the ball, White, who has acquired the nickname "Takeaway Tre," has proven to be particularly adept at making game-changing plays during the latter stages of contests, with Leslie Frazier saying, "He finds a way to come up with big plays in some tough moments. There's no situation too big for him, no circumstance that scares him."

Expressing similar sentiments, teammate Micah Hyde stated, "Big-time players make big-time plays in big-time moments, and he's a big-time player since he got here. That's just Tre. What's he call himself? Fourth-quarter Tre? That's when he starts playing really well."

White continued to perform well for the Bills in 2021, before a torn ACL he sustained during a 31-6 win over the New Orleans Saints on Thanksgiving Day forced him to miss the rest of the season. But the popular White, who holds his hometown of Shreveport close to his heart, giving back to the community through many charitable causes, soon found his spirits being lifted by the Bills Mafia, which displayed its affection for him by donating more than $100,000 to the Food Bank of Northwest Louisiana.

In discussing the philanthropic gesture, Lara McKee, who is the VP of the Bills Mafia Babes, stated in a press release, "What differentiates our fanbase from all others is our connection with players. Tre'Davious White exemplifies everything it means to be a Buffalo Bill. We wanted to show our appreciation of him by giving to a cause that's near and dear to his heart. Thousands of lives will be touched by the generosity of this fanbase. Football truly is family, especially when you are a Bills fan."

Expressing his appreciation to the fans of Buffalo for the kindness they showed toward him, White said, "I am at a loss for words for what the Bills Mafia has done for me and my hometown. It truly means the world to me to have my fans support me in this way, by giving back to my community."

After being deactivated for the first ten games of the 2022 season to allow him to fully recover from his injury, White returned to the Bills lineup on Thanksgiving, after which he spent the remainder of the year starting at his familiar position of left cornerback. Recording one interception and 20 tackles in his six games with the Bills this past season, White will enter the 2023 campaign with career totals of 17 interceptions, 208 interception-return yards, 299 tackles, 5 forced fumbles, 5 fumble recoveries, 3 sacks, and 1 touchdown scored on defense.

## CAREER HIGHLIGHTS

### Best Season

White had his finest season to this point in his career in 2019, when he earned First-Team All-Pro and First-Team All-AFC honors, his first Pro Bowl selection, and a tie for fifth place in the NFL Defensive Player of the Year voting by tying for the league lead with 6 interceptions, recording 58 tackles, forcing 2 fumbles, and going the entire year without allowing opposing wide receivers to score a single touchdown against him.

### Memorable Moments/Greatest Performances

- Recorded the first interception of his career when he picked off a Trevor Siemian pass during a 26-16 win over the Denver Broncos on September 24, 2017.
- Scored his only touchdown as a pro one week later when he ran 52 yards to paydirt after recovering a fumble during a 23-17 victory over the Atlanta Falcons on October 1, 2017.
- Helped preserve a 16-10 victory over the Chiefs on November 26, 2017, when he picked off an Alex Smith pass at the Buffalo 27-yard line with just over one minute left in regulation and subsequently returned the ball 63 yards, deep into Kansas City territory.

- Had a huge hand in the Bills' 21-17 win over Cincinnati on September 22, 2019, forcing a fumble deep inside Buffalo territory on the final play of the first half and recording a pair of interceptions, with his pick of a tipped Andy Dalton pass at the Buffalo 10-yard line with just twelve seconds left in regulation sealing the victory.
- Earned AFC Defensive Player of the Week honors by intercepting a Ryan Fitzpatrick pass and forcing a fumble during a 31-21 win over the Miami Dolphins on October 20, 2019.
- Earned that distinction again by recording a pair of interceptions during a 17-10 victory over the Pittsburgh Steelers on December 15, 2019, returning his two picks a total of 49 yards.

### Notable Achievements

- Has scored 1 defensive touchdown
- Led NFL with 6 interceptions in 2019
- Has led Bills in interceptions twice
- Three-time division champion (2020, 2021, and 2022)
- Member of 2017 NFL All-Rookie Team
- Two-time AFC Defensive Player of the Week
- Two-time Pro Bowl selection (2019 and 2020)
- 2019 First-Team All-Pro selection
- 2020 Second-Team All-Pro selection
- Two-time First-Team All-AFC selection (2019 and 2020)

# SUMMARY AND HONORABLE MENTIONS

## (THE NEXT 25)

Having identified the fifty greatest players in Buffalo Bills history, the time has come to select the best of the best. Based on the rankings contained in this book, the members of the Bills' all-time offensive and defensive teams are listed below. Our squads include the top player at each position, with the offense featuring the two best wide receivers, running backs, tackles, and guards, as well as the top quarterback, tight end, and center. Meanwhile, the defense features two ends, two tackles, three linebackers, two cornerbacks, and a pair of safeties. Special teams have been accounted for as well, with a placekicker, punter, kickoff returner, punt returner, and cover man also being included, some of whom were taken from the list of honorable mentions that will soon follow.

| OFFENSE | | DEFENSE | |
|---|---|---|---|
| PLAYER: | POSITION: | PLAYER: | POSITION: |
| Jim Kelly | QB | Ron McDole | LE |
| O. J. Simpson | RB | Fred Smerlas | LT |
| Thurman Thomas | RB | Tom Sestak | RT |
| Ernie Warlick | TE | Bruce Smith | RE |
| Andre Reed | WR | Cornelius Bennett | LB |
| Eric Moulds | WR | Darryl Talley | LB |
| Stew Barber | LT | Mike Stratton | LB |
| Billy Shaw | LG | Nate Odomes | LCB |
| Kent Hull | C | George Saimes | SS |
| Joe DeLamielleure | RG | Tony Greene | FS |
| Joe Devlin | RT | Butch Byrd | RCB |

| Steve Christie | PK | Brian Moorman | P |
|---|---|---|---|
| Terrence McGee | KR | Roscoe Parrish | PR |
| | | Steve Tasker | ST |

Although I limited my earlier rankings to the top fifty players in Bills history, many other fine players have donned the team's colors through the years, some of whom narrowly missed making the final cut. Following is a list of those players deserving of an honorable mention. These are the men I deemed worthy of being slotted into positions 51 to 75 in the overall rankings. Where applicable and available, the statistics they compiled during their time in Buffalo are included, along with their most notable achievements while playing for the Bills.

### 51 - ROBERT JAMES (DB; 1969-1974)

**Career Numbers**

9 interceptions, 38 interception-return yards, 6 fumble recoveries, 1 TD

**Notable Achievements**

- Missed just one game in six seasons, appearing in eighty-three of eighty-four contests
- Led Bills with 4 interceptions in 1971
- Three-time Pro Bowl selection (1972, 1973, and 1974)
- Two-time First-Team All-Pro selection (1973 and 1974)
- Three-time First-Team All-AFC selection (1972, 1973, and 1974)
- Inducted into Bills Wall of Fame in 1998

### 52 - CHARLES ROMES (DB; 1977-1986)

**Bills Numbers**

28 interceptions, 493 interception-return yards, 8 fumble recoveries, 2 TDs

**Notable Achievements**

- Never missed a game in ten seasons, appearing in 151 straight contests
- Recorded at least 5 interceptions twice
- Amassed more than 100 interception-return yards twice
- Finished fourth in NFL with 7 interceptions in 1985
- Led Bills in interceptions three times
- Ranks among Bills career leaders in interceptions (4th) and interception-return yards (4th)
- 1980 division champion
- 1986 Week 13 AFC Defensive Player of the Week

## 53 - TED WASHINGTON (NT; 1995-2000)

**Bills Numbers**

19.5 sacks, 378 tackles, 3 forced fumbles, 1 fumble recovery, 1 interception

**Notable Achievements**

- Never missed a game in six seasons, starting 96 consecutive contests
- Recorded 92 tackles in 1996
- Led Bills defensive linemen in tackles twice
- 1995 division champion
- Three-time Pro Bowl selection (1997, 1998, and 2000)
- 1997 Second-Team All-Pro selection
- Two-time First-Team All-AFC selection (1997 and 1998)

## 54 - JAIRUS BYRD (DB; 2009-2013)

**Bills Numbers**

22 interceptions, 409 interception-return yards, 356 tackles, 3 sacks, 11 forced fumbles, 5 fumble recoveries, 2 TDs

Courtesy of Guy Harbert

**Notable Achievements**

- Recorded at least 5 interceptions twice
- Amassed more than 100 interception-return yards once
- Recorded 98 tackles in 2011
- Led NFL with 9 interceptions in 2009
- Led Bills in interceptions three times
- Ranks among Bills career leaders in interceptions (tied for 10th), interception-return yards (8th), and forced fumbles (7th)
- Member of 2009 NFL All-Rookie Team
- 2012 Week 6 AFC Defensive Player of the Week
- Three-time Pro Bowl selection (2009, 2012, and 2013)
- Two-time Second-Team All-Pro selection (2012 and 2013)
- Two-time First-Team All-AFC selection (2009 and 2012)

### 55 - LONDON FLETCHER (LB; 2002-2006)

**Bills Numbers**

730 tackles, 14.5 sacks, 5 interceptions, 50 interception-return yards, 5 forced fumbles, 7 fumble recoveries, 2 TDs

### Notable Achievements

- Never missed a game in five seasons, starting eighty consecutive contests
- Recorded more than 130 tackles five times
- Finished third in NFL in tackles three times
- Led Bills in tackles five times and interceptions once
- Ranks fifth in franchise history in tackles

## 56 - JORDAN POYER (DB; 2017-2022)

### Bills Numbers

22 interceptions, 151 interception-return yards, 582 tackles, 10 sacks, 7 forced fumbles, 6 fumble recoveries, 1 TD

**Notable Achievements**

- Has recorded 5 interceptions twice
- Has recorded at least 100 tackles three times
- Has led Bills in interceptions four times and tackles twice
- Ranks among Bills career leaders in interceptions (tied for 10th) and tackles (8th)
- Three-time division champion (2020, 2021, and 2022)
- 2022 Week 4 AFC Defensive Player of the Week
- December 2017 AFC Defensive Player of the Month
- 2021 First-Team All-Pro selection
- 2021 First-Team All-AFC selection

## 57 - BOB CHANDLER (WR; 1971-1979)

**Bills Numbers**

295 receptions, 3,999 receiving yards, 34 touchdown receptions

### Notable Achievements

- Surpassed 50 receptions three times
- Finished second in NFL in receptions twice
- Finished third in NFL with 10 touchdown receptions in 1976
- Led Bills in receptions five times and receiving yards four times
- Ranks among Bills career leaders in receptions (10th), receiving yards (9th), touchdown receptions (5th), and touchdowns (tied for 10th)
- Two-time Second-Team All-AFC selection (1975 and 1977)

## 58 – HENRY JONES (DB; 1991–2000)

### Bills Numbers

18 interceptions, 455 interception-return yards, 4 touchdown-interceptions, 663 tackles, 5 sacks, 7 forced fumbles, 9 fumble recoveries, 1 safety, 41 kickoff-return yards, 1 kickoff-return touchdown

### Notable Achievements

- Led NFL with 8 interceptions and 263 interception-return yards in 1992

- Led Bills with 81 tackles in 1997
- Ranks among Bills career leaders in interception-return yards (5th), touchdown interceptions (4th), and tackles (6th)
- Three-time division champion (1991, 1993, and 1995)
- Three-time AFC champion (1991, 1992, and 1993)
- 1992 Pro Bowl selection
- 1992 First-Team All-Pro selection
- 1992 First-Team All-AFC selection

### 59 - TERRENCE MCGEE (DB/KR; 2003-2012)

**Career Numbers**

17 interceptions, 166 interception-return yards, 521 tackles, 3 sacks, 3 forced fumbles, 4 fumble recoveries, 2 defensive TDs, 5,450 kickoff-return yards, 5,722 all-purpose yards, 5 kickoff-return TDs, 7 TDs

Courtesy of Mark Cromwell

### Notable Achievements

- Amassed more than 1,000 all-purpose yards four times
- Led NFL in kickoff-return touchdowns once, kickoff-return average once, and passes defended once
- Finished third in NFL in kickoff-return yards once and kickoff-return average once
- Led Bills in interceptions three times
- Holds Bills career record for most kickoff-return yards
- Ranks 10th in franchise history in all-purpose yards
- Three-time AFC Special Teams Player of the Week
- 2004 Pro Bowl selection
- Two-time Second-Team All-Pro selection (2004 and 2005)
- 2004 First-Team All-AFC selection

## 60 - WILL WOLFORD (OT/G; 1986-1992)

### Notable Achievements

- Missed just three nonstrike games in seven seasons, starting 102 out of 105 contests

Courtesy of Mark Cromwell

- Four-time division champion (1988, 1981, 1990, and 1991)
- Three-time AFC champion (1990, 1991, and 1992)
- Member of 1986 NFL All-Rookie Team
- Two-time Pro Bowl selection (1990 and 1992)

## 61 – TOM JANIK (DB; 1965–1968)

**Bills Numbers:** 21 interceptions, 495 interception-return yards, 5 touchdown-interceptions

### Notable Achievements

- Recorded three interceptions vs. Patriots on December 9, 1967
- Recorded at least 8 interceptions twice
- Amassed more than 100 interception-return yards three times
- Led AFL with 10 interceptions in 1967
- Finished second in AFL with 222 interception-return yards in 1967
- Finished third in AFL with 8 interceptions and 136 interception-return yards in 1966
- Led Bills in interceptions twice

- Holds share of franchise record for most touchdown-interceptions
- Ranks third in franchise history in interception-return yards
- Two-time division champion (1965 and 1966)
- 1965 AFL champion
- Three-time AFL Defensive Player of the Week
- Two-time AFL All-Star selection (1965 and 1967)

### 62 - MICAH HYDE (DB; 2017-2022)

**Bills Numbers**

14 interceptions, 172 interception-return yards, 363 tackles, 1 sack, 3 forced fumbles, 3 fumble recoveries, 2 TDs

Courtesy of Keith Allison

**Notable Achievements**

- Has recorded five interceptions twice
- Has led Bills in interceptions twice
- Three-time division champion (2020, 2021, and 2022)
- October 2017 AFC Defensive Player of the Month
- 2017 Pro Bowl selection
- Two-time Second-Team All-Pro selection (2017 and 2021)

### 63 - FRANK LEWIS (WR; 1978-1983)

**Bills Numbers**

269 receptions, 4,638 receiving yards, 24 touchdown receptions

**Notable Achievements**

- Surpassed 50 receptions twice, catching 70 passes in 1981
- Surpassed 1,000 receiving yards twice
- Averaged 20 yards per reception in 1979
- Recorded longest reception in NFL in 1978 (92 yards)
- Finished third in NFL in receiving yards once and yards per reception once
- Led Bills in receptions twice and receiving yards three times
- Ranks among Bills career leaders in receiving yards (5th), yards from scrimmage (10th), and touchdown receptions (11th)
- 1980 division champion
- 1981 Pro Bowl selection
- 1981 First-Team All-AFC selection

## 64 - MARIO WILLIAMS (DE; 2012-2015)

**Bills Numbers**

43 sacks, 145 tackles, 5 forced fumbles, 2 fumble recoveries

**Notable Achievements**

- Finished in double digits in sacks three times
- Finished fourth in NFL in sacks twice and tackles for loss once
- Led Bills in sacks four times
- Ranks ninth in Bills history in sacks
- Two-time AFC Defensive Player of the Week
- November 2014 AFC Defensive Player of the Month
- Two-time Pro Bowl selection (2013 and 2014)
- 2014 First-Team All-Pro selection
- 2013 Second-Team All-Pro selection
- 2014 First-Team All-AFC selection

Courtesy of Matthew D. Britt

## 65 - BOOKER EDGERSON (DB; 1962-1969)

**Bills Numbers**

23 interceptions, 421 interception-return yards, 4 fumble recoveries, 3 TDs

**Notable Achievements**

- Recorded at least 5 interceptions twice
- Amassed more than 100 interception-return yards three times
- Led AFL in fumble-return yards once and TD interceptions once
- Ranks among Bills career leaders in interceptions (tied for 7th) and interception-return yards (7th)
- Three-time division champion (1964, 1965, and 1966)

- Two-time AFL champion (1964 and 1965)
- 1969 Week 11 AFL Defensive Player of the Week
- 1965 AFL All-Star selection
- 1969 Second-Team All-AFL selection
- Inducted into Bills Wall of Fame in 2010

## 66 - MARCELL DAREUS (DT; 2011-2017)

**Bills Numbers**

35 sacks, 292 tackles, 2 forced fumbles, 2 fumble recoveries

Courtesy of Jeffrey Beall

### Notable Achievements

- Recorded 10 sacks in 2014
- Recorded 71 tackles in 2013
- Led Bills in sacks once
- Led Bills defensive linemen in tackles once
- Ranks 12th in Bills history in sacks
- Member of 2011 NFL All-Rookie Team
- 2014 Week 5 AFC Defensive Player of the Week
- Two-time Pro Bowl selection (2013 and 2014)
- 2014 First-Team All-Pro selection
- 2014 First-Team All-AFC selection

## 67 - C. J. SPILLER (RB/PR/KR; 2010-2014)

**Bills Numbers**

3,321 yards rushing, 158 receptions, 1,195 receiving yards, 4,516 yards from scrimmage, 302 punt-return Yards, 1,463 kickoff-return yards, 6,281 all-purpose yards, 12 rushing TDs, 6 TD receptions, 2 kickoff-return TDs, 20 TDs, 5.0 rushing average

**Notable Achievements**

- Rushed for more than 1,000 yards once (1,244 in 2012)
- Amassed more than 1,000 yards from scrimmage twice, topping 1,500 yards once (1,703 in 2012)
- Amassed more than 1,000 all-purpose yards four times, topping 1,500 yards twice
- Averaged more than 5 yards per carry twice
- Finished second in NFL with an average of 6.0 yards per carry in 2012

Courtesy of Mark Cromwell

- Led Bills in rushing twice
- Ranks among Bills career leaders in rushing yards (9th), kickoff-return yards (8th), and all-purpose yards (8th)
- Two-time AFC Special Teams Player of the Week
- 2012 Pro Bowl selection

### 68 - MARIO CLARK (DB; 1976-1983)

**Bills Numbers**

25 interceptions, 438 interception-return yards, 9 fumble recoveries.

**Notable Achievements**

- Recorded at least 5 interceptions four times
- Amassed more than 100 interception-return yards twice
- Finished fourth in NFL with 7 interceptions in 1977

- Finished fifth in NFL with 151 interception-return yards in 1977
- Led Bills in interception twice
- Ranks among Bills career leaders in interceptions (6th) and interception-return yards (6th)
- 1980 division champion
- Member of 1976 NFL All-Rookie Team
- 1981 Second-Team All-AFC selection

## 69 - JERRY HUGHES (DE/LB; 2013-2021)

### Bills Numbers

53 sacks, 350 tackles, 16 forced fumbles, 5 fumble recoveries, 1 TD

Courtesy of Keith Allison

**Notable Achievements**

- Recorded 10 sacks twice
- Led Bills in sacks three times
- Led Bills' defensive linemen in tackles four times
- Ranks among Bills career leaders in sacks (4th) and forced fumbles (5th)
- Two-time division champion (2020 and 2021)

### 70 - STEVE JOHNSON (WR; 2008-2013)

**Bills Numbers**

301 receptions, 3,832 receiving yards, 28 touchdown receptions

**Notable Achievements**

- Surpassed 75 receptions three times

Courtesy of Jeffrey Beall

- Surpassed 1,000 receiving yards three times
- Made 10 touchdown receptions in 2010
- Led Bills in receptions and receiving yards three times each
- Ranks among Bills career leaders in receptions (9th), receiving yards (10th), and touchdown receptions (8th)

### 71 – ROSCOE PARRISH (WR/PR/KR; 2005–2011)

**Bills Numbers**

134 receptions, 1,502 receiving yards, 7 TD receptions, 71 rushing yards, 1 rushing TD, 1,573 yards from scrimmage, 1,622 punt-return yards, 685 kickoff-return yards, 3,880 all-purpose yards, 3 punt-return TDs, 11 TDs

Courtesy of Mark Cromwell

**Notable Achievements**

- Led NFL in punt-return average twice
- Finished third in NFL in punt-return average once and punt-return yards once
- Holds Bills career record for most punt-return yards
- Two-time AFC Special Teams Player of the Week
- 2007 First-Team All-AFC selection

## 72 - STEVE FREEMAN (DB; 1975-1986)

**Bills Numbers**

23 interceptions, 329 interception-return yards, 8 fumble recoveries, 3 sacks, 3 touchdowns

**Notable Achievements**

- Recorded 7 interceptions in 1980
- Amassed more than 100 interception-return yards once
- Led Bills in interceptions twice
- Ranks among Bills career leaders in interceptions (tied for 7th), interception-return yards (10th), and games played (178; 8th)
- 1980 division champion

### 73 - RIAN LINDELL (K; 2003-2012)

**Bills Numbers**

225 field goals, 305 extra points, 980 points, 83.3 field-goal percentage

**Notable Achievements**

- Scored more than 100 points six times, topping 120 points once

Courtesy of Mark Cromwell

- Converted more than 80 percent of field goal attempts seven times, surpassing 90 percent once
- Finished third in NFL in field-goal percentage once
- Ranks second in Bills history in points scored, field goals made, and extra points made
- Three-time AFC Special Teams Player of the Week

### 74 - MATT MILANO (LB; 2017-2022)

**Career Numbers**

458 tackles, 8 interceptions, 140 interception-return yards, 10.5 sacks, 2 forced fumbles, 8 fumble recoveries, 2 touchdowns

### Notable Achievements

- Has recorded more than 100 tackles once
- Three-time division champion (2020, 2021, and 2022)
- Two-time AFC Defensive Player of the Week
- 2022 First-Team All-Pro selection

## 75 - BRYCE PAUP (LB; 1995-1997)

### Bills Numbers

33 sacks, 215 tackles, 2 interceptions, 7 forced fumbles, 2 fumble recoveries

### Notable Achievements

- Led NFL with 17.5 sacks in 1995
- 1995 division champion

- Three-time AFC Defensive Player of the Week
- November 1995 AFC Defensive Player of the Month
- 1995 NFL Defensive Player of the Year
- Three-time Pro Bowl selection (1995, 1996, and 1997)
- 1995 First-Team All-Pro selection
- 1995 First-Team All-AFC selection
- 1996 Second-Team All-AFC selection

# GLOSSARY

## ABBREVIATIONS AND STATISTICAL TERMS

**C** Center.

**COMP %** Completion percentage: the number of successfully completed passes divided by the number of passes attempted

**FS** Free safety

**INTS** Interceptions: passes thrown by the quarterback that are caught by a member of the opposing team's defense

**KR** Kickoff returner

**LCB** Left cornerback

**LE** Left end

**LG** Left guard

**LT** Left tackle

**NT** Nose tackle

**P** Punter

**PK** Placekicker

**PR** Punt returner

**QB** Quarterback

**QBR** Quarterback rating

**RB** Running back

**RCB** Right cornerback

**RE** Right end

**RG** Right guard

**RT** Right tackle

**SS** Strong Safety

**ST** Special teams

**TD PASSES** Touchdown passes

**TD RECS** Touchdown receptions

**TDS** Touchdowns

**TE** Tight end

**WR** Wide receiver

# BIBLIOGRAPHY

## Books

Felser, Larry. 2008. *The Birth of the New NFL: How The 1966 NFL/AFL Merger Transformed Pro Football.* Guilford, CT: Lyons Press.

Gehman, Jim. 2008. *"Then Levy Said to Kelly...": The Best Buffalo Bills Stories Ever Told.* Chicago: Triumph Books.

Jones, Danny. 2006. *More Distant Memories: Pro Football's Best Ever Players of the 50's, 60's, and 70's.* Bloomington, IN: AuthorHouse.

Miller, Jeffrey J. 2012. *100 Things Bills Fans Should Know & Do Before They Die.* Chicago: Triumph Books.

Pitoniak, Scott. 2007. *The Good, The Bad, and The Ugly: Heart-Pounding, Jaw-Dropping, and Gut-Wrenching Moments in Buffalo Bills History.* Chicago: Triumph Books.

Schultz, Randy. 2015. *Legends of the Buffalo Bills: Marv Levy, Bruce Smith, Thurman Thomas, and Other Bills Stars.* Champaign, IL: Sports Publishing.

Tasker, Steve, with Scott Pitoniak. 2006. *Steve Tasker's Tales from the Buffalo Bills.* Champaign, IL: Sports Publishing.

## Websites

www.buffalobills.com
http://sports.espn.go.com
www.newsday.com
www.nydailynews.com/new-york
www.nytimes.com
http://profootballtalk.nbcsports.com
http://www.sptimes.com

www.starledger.com
http://articles.sun-sentinel.com
http://www.pro-football-reference.com/players